THE

LATIN

Enrique Caracciol
1932 and has live
graduated at the U
where he later became Associate Professor of English and American Literature. His books are *William Blake: Poemas y profecías* (1957), the first comprehensive translation of Blake into Spanish; *Los poetas metafísicos ingleses del siglo XVII* (1962); and *Hawthorne, Melville y el pasado puritano* (1963). His essays and reviews on Latin American literature have been published both in Europe and Latin America. Since 1962 he has lived intermittently in this country. He taught Latin American studies at Bristol University and, interested in comparative literature, joined the Department of Literature at the University of Essex, where he is a lecturer, in 1967. He is married and has one son.

THE PENGUIN BOOK OF

LATIN AMERICAN VERSE

EDITED BY

E. CARACCIOLO-TREJO

INTRODUCED BY

HENRY GIFFORD

*

WITH PLAIN PROSE TRANSLATIONS

PENGUIN BOOKS

Penguin Books Ltd, Harmondsworth, Middlesex, England
Penguin Books Inc., 7110 Ambassador Road, Baltimore Maryland 21207, U.S.A.
Penguin Books Australia Ltd, Ringwood, Victoria, Australia

—

First published 1971

—

—

Made and printed in Great Britain
by Richard Clay (The Chaucer Press) Ltd
Bungay, Suffolk
Set in Monotype Fournier

CONTENTS*

---

*For explanation of movements, etc. referred to in the contents, please see *Appendix: An Explanatory Guide to Movements in Latin-American Poetry*, p. 395.

primavera (1952), a farce, and *Dulioto* (1953). He has published poems and articles in many literary magazines, both in Latin America and in Europe. His books *En común* (1954) and *La vigilia y el viejo* (1961) contain most of his poetry up to 1960. The two poems included here are more recent.

ALBERTO GIRRI (b. 1919) has contributed to the review *Sur* for many years. His poems have appeared in international publications and he is well known outside Argentina. His poems are tense and precise. He has translated poetry from English and Italian. His books include *Playa sola* (1946), *Examen de nuestra causa* (1956), *Propiedades de la magia* (1959), *Elegías italianas* (1962), *Envíos* (1967). A useful collection of his work is *Poemas elegidos* (1965).

RAÚL GUSTAVO AGUIRRE (b. 1927) edited the review *Poesía Buenos Aires* for many years. He has translated the work of many poets into Spanish, including Emily Dickinson, Guillaume Apollinaire, and René Char. He is the leading figure of the Argentine Surrealist movement. His books include *El tiempo de la rosa* (1945), *La danza nupcial* (1951), and *alguna memoria* (1960).

BOLIVIA

RICARDO JAIMES FREYRE (1868–1933) was born in Bolivia but spent most of his life in the Argentine, where he met and was influenced by Rubén Darío. He was a *modernista* poet with a fascination for the exotic – in his case, Northern European legends – characteristic of Modernismo. Echoes of Leconte de Lisle, Carducci and, fundamentally, of Wagner, are to be found in his poetry. His book *Castalia Bárbara* (1897) gained for him continental recognition.

CONTENTS

BRAZIL

a unique quality. His main published work includes *La muerte de Narciso* (1937), *Enemigo rumor* (1941), *Aventuras sigilosas* (1945), and *Dador* (1960). His novel, *Paradiso* (1966), is one of the most important works of Spanish-American fiction.

ROBERTO FERNÁNDEZ RETAMAR (b. 1930) One of the most accomplished of the younger generation of Cuban poets. He studied in Cuba, Paris, and London and has taught both in his own country and in the United States. Since the Revolution he has played an active role in the intellectual life of Cuba. At present he is the editor of the magazine *Casa de las Américas*. Fernández Retamar's books of poetry include *Elegía como un himno* (1950), *Alabanzas, conversaciones* (1955), *Vuelta a la antigua esperanza* (1959) and an anthology, *Con las mismas manos* (1962). He has also written excellent criticism.

PABLO ARMANDO FERNÁNDEZ (b. 1930) lived in the United States for fifteen years and returned to Cuba after the Revolution. *Toda la poesía* (1962) is a collection that includes poems from all his previous books. In the section *Poemas apócrifos de Adriano*, Fernández reaches a great concentration, combining old themes with new experience. In 1964 he published *El libro de los héroes*, a collection of poems about the recent political events in his country. He has also written fiction: *Los niños se despiden* (1968) won the Casa de las Américas prize.

ECUADOR

JOSÉ JOAQUÍN DE OLMEDO (1780–1847) devoted his life to the cause of the independence of his country, and later to the consolidation and organization of the Republic. His best

González Martínez reveals himself as the spokesman for a new attitude towards poetry, defined in his famous sonnet: 'Twist the neck of the swan of deceitful plumage/striking a white note on the blue of the fountain/sporting its grace only, but not feeling/the soul of things created.' In his long life he worked as doctor, politician, and diplomat. His memoirs were published under the titles *El hombre del buho* (1944) and *La apacible locura* (1951). His other books include *Silenter* (1909), *La muerte del cisne* (1915), and *El nuevo narciso* (1952, published posthumously).

JOSÉ JUAN TABLADA (1871–1945) was born in Mexico and died in New York. He led a very active life and travelled extensively. In 1900 he visited Japan, and later introduced the 'haiku' into Spanish poetry. He was a friend of the poet Ramón López Velarde, whom he guided and inspired. He must be considered an *ultraísta* because of the freedom of his metaphors, but he had no connection with the *ultraísta* groups of Madrid and Buenos Aires. He composed 'calligrammes' at almost the same time as Apollinaire. Tablada's books include *El florilegio* (1899, 1904, and 1918), *Al sol y bajo la luna* (1918), *Un día . . .* (1919), *Li-po y otros poemas* (1920), *La feria* (1928), and *Los mejores poemas de José Juan Tablada* (1943).

RAMÓN LÓPEZ VELARDE (1888–1921) was born in Zacatecas. With López Velarde, Mexican poetry abandoned Modernismo and entered a new phase: his use of colloquial language sounds new compared to the *modernista* preciousness, although occasionally those refinements he was reacting against crept into his own poetry. His books include *La sangre devota* (1916), *Zozobra* (1919), and *El son del corazón* (1932). A useful

NICARAGUA

RUBÉN DARÍO (1867–1916) is today regarded as the most important poet of the *modernista* movement. His work marks a turning point in Spanish poetry because, through him, Latin America began to influence Spain. He travelled extensively, and lived in Guatemala, El Salvador, Costa Rica, Chile, Argentina, Spain, and France. At a time when communications between Latin-American countries were particularly difficult, the fact that he travelled so much is not unrelated to his becoming the centre and the spokesman of the new aesthetic ideas for which he coined the name Modernismo. Modernismo was little more than a reaction to established literary standards and forms that had dominated Latin-American poetry until then: classicist Spanish peninsularism, moralistic attitudes, rhetorical over-ornamentation. In *Azul* (1888 and 1890), which includes poems, prose poems and short stories, Darío already showed himself to be a pioneer. *Prosas profanas* (1896) best illustrates Darío's innovations of rhythm and metre. His other books include *Cantos de vida y esperanza* (1905), *El canto errante* (1907), *Poema del otoño y otros poemas* (1910), and *Canto a la Argentina y otros poemas* (1914). His *Poesía* is in the series *Biblioteca Americana* of Fondo de Cultura Económica, Mexico, 1952.

ERNESTO CARDENAL (b. 1925) He studied in Mexico and the United States, where he attended courses in theology. A disciple of Thomas Merton, he later lived in a Benedictine monastery in Mexico. He has recently founded a contemplative order on an island in the Gran Lago, Nicaragua. Cardenal's books include *La Hora O* (1960), *Epigramas* (1961), *Salmos*

most of his books were published in his lifetime, a just recognition of his significance as a poet came late. Vallejo's first book, *Los heraldos negros* (1918), is deeply religious, and there are many biblical references. *Trilce* (1922) is his most ambitious book, and it is crucial in his development as a poet. In the thirties, Vallejo became a militant communist, was expelled from France, where he had lived since 1923, and went to Spain. He also made two journeys to the Soviet Union. The Spanish Civil War was to him a momentous experience which he described with particular pathos in *Poemas humanos*, published posthumously in 1939. There are two volumes of collected poems: *Poesías completas*, Losada, 1949, and *Obra poética completa*, Moncloa, Lima, 1968.

MARTÍN ADÁN (b. 1908) is the pseudonym of Rafael de la Fuente Benavides. He published *La casa de cartón*, a vanguard, poematic novel, in 1928. He was interested in Novalis, Hölderlin, and the French Parnassians and Symbolists, and his poetry achieves a mystic quality in *Travesía de extramares* (1950). His second volume is *La mano desasida* (1964).

CARLOS GERMÁN BELLI (b. 1927) One of the foremost young poets in Latin America today. Belli's sense of despair is controlled by a fine irony, reminiscent at times of the great Spanish poet Quevedo. His volume *El pie sobre el cuello* (1967) includes poems from previous books: *Poemas* (1958), *¡Oh hada cibernética!* (1962), *El pie sobre el cuello* (1964), and *Por el monte abajo* (1966).

PUERTO RICO

LUIS LLORÉNS TORRES (1878–1944) introduced Modernismo in Puerto Rico, and in particular the aspect of Modernismo which seeks a national identity: hence his interest in historical themes. But his main contribution is in his use of the demotic language, which gives a musical quality to his poetry. *Al pie de la Alhambra* (1899) was published in Spain. *Sonetos sinfónicos* (1914) and *Voces de la campana mayor* (1935) are his *modernista* books. A useful collection of his poetry is *Alturas de América* (1940). He also wrote prose.

LUIS PALÉS MATOS (1898–1959) After a first book in the *modernista* manner, *Azaleas* (1915), he began to experiment in Negro themes and rhythms. His Negro poetry was gathered in *Tuntún de pasa y grifería* (1937). *Poesía 1915–1956* (1957), introduced by Frederico de Onís, shows the variety of phases of his poetry.

URUGUAY

JULIO HERRERA Y REISSIG (1875–1910) is representative of the *modernista* school in Uruguay. The Latin-American critic, Pedro Henríquez Ureña, has written of him: 'The baroque tendency grew with J. Herrera y Reissig, whose imagery soon became startling, even delirious at times.' His books include *Las pascuas del tiempo* (1900, his first book), *Los maitines de la noche* (1902), *Los éxtasis de la montaña* (1904, 1910, perhaps his best collection), and *La torre de las Esfinges* (1909). His *Poesías completas* were published by Losada, Buenos Aires, in 1942.

ACKNOWLEDGEMENTS

I am indebted to many friends who have helped me with this book: first to Sr Pablo Armando Fernández, with whom I began preparing this anthology; to Mr J. M. Cohen, Mr Alastair Reid and Professor Jean Franco, for their useful suggestions; to Mr John Hill and Dr Simon Collier of the Department of Literature of the University of Essex, for their most generous help; and to the staff of Canning House, for obtaining a number of books for my use. I am grateful to Sr Fernando Sabino and Sr Claudio Leal, with whom I discussed matters relating to the Brazilian section; to the Chilean poet Nicanor Parra, for his wonderful hospitality as well as for his advice; to José Miguel Oviedo of Peru, who drew my attention to the work of Martín Adán; and to many friends who, sometimes without knowing it, contributed to the book. I am particularly grateful to the translators, Mr John Hill, Mr Tom Raworth, Mr Michael Gonzalez and Mr Peter Standish, whose infinite patience I put to repeated tests when we discussed the translations; and to Miss Mary Hodges, Miss Mary Bonner and Mrs Marjorie MacGlashan who prepared the typescripts.

E. CARACCIOLO-TREJO

Layer-de-la-Haye, Essex,
October 1970

For permission to reprint poems in copyright, thanks are due to the following:

MARTÍN ADÁN: to the author.
RAÚL GUSTAVO AGUIRRE: 'El mutilado' from *Señales de vida*, and 'Y bien' from *Poesía argentina*, to the author.
MÁRIO DE ANDRADE: from *Obras de Mário de Andrade*, to Maria de Lourdes Moraes Andrade and Livraria Martins Editoras S.A.
ENRIQUE BANCHS: from *Enrique Banchs*, in the collection *Argentinos en las letras*, to the estate of Enrique Banchs.
MANUEL BANDEIRA: from *Poesia e prosa*, to Maria de Lourdes de Souza.
EDGAR BAYLEY: 'cuestión de tiempo' from *ni razón ni palabra* and 'la violencia' from *Poesía argentina*, to the author.

CARLOS GERMÁN BELLI: from *El pie sobre el cuello*, to the author.
JORGE LUIS BORGES: from *Poemas 1922–1943*, to the author and Editorial Losada S.A.
JOÃO CABRAL DE MELO NETO: from *Poesias completas*, to the author.
ERNESTO CARDENAL: from *Gethsemani, KY.*, *Salmos*, to the author.
LUIS CARDOZA Y ARAGÓN: from *Poesía*, to the author.
SALVADOR DÍAZ MIRÓN: from *Poesías completas*, to Editorial Porrúa S.A.
CARLOS DRUMMOND DE ANDRADE: from *Poemas*, to the author.
ANDRÉS ELOY BLANCO: from *Giraluna*, to the estate of Andrés Eloy Blanco and Editorial Yocoima.
PABLO ARMANDO FERNÁNDEZ: 'Trajano' from *Toda la poesía*, and 'Los héroes' from *El libro de los héroes*, to the author.
BALDOMERO FERNÁNDEZ MORENO: 'Dalmira' from *Antología 1915–1940* and 'Soneto (No hay nada comparable a este momento)' from *Las cien mejores poesías*, to the estate of Baldomero Fernández Moreno.
ROBERTO FERNÁNDEZ RETAMAR: from *Con las mismas manos*, to the author.
EUGENIO FLORIT: from *Antología poética 1930–1955*, to the author.
EMILIO FRUGONI: from *La elegía unánime*, to Editorial Losada S.A.
OLIVERIO GIRONDO: 'Café-concierto' from *Veinte poemas para ser leídos en el tranvía* and poem 18 from *Espantapájaros*, to Centro Editor de América Latina.
ALBERTO GIRRI: from *Poemas elegidos*, to the author and Editorial Losada S.A.
ENRIQUE GONZÁLEZ MARTÍNEZ: from *Poesia 1898–1938*, to Héctor González Rojo.
LÉON DE GREIFF: from *Obras completas*, to the author.
NICOLÁS GUILLÉN: 'Caminando' from *Sóngoro cosongo* and 'No sé por qué piensas tú' from *El son entero*, to Editorial Losada S.A.
VICENTE HUIDOBRO: from *Obras completas de Vicente Huidobro*, vol. 1, to the estate of Vicente Huidobro and Empresa Editora Zig-Zag S.A.
RICARDO JAIMES FREYRE: from *Poesías completas*, to the Ministerio de Educatión y Bellas Artes, La Paz, Bolivia.

JOSÉ LEZAMA LIMA: 'Pez nocturno' and 'Llamado del deseoso' from *Orbita de Lezama Lima* and 'Fragmentos' and extracts from 'Primera glorieta de la amistad' ('Para Fina García Marruz' and 'Para Octavio Smith') from *Dador*, to the author.

ENRIQUE LIHN: from *La pieza oscura*, to the author and Editorial Universitaria de Chile.

JORGE DE LIMA: from *Obra completa*, vol. 1, to Adila Alves de Lima.

RAMÓN LÓPEZ VELARDE: from *Poesías completas*, to Editorial Porrúa S.A.

LEOPOLDO LUGONES: from *Antología poética*, to Compañía Editora Espasa-Calpe, Argentina.

EZEQUIEL MARTÍNEZ ESTRADA: from *Poesía*, to the estate of Ezequiel Martínez Estrada and Editorial Universitaria de Buenos Aires.

CECÍLIA MEIRELES: from *Obra poética*, to Heitor Grillo.

MURILO MENDES: from *Poesías*, to the author.

ENRIQUE MOLINA: from *Fuego libre*, to the author.

RICARDO E. MOLINARI: from *Mundos de la madrugada*, to the author and Editorial Losada S.A.

MARCO ANTONIO MONTES DE OCA: from *Delante de la luz cantan los pájaros*, to the author.

VINÍCIUS DE MORAES: from *Cinco elegías*, to the author.

ÁLVARO MUTIS: from *Los elementos del desastre*, to the author.

PABLO NERUDA: 'Bruselas' from *Tercera residencia*, 'Walking Around' from *Residencia en la tierra* and 'Alturas de Macchu Picchu' from *Canto general*, to the author.

SALVADOR NOVO: from *Poesía*, to the author.

EMILIO ORIBE: from *Poesía*, to the author.

JOSÉ EMILIO PACHECO: from *No me preguntes cómo pasa el tiempo*, to the author.

LUIS PALÉS MATOS: from *Poesía 1915–1956*, third edition 1968 © University of Puerto Rico Press. Reprinted with permission.

NICANOR PARRA: from *Poemas y antipoemas*, to the author.

OCTAVIO PAZ: 'Temporal', 'Complementarios', 'Alba última', 'Ustica' and 'Ida y vuelta' from *Salamandra*, and 'Cuento de dos jardines' from *Ladera este*, to the author.

CARLOS PELLICER: from *Material poético 1918–1961*, to the author and Universidad Nacional Autónoma de México.

ALFONSO REYES: from *Obra poética*, to Alicia Reyes.
CASSIANO RICARDO: to the author.
CARLOS SABAT ERCASTY: 'Interludios al modo antiguo – LVI' from *Los adioses*, and poems LXXXVII and LXXXVIII from *Las sombras diáfanas*, to the author.
JAIME SABINES: from *Tarumba*, to the author.
JOSÉ JUAN TABLADA: to Nina Cabrera de Tablada.

NOTE

Unless otherwise stated, translations are by the following:

Tom Raworth:
Argentina, Bolivia, Chile, Peru

Peter Standish:
Brazil

John Hill:
Cuba, Colombia, Guatemala

Michael Gonzalez:
Ecuador, Mexico, Nicaragua, Puerto Rico, Uruguay, Venezuela

INTRODUCTION

THIS anthology of Latin-American verse includes poems from thirteen countries in which the literary language is Spanish and from one, Brazil, in which it is Portuguese.

The term 'Latin-American' needs closer inspection than perhaps we normally give it. Spain and Portugal form part of that Latin world sometimes called 'Romania'. Thus we may expect to hear in their poetry certain notes which derive from Lucretius or Virgil, Horace or Martial; from the Latin Middle Ages; from Petrarch and the Renaissance. The former colonies of Spain and Portugal had been compelled to take the language and the religion of their conquerors; and both are still there, when the imperial power has gone. How far, we may ask, will their poetry – and above all their modern poetry, no longer imitative and dependent – resemble the 'Latin' poetry that we know in Europe? The term 'American' also calls for definition. Central and South America share with North America a geographical name; to some extent they share a situation ('the New World'); and to some extent certain attitudes. Thus Pablo Neruda, a Chilean, addresses Walt Whitman:

tú
me enseñaste
a ser
americano.

'You taught me to be American.' There are Latin-American writers, Jorge Luis Borges has noted, who claim, as so many North Americans have done, that they have been 'cut off from the past' to find themselves 'in a situation like that of the first days of Creation'. This is the familiar myth, cherished in the United States for so long, of the American Adam. But Neruda, the self-confessed pupil of Whitman, could read a different lesson from the ruins of a pre-Columbian city, Macchu Picchu:

El reino muerto vive todavía.

The dead kingdom lives on, Central and South America cannot

escape from memories of the dead kingdom; or if an Argentine may, it is impossible for a Mexican or a Peruvian.

Thus to be American means something different south of the Rio Grande. But at least Latin Americans share with North Americans the problem of self-expression in an imported language. Spanish and Portuguese, like English, for a long time constrained the writers of the New World to observe literary traditions that were becoming increasingly remote from them. In Brazil, where the native peoples were to perish silently without history or monuments, and where the political break with Portugal was neither abrupt nor violent, the cultural problem may have been less acute. For the Spanish-speaking countries, however, relationship with Spain has often proved difficult and oppressive. At the time of the Counter-Reformation Spain withdrew into itself, and as Europe grew ever more infidel almost every window and door in Spain was barred against it. In 1898 the last colonies of Spain in the Americas were lost, and a new beginning was made with the reappraisal of Spanish culture by a generation that wanted to find Spain her place in the modern world. And this meant also the opening of a dialogue between Spain and Spanish America, a dialogue in which, according to Octavio Paz, the participants were 'Darío and Jiménez, Machado and Lugones, Huidobro and Guillén, Neruda and García Lorca'. There can be no dialogue, of course, where there is not divergence – and those in it must meet as equals. With the twentieth century, Latin-American literature, like North American literature, has gained its freedom from Europe, and a confidence in its own destiny.

Needless to say, political liberation came long before that of the poet's tongue. To celebrate victory over the Spaniards an early nineteenth-century Ecuadorian patriot, José Joaquín de Olmedo, produced the kind of formal ode that could have been written anywhere in Europe. Until the appearance of the Nicaraguan prodigy Rubén Darío, Latin-American poets were all too conscious of European primacy; and even Darío, for all his vibrant and unfamiliar tone, was not a Latin American to the marrow like César Vallejo or Pablo Neruda. His novelty derived in large part from the latter phase of French romanticism. There is no denying his powerful effect in both Spain and Latin America. Juan Ramón Jiménez has pointed to the accent, the metre, and themes of Darío in Antonio Machado's *Galerías* and *Campos de Castilla* – and these are the principal works of the poet whom many would call the greatest to have been produced by Spain in this century. Darío achieved what he had set out to do: he gave 'colour and life and air and flexibility to the ancient verse' too long cramped in the Spanish mould – but neither he, nor those other poets of *modernismo* who catch his tone and rhythm, the Argentine Leopoldo Lugones and Herrera y Reissig of Uruguay, write verse which can truly claim to be American. Darío is ultimately a provincial poet; whereas Vallejo, Neruda, and Octavio Paz in our century are universal poets – universal because they write from the centre of their own being and hence of the culture that bred them.

This marks the final stage in a process which can be illustrated by looking at one or two landscape poems. The Latin-American writer, deferential though he might be to European taste, knew that his native scene was overwhelmingly novel. He wanted to celebrate this grandeur in the appropriate terms – and the terms he chose to begin with were all too conventional. Andrés Bello of Venezuela writes, in the 1820s, a georgic description of the torrid zone:

> . . . la prócera palma
> su vario feudo cría,
> y el ananás sazona su ambrosía;
> su blanco pan la yuca,
> sus rubias pomas la patata educa . . .

'The noble palm brings forth its varied fee and the pineapple-tree ripens its ambrosia; the yucca-tree grows its white bread and the potato plant its golden fruit' – and so on, elevated and indistinct. Not much later Esteban Echeverría tries an Argentine scene:

¡ Cuántas, cuántas maravillas
Sublimes y a par sencillas
Sembró la fecunda mano
De Dios allí! ¡Cuánto arcano
Que no es dado al mundo ver!
La humilde yerba, el insecto,
La aura aromática y pura;
El silencio, el triste aspecto
De la grandiosa llanura,
El pálido anochecer.

'How many, many marvels, sublime and at the same time simple, did the fertile hand of God scatter there! How many secrets not given to the world to see! The humble weed; the insect; the pure and aromatic breeze. The silence; the sad aspect of the great plain; the pale dusk.' This is poetic in the way of Chateaubriand, which has more sentiment than observation (despite the pale dusk). Only with a Mexican poet of the same century, Othón, does landscape become properly seen and felt. He describes 'A Steppe on the Nazas':

. . . al raz del horizonte, el sol poniente,
cual la boca de un horno, reverbera.

. . . esta grama gris que no abrillanta
ningún color; aquí, do el aire azota
con ígneo soplo la reseca planta . . .

'At the edge of the horizon, the dying sun reverberates like the mouth of a furnace . . . this grey and lifeless grass that no colour brightens; here, where the wind whips the dry plants with burning breath . . . '. *Here* – perhaps for the first time – a place is made actual. The diction however and the form remain, as Octavio Paz has commented, purely conventional; but the scene becomes 'a mirror of the poet's exhausted being'. He recognizes in the Mexican plain his own interior landscape.

There had of course been attempts by Latin-American poets before Othón to render what was specific in their world, and they used images and tones which would convey local colour. Thus in the 1870s José Hernández presented the Argentine gaucho, who reveals himself in *Martín Fierro* through what purports to be the popular idiom. The hero of this ballad-epic declares:

> Soy gaucho, y entiendanló
> Como mi lengua lo esplica . . .

'I am a gaucho, and let it be understood the way I tell it.' The way of telling requires that his speech be recorded as in a dialect survey, with *naides* for *nadie*, *ande* for *donde*, *alversidá* for *adversidad.* Hernández was a journalist; and all this makes the poem picturesque rather than inevitably Argentine. Borges has said:

> The idea that Argentine poetry should abound in differential Argentine traits and Argentine local colour seems to me a mistake. If we are asked which book is more Argentine, *Martín Fierro* or the sonnets in Enrique Banchs's *La urna*, there is no reason to say that it is the first.

He then admits that the imagery of Banchs has nothing about it specifically Argentine, quoting a poem that speaks of the sun on slanting roofs – but these are flat in the suburbs of Buenos Aires where Banchs wrote *La urna* – and of nightingales, which belong to Greek and Germanic tradition. Nonetheless he holds it significant that the poet should turn to these borrowed images: 'significant of Argentine reserve, distrust and reticence, of the difficulty we have in making confessions, in revealing our intimate nature'.

A dozen years ago there appeared *An Anthology of Mexican Poetry** selected by Octavio Paz and translated by Samuel Beckett. Mexican verse in Spanish has a tradition extending over three centuries. It includes two notable seventeenth-century poets, Guevara and the boldly speculative Sor Juana. Yet it was not until the present century, with Ramón López Velarde, that Paz considers 'Mexican poetry proper' to have begun. López Velarde achieved new forms, and his use of language was both highly original and yet true to the idiom of the Mexican people.

* Thames & Hudson, London, 1958.

Thereby, in Paz's words, he was enabled 'to discover his own inner self and that of his country'.

These words apply to César Vallejo, whose attempt to feel down to the roots of language and the roots of man, especially in *Trilce* (1922), brought about the finest poetry yet to be written in Latin America. *Trilce* appeared at the same time as Joyce's *Ulysses*; it is more profound because Vallejo suffered more seriously than Joyce, lived with a greater intensity and encountered more. *Trilce* expresses a deeply personal theme:

> ... entre mi donde y mi cuando,
> esta mayoría inválida de hombre.

'Between my where and my when ... this crippled coming of age of a man': Vallejo realizes for us the *where* – a little town in the Andes; his patrimony that is both Spanish and Indian; and the *when* – cast out from a childhood which can still return, totally, once he invokes the mother, time past being contained in time present, reabsorbing it. The language enables him to expose the hidden nerves of his experience, and to register sensations, presences, terror and loneliness and gratitude, as they are felt by the child, in part below the level of speech. The whole experiment demands that language should be dismantled, and put to use brokenly, as it forms under stress or in moments of intense solitude. Vallejo interrogates it, as he interrogates himself: he is showing how words disengage from the toils of experience, how they yield up the secrets of the innermost self and so of common humanity. César Vallejo came to acquire a passionate feeling for Spain. Through his poetry a new spiritual realm had been discovered, in which ultimately the Amerindian and the Castilian were at one. The Spanish poet José Bergamín emphasized that Vallejo's work had its roots in the Castilian language, while also affirming that its idiom was entirely personal. This is true: Vallejo succeeded in taking the words back to their childhood, thus renewing them and for the first time admitting an American sensibility into the fullest possession of the peninsular tongue.

Bergamín in the preface from which I quoted also mentions Neruda, whose poetry he finds 'denser, and perhaps richer in tones', but also 'less inventive, less flexible, less agile'. Neruda's collected poems now fill an exceedingly bulky volume. He contains multitudes, like Whitman; he is more obviously American than César Vallejo. His poem from which *The Heights of Macchu Picchu* was taken, *Canto general*, belongs to the genre of Hart Crane's *The Bridge*; like it, and like William Carlos Williams's *In the American Grain*, it seeks to interpret the history of the race. Neruda is essentially a lyric poet with epic ambitions; and in this he resembles Mayakovsky. *Walking Around*, the first poem by him in this collection, recalls the earlier Mayakovsky of *A Cloud in Trousers*, with its ache of weariness and the gusto behind the boredom, and its outrageous images:

> Sin embargo sería delicioso
> asustar a un notario con un lirio cortado
> o dar muerte a una monja con un golpe de oreja.
> Sería bello
> ir por las calles con un cuchillo verde
> y dando gritos hasta morir de frío.

'Nonetheless, it would be delicious to frighten a notary with a cut lily, or to kill a nun by a blow with the ear. It would be beautiful to go through the streets with a green knife shouting until I died of cold.' And in those streets he notices what Mayakovsky would have noticed: the suspended washing, 'underpants, towels and shirts that weep slow, dirty tears'.

The Heights of Macchu Picchu is a personal confession leading to the discovery of the 'stone mother', *madre de piedra*, this Inca ruin which reveals Neruda to himself as the descendant of its unknown builders: he imagines

> ... un rostro
> que miró con mis ojos las lámparas terrestres,
> que aceitó con mis manos las desaparecidas
> maderas ...

'a face that watched earth's lanterns with my eyes, that oiled the vanished timbers with my hands'. Macchu Picchu is for him the 'dome of silence, pure fatherland'; he feels 'the old heart of the forgotten one' beat in his hand 'like a bird imprisoned for a thousand years'; and resurrects in himself Juan Cortapiedras, Juan Comefrío, Juan Piesdescalzos – John Stonehewer, John Starveling, John Barefoot – the slaves buried by Macchu Picchu. In both Neruda and Vallejo the tribune is primarily a man who bears his own wounds: from personal anguish he moves to a broader vision of suffering humanity. With Vallejo that vision was there from the beginning: with Neruda it grew more slowly.

Neruda is a great natural force, palpitating with the immediate moment: Octavio Paz is a poetic intelligence (and capable too of sustained and subtle disquisition in prose). The beautifully balanced 'Fable of Two Gardens' which concludes the selection of his poetry here will strike the English reader by its affinities with Eliot:

Una casa, un jardín,
No son lugares:
Giran, van y vienen.
Sus apariciones
Abren en el espacio
Otro espacio,
Otro tiempo en el tiempo.
Sus eclipses
No son abdicaciones:
Nos quemaría
La vivacidad de uno de esos instantes
Si durase otro instante . . .

'A house, a garden, are not places. They spin, come and go. Their apparitions unfold in space other space, other time within time. Their eclipses are not abdications. We would be scorched by the vitality of one of those moments if it lived a moment longer . . .' Here the careful distinctions, the hovering motion, the culminating insight all bring to mind the opening of *Burnt Norton*. But Paz has a richer joy in 'the substance of time and its inventions' than Eliot. His poem is a celebration of life – the two gardens in Mexico and India, 'the girl in the fable' whom he has called Almendrita, the breaking wave at sea and the vision of 'Delhi and her red stones'. The last word in the poem is *claridad.* This would seem to be the quality most desired by Paz. The search for it has impelled him to much exploration in criticism, seeking the contours of the Latin-American consciousness. And here too he resembles Eliot: his habit of mind is tirelessly critical.

In *The Labyrinth of Solitude* Octavio Paz reflects on the position today of the Mexican (to all intents the Latin American). It is no longer marginal to humanity: 'we are, for the first time in our history, the contemporaries of all men'. An 'open solitude' has become the universal condition. The predominance of Europe in literature is now ended. During the present century Latin-American poets have participated fully in all its movements – in symbolism, surrealism, proletarian verse. Huidobro, like Williams, was keenly aware of Cubist painting – José Juan Tablada mastered the Japanese *haiku* like the Imagists in England and the United States. Poets of Brazil, Ecuador, Guatemala have been strikingly original in the confidence of a literature that has found itself. And it has gathered new tones – for example that of 'Negro' poetry in the work of the Brazilian Jorge de Lima and the Cuban Nicolás Guillén. The possession of a continental language – from which the Portuguese of Brazil is not widely separated – would seem to offer immense opportunities. The voices of Latin America, however various, can be harmonized in a developing symphony. Perhaps the future of poetry is more hopeful in these countries than anywhere else in the world.

HENRY GIFFORD

ARGENTINA

ESTEBAN ECHEVERRÍA (1805–51)

from *La cautiva*

El desierto

Ils vont. L'espace est grand. – Hugo

ERA la tarde, y la hora
En que el sol la cresta dora
De los Andes. El Desierto
Inconmensurable, abierto,
Y misterioso a sus pies
Se extiende; triste el semblante,
Solitario y taciturno
Como el mar, cuando un instante
Al crepúsculo nocturno,
Pone rienda a su altivez.

Gira en vano, reconcentra
Su inmensidad, y no encuentra
La vista, en su vivo anhelo,
Do fijar su fugaz vuelo,
Como el pájaro en el mar.

from *The Captive*

The Desert

IT was evening, and the hour when the sun gilds the peak of the Andes. At their feet, unmeasurable, open, and mysterious, stretches the Desert; its aspect sad, solitary and taciturn, like the sea when a moment of twilight seems to restrain its arrogance.

It spins in vain, reconcentrates its immensity, and sight does not find – however fervent its wish – a place to rest its fugitive flight; like a bird over the sea. Anywhere in fields and estates, lairs of bird

Doquier campos y heredades
Del ave y bruto guaridas,
Doquier cielo y soledades
De Dios sólo conocidas,
Que Él sólo puede sondar.

A veces la tribu errante,
Sobre el potro rozagante,
Cuyas crines altaneras
Flotan al viento ligeras,
Lo cruza cual torbellino,
Y pasa; o su toldería
Sobre la grama frondosa
Asienta, esperando el día
Duerme, tranquila reposa,
Sigue veloz su camino.

¡Cuántas, cuántas maravillas,
Sublimes y a par sencillas,
Sembró la fecunda mano
De Dios allí! ¡Cuánto arcano
Que no es dado al mundo ver!
La humilde yerba, el insecto,

and beast. Anywhere in skies and solitary places known only to God. [Places] only He can fathom.

Sometimes the wandering tribe, on lively colts whose proud manes drift lightly in the wind, cross it like a whirlwind and pass; or site their camp on the luxuriant grass, sleep, await day in quiet repose, then continue quickly on their way.

How many, many marvels, sublime and at the same time simple, did the fertile hand of God scatter there! How many secrets not given to the world to see! The humble weed; the insect; the

La aura aromática y pura;
El silencio, el triste aspecto
De la grandiosa llanura,
El pálido anochecer.

. . . .

El crepúsculo, entretanto,
Con su claroscuro manto,
Veló la tierra; una faja,
Negra como una mortaja,
El occidente cubrió;
Mientras la noche bajando
Lenta venía, la calma
Que contempla suspirando,
Inquieta a veces el alma,
Con el silencio reinó.

Entonces, como el ruido,
Que suele hacer el tronido
Cuando retumba lejano,
Se oyó en el tranquilo llano
Sordo y confuso clamor;
Se perdió . . . y luego violento,
Como baladro espantoso

pure and aromatic breeze. The silence; the sad aspect of the great plain; the pale dusk.

. . . .

Meanwhile the twilight veiled the earth with its mantle of light and shade; a black sash like a shroud covered the west. While night was slowly descending, the calm, sighing in contemplation, sometimes with anxious soul, reigned with the silence.

Then, like the noise sometimes made by thunder rumbling in the distance, a muffled and confused clamour was heard amid the quiet plain; it dwindled . . . and then violent, like the frightening outcry

De turba inmensa, en el viento
Se dilató sonoroso,
Dando a los brutos pavor.

Bajo la planta sonante
Del ágil potro arrogante
El duro suelo temblaba,
Y envuelto en polvo cruzaba
Como animado tropel,
Velozmente cabalgando;
Víanse lanzas agudas,
Cabezas, crines ondeando,
Y como formas desnudas
De aspecto extraño y cruel.

¿Quién es? ¿Qué insensata turba
Con su alarido perturba
Las calladas soledades
De Dios, do las tempestades
Sólo se oyen resonar?
¿Qué humana planta orgullosa
Se atreve a hollar el desierto
Cuando todo en él reposa?
¿Quién viene seguro puerto
En sus yermos a buscar?

of an immense crowd, spread out sonorously on the wind, making the beasts fearful.

The hard ground trembled beneath the ringing hooves of the agile, haughty colts, and shrouded in dust they crossed, like a vigorous throng, galloping fast. Sharp lances, heads, undulating manes are seen; like naked shapes of strange and cruel aspect.

Who is it? What mad crowd disturbs the silent solitary places of God with its cry? [Places] where the storms alone are heard to sound. What proud human foot dares to trample upon the desert when everything there is at rest? Who comes to seek a safe harbour in its wilderness?

¡Oíd! Ya se acerca el bando
De salvajes, atronando
Todo el campo convecino.
¡Mirad! Como torbellino
Hiende el espacio veloz.
El fiero ímpetu no enfrena
Del bruto que arroja espuma;
Vaga al viento su melena,
Y con ligereza suma
Pasa en ademán atroz.

¿Dónde va? ¿De dónde viene?
¿De qué su gozo proviene?
¿Por qué grita, corre, vuela,
Clavando al bruto la espuela,
Sin mirar alrededor?
¡Ved que las puntas ufanas
De sus lanzas, por despojos,
Llevan cabezas humanas,
Cuyos inflamados ojos
Respiran aún furor!

Así el bárbaro hace ultraje
Al indomable coraje

Listen! Now the band of savages draws near making the surrounding countryside tremble. See! Like a rapid whirlwind they cut through the air. They do not restrain the fierce rush of the beasts that spray out spume. Their hair flies in the wind, and with terrible gesture they pass speedily by.

Where are they going? Where do they come from? From what do they derive their joy? Why do they shout, run, fly, spurring on the beasts without looking round? See how for spoils the proud points of the lances carry human heads whose swollen eyes still breathe fury!

Thus the barbarian shows contempt for the indomitable courage

Que abatió su alevosía;
Y su rencor todavía
Mira, con torpe placer,
Las cabezas que cortaron
Sus inhumanos cuchillos,
Exclamando: – «Ya pagaron
Del cristiano los caudillos
El feudo a nuestro poder.

Ya los ranchos do vivieron
Presa de las llamas fueron,
Y muerde el polvo abatida
Su pujanza tan erguida.
¿Dónde sus bravos están?
Vengan hoy del vituperio,
Sus mujeres, sus infantes,
Que gimen en cautiverio,
A libertad, y como antes,
Nuestras lanzas probarán».

Tal decía, y bajo el callo
Del indómito caballo,
Crujiendo el suelo temblaba;

that his treachery overthrew, and his anger still looks with dull pleasure at the heads cut off by his inhuman knives, exclaiming: 'The leaders of the Christians have already paid tribute to our might.

'Already the huts where they lived have been the prey of flames and their once proud might, overthrown, now bites the dust. Where are their warriors? Should their women and children, now groaning in captivity, today be freed, they will taste our lances as before.'

Thus he spoke, and beneath the shoe of the indomitable horse the ground trembled and creaked. His cry rumbled, hollow and

Hueco y sordo retumbaba
Su grito en la soledad.
Mientras la noche, cubierto
El rostro en manto nubloso,
Echó en el vasto desierto,
Su silencio pavoroso,
Su sombría majestad.

muffled in the solitude. While the night, its face wrapped in a cloudy mantle, spread over the desert its fearful silence, its sombre majesty.

JOSÉ HERNÁNDEZ (1834–86)

from *Martín Fierro*

SOY gaucho, y entiendanló
Como mi lengua lo esplica –
Para mí la tierra es chica
Y pudiera ser mayor –
Ni la víbora me pica
Ni quema mi frente el Sol.

Nací como nace el peje
En el fondo de la mar –
Naides me puede quitar
Aquello que Dios me dió –
Lo que al mundo truje yo
Del mundo lo he de llevar.

Mi gloria es vivir tan libre
Como el pájaro del Cielo,
No hago nido en este suelo
Ande hay tanto que sufrir;
Y naides me ha de seguir
Cuando yo remonto el vuelo.

from *Martín Fierro*

I AM a gaucho, and let it be understood the way I tell it. For me the world is small, and could be bigger. The viper doesn't sting me, nor the sun burn my forehead.

I was born as a fish is born in the bottom of the sea. No one can take from me what God gave me. What I brought into the world I will also take away with me.

My glory is to live as free as the birds in the sky. I make no nest on this earth where there is so much to be suffered, and nobody will be able to follow me when I take flight again.

Yo no tengo en el amor
Quien me venga con querellas,
Como esas aves tan bellas
Que saltan de rama en rama –
Yo hago en el trébol mi cama
Y me cubren las estrellas.

Y sepan cuantos escuchan
De mis penas el relato,
Que nunca peleo ni mato
Sinó por necesidá;
Y que a tanta alversidá
Sólo me arrojó el mal trato.

Y atiendan la relación
Que hace un gaucho perseguido,
Que padre y marido ha sido
Empeñoso y diligente,
Y sin embargo la gente
Lo tiene por un bandido.

I have no one to love who will quarrel with me, like those birds that are so beautiful, jumping from branch to branch – I make my bed in the clover and the stars cover me.

And all of you who listen shall know the story of my sorrows, that I never quarrel, nor kill, except when it's needed; and that only bad treatment threw me into such adversity.

And hear the story of a persecuted gaucho, who has been a careful and attentive father and husband, and yet is still thought of by people as a bandit.

LEOPOLDO LUGONES (1874–1938)

Plegaria de carnaval

OH luna que diriges como *sportswoman* sabia
Por zodíacos y eclípticas tu lindo cabriolé:
Bajo la ardiente seda de tu cielo de Arabia,
Oh luna, buena luna, quién fuera tu Josué.

Sin cesar encantara tu blancura mi tienda,
Con desnudez tan noble que la agraviara el tul;
O extasiado en un pálido antaño de leyenda,
Tu integridad de novia perpetuara el azul.

Luna de los ensueños, sobre la tarde lila
Tu oro viejo difunde morosa enfermedad,
Cuando en un solitario confín de mar tranquila,
Sondeas como lúgubre garza la eternidad.

En tu mística nieve baña sus pies María,
Tu disco reproduce la mueca de Arlequín,
Crimen y amor componen la hez de tu poesía
Embriagadora y pálida como el vino del Rhin.

A Carnival Prayer

OH moon, driving your fine cabriolet like a wise sportswoman through zodiacs and ecliptics beneath the burning silk of your Arabian sky, oh moon, good moon, who might your Joshua be.

Ceaselessly your whiteness enchanted my tent with a nakedness so noble that tulle would mar it; oh, carried away in a pale legendary yesteryear, your bridal integrity will perpetuate the blue.

Moon of illusions, above the lilac evening your old gold spreads slow sickness, when at a solitary limit of the tranquil sea you fathom eternity like a lugubrious heron.

In your mystical snows Mary bathes her feet. Your disc mimics Harlequin's grimace. Crime and love comprise the dregs of your poetry, as intoxicating and pale as Rhine wine.

Y toda esta alta fama con que elogiando vengo
Tu faz sietemesina de bebé en alcohol,
Los siglos te la cuentan como ilustre abolengo,
Porque tú eres, oh, luna, la máscara del sol.

Nocturno

I

EN la ribera
De la laguna,
Sale la luna
De primavera.

Derrama su orto
Sutil topacio
Por el espacio
Tibio y absorto.

Un vago cirro
De medio luto,
Le da un astuto
Ceño de esbirro.

And the centuries recount all this high fame with which I come in praise of your premature face, like a baby in alcohol, as your illustrious heritage; for you are, oh moon, the mask of the sun.

Nocturne

ON the banks of the lagoon the spring moon rises.

Its rising spreads a subtle topaz through space warm and lost in thought.

A vague cirrus, in half mourning, gives it the shrewd frown of a servant.

Blancor de polo
Su disco ampara
Como una cara
Que ardió el vitriolo.

En los jirones
De la tiniebla
Traza y amuebla
Largos salones;

Donde con yerros
De vano alarde,
Hasta muy tarde
Ladran los perros.

Adagio

OH, carbón del delirio que, en morosa
Desolación, los párpados enluta:
Frase de teclas negras que transmuta
El suspiro en celeste mariposa:

Whiteness of the pole, its disc shelters like a face burned by vitriol.

In the tatters of the mist it traces and furnishes long drawing-rooms;

Where with the faults of vain boasting the dogs howl until very late.

Adagio

OH, [you] coal of delirium that in slow desolation puts the eyelids into mourning; phrase of black notes that transforms the sigh into a heavenly butterfly;

Sabor de húmedos pétalos de rosa,
Que embriaga de frescor la boca enjuta:
Ingenua dicha de perder la ruta
Por encontrar los labios de la Esposa:

Temas de amor, si estás de manifiesto
Lo pálido y dichoso que me han puesto,
Mi humilde flauta a su alabanza obligo.

Y en la tarde, al bogar de la piragua,
Con un dedo pueril rayando el agua,
Mi dulce bien los cantará conmigo.

El lucero

SOBRE la nave temprana
Que surca la onda serena,
Va meciéndose en la entena
La estrella de la mañana.

El mar, entre vagos tules,
Con suavísimo desmayo,
Parece abrir en su rayo
Sus torvas cejas azules.

Taste of moist rose petals that intoxicates the arid mouth with freshness; naïve happiness in losing one's way, to find the lips of the Wife;

Themes of love, if you are aware of how pale and happy they have made me, my humble flute will sing in praise.

And in the evening, as the piragua sails, marking the water with a childlike finger, my sweetheart will sing them with me.

The Morning Star

OVER the early ship that furrows the serene wave the morning star swings in the lateen yard.

The sea, amid vague nets, seems to open in its track its stern blue brows with a very gentle swoon.

Y aquietando su hondo afán,
Como tu amor en mi vida,
La estrella cae dormida
En el seno del titán.

La granizada

SOBRE el repicado cinc del cobertizo,
Y el patio que, densa, la siesta calcina,
En el turbio vértigo de la ventolina
Ríen los sonoros dientes del granizo.

Ríen y se comen la viña y la huerta,
Rechiflan el vidrio que frágil tirita,
Y escupen chisguetes de saltada espita
Por algún medroso resquicio de puerta.

Junto al marco rústico, donde pía en vano,
Refúgiase un pollo largo y escurrido.
Volcado en el suelo yace un pobre nido.
En el agua boya la flor de manzano.

And, soothing its deep anxiety, the star falls asleep in the bosom of the titan, like your love in my life.

The Hailstorm

IN the turbid vortex of the gale, the sonorous teeth of the hail laugh on the ringing metal roof of the shelter, and on the patio that the dense siesta burns.

They laugh and they eat the vineyard and the orchard, jeering and hissing on the fragile trembling glass, spitting water from jumping spigots through timid crevices of the door.

By the rustic frame, a thin and drenched chicken shelters, clucking in vain. Fallen on the ground lies a poor nest. On the water floats the flower of the apple-tree.

Con frescor de páramo el chubasco azota.
Cenizas de estaño la nube condensa.
Y al lúgubre fondo de la pampa inmensa,
Desgreñados sauces huyen en derrota.

With the freshness of the paramo the squall lashes. The cloud drips leaden ashes. Dishevelled willow-trees fly in defeat towards the lugubrious depths of the immense pampa.

BALDOMERO FERNÁNDEZ MORENO
(1886–1950)

Dalmira

Tu nombre es terso, claro, deslumbrante,
como la hoja desnuda de una espada.
En el aire se aguza como el aire
y en el agua se estría como el agua.

Para ser suspirado entre palmeras,
al fondo del harén, a una sultana,
entre un rebaño pálido de eunucos
y el brillo corvo de las cimitarras.

Soneto

No hay nada comparable a este momento
matinal, indeciso, solitario,
en que tu propia sábana es sudario,
borda tu lecho el agua y firmamento.

Dalmira

Your name is smooth, bright, dazzling, like the naked blade of a sword. In the air it is sharpened like the air, and in the water it is grooved like the water.

To be sighed amid palm-trees, in the depths of the harem, to a sultana, amid a pale flock of eunuchs and the curved brilliance of the scimitars.

Sonnet

There is nothing to compare with this morning moment, indecisive, solitary, when your own sheet is a shroud; water and sky the embroidery of your bed.

Sólo falta la bala, sólo el lento
empujón hacia el mar único y vario,
e irse al fondo del eterno acuario,
por un sendero vertical de viento.

Y mientras vuela el barco tras su puerto
entre espumas y nubes de colores,
permanecer en los abismos, muerto.

No más correr tras ilusorias flores,
sino aspirar la de un coral abierto:
candelabro de rojos resplandores.

All it needs is the bullet, only the slow push towards the unique and various sea, and to go into the depths of the eternal aquarium by a vertical path of wind.

And while the ship flies after its port among foam and coloured clouds to remain in the depths, dead.

No longer to run after illusory flowers, but to wish for that of an open coral; candelabra of red splendours.

ENRIQUE BANCHS (1888-1968)

Diminuto dolor

FUERON un tiempo mi apagada suerte
diminuto dolor, dicha menuda:
la vida a un lado me dejó, sin duda;
sin duda, a un lado me dejó la muerte . . .

Temí esa paz que sordamente anuda
el nervio fino más vibrante y fuerte;
temí que el alma, poco a poco inerte,
se me quedara para siempre muda.

Pero el silencio, roto apenas, era
acecho inmóvil de escondida fiera . .
Saltó de pronto en la callada ruta

y supe entonces del vivir bravío,
tanto, que ahora solamente ansío
dolor menudo y dicha diminuta.

A Small Pain

ONCE my dull luck was a small pain, a small happiness: life left me on one side, without doubt; without doubt death left me on one side . . .

I feared that peace that secretly knots the most vibrant and strongest fine nerve: I feared that my soul, more and more inert, would remain silent for ever.

But the silence, scarcely broken, was the motionless lurking of a hidden beast. . . . [It] jumped suddenly onto the silent path.

And then I learned so much of untamed living, that now all I wish for is a small pain and a small happiness.

Veterrima laurus

MUERTA suntuosidad, marchitos oros,
púrpura desteñida, pompa inmota,
corona seca en la columna rota
del templo solo, silenciosos foros;

parques que el olifante hizo sonoros,
caída estatua en la que puso cota
sombría el musgo, pátina que embota
el brillo agudo en bruma de tesoros:

Morada son dilecta de mi alma
que, alumna secular, prefiere ruinas
próceres, a la de hoy menguada palma,

y pliega, entre el fragor de vanos vientos,
las inútiles alas aquilinas
en las cenizas de los monumentos.

Veterrima Laurus

DEAD luxury, faded golds, discoloured purple, unmoved pomp, dry crown on the broken column of the lonely temple, silent forums;

Parks that the oliphant made resound, fallen statue on which moss formed as a dark coat of mail, patina that dulls the sharp brilliance in the haze of riches;

These are the favourite dwellings of my soul – a secular pupil preferring lofty ruins to the waning palm of today,

And folding its useless aquiline wings amid the clamour of vain winds in the ashes of the monuments.

OLIVERIO GIRONDO (1891–1965)

Café-concierto

LAS notas del pistón describen trayectorias de cohete, vacilan en el aire, se apagan antes de darse contra el suelo.

Salen unos ojos pantanosos, con mal olor, unos dientes podridos por el dulzor de las romanzas, unas piernas que hacen humear el escenario.

La mirada del público tiene más densidad y más calorías que cualquier otra, es una mirada corrosiva que atraviesa las mallas y apergamina la piel de las artistas.

Hay un grupo de marineros encandilados ante el faro que un «maquereau» tiene en el dedo meñique, una reunión de prostitutas con el relente a puerto, un inglés que fabrica niebla con sus pupilas y su pipa.

La camarera me trae, en una bandeja lunar, sus senos semidesnudos ... , unos senos que me llevaría para

Café-Concert

THE notes of the trumpet describe a rocket's flight, they vacillate in the air, they go out before they thud on the floor.

Swampy eyes with a bad smell emerge, teeth rotted by the sweetness of romances legs that make the scenery smoke.

The public's look has more calories and is denser than any other; it is a corrosive look that goes through tights and dries up the skin of the artistes.

There is a group of dazzled sailors in front of the lamp that a *maquereau* wears on his little finger, a meeting of prostitutes with the slyness of the port, an Englishman who manufactures fog with the pupils of his eyes and his pipe.

The waitress brings me, on a lunary tray, her half-naked breasts

calentarme los pies cuando me acueste.

El telón, al cerrarse, simula un telón entreabierto.

from *Espantapájaros*

18

LLORAR a lágrima viva. Llorar a chorros. Llorar la digestión. Llorar el sueño. Llorar ante las puertas y los puertos. Llorar de amabilidad y de amarillo.

Abrir las canillas, las compuertas del llanto. Empaparnos el alma, la camiseta. Inundar las veredas y los paseos, y salvarnos, a nado, de nuestro llanto.

Asistir a los cursos de antropología, llorando. Festejar los cumpleaños familiares, llorando. Atravesar el África, llorando.

Llorar como un cacuy, como un cocodrilo ... si es verdad que los cacuies y los cocodrilos no dejan nunca de llorar.

Llorarlo todo, pero llorarlo bien. Llorarlo con la

... breasts that I would take with me to keep my feet warm when I go to bed.

The curtain, when it closes, pretends to be a half-open curtain.

from *Scarecrow*

TO weep with a lively tear. To weep in floods. To weep of digestion. To weep the dream. To weep before doors and ports. To weep of kindness and yellowness.

To open the taps, the floodgates of tears. To drench the soul, the vest. To flood the paths and the avenues and to save ourselves, by swimming, from our tears.

To attend courses in anthropology crying. To celebrate family birthdays crying. To cross Africa crying.

To cry like a cacuy, like a crocodile ... if it is true that cacuys and crocodiles never stop crying.

To weep over everything, but to weep well. To weep with the

nariz, con las rodillas. Llorarlo por el ombligo, por la boca.

Llorar de amor, de hastío, de alegría. Llorar de frac, de flato, de flacura. Llorar improvisando, de memoria. ¡Llorar todo el insomnio y todo el día!

nose, with the knees. To weep through the navel, through the mouth.

To weep of love, of tediousness, of happiness. To weep of [in] a tail-coat, of wind, of skinniness. To weep improvising, or by heart. To weep all through insomnia and all through the day!

EZEQUIEL MARTÍNEZ ESTRADA (1895–1964)

Cuarto menguante

UN descender de araña por su hilo,
una provecta calma;
hacer del alma
un asilo.

Indiferencia, tal vez;
la vida, un filosofema,
o cuando más un problema
de ajedrez.

Las virtudes del hogar
que cualquier aire constipa;
el corazón en la pipa
de soñar.

La noche mejor que el día;
naipes, charla, tilo, coca,
pantuflas y risa y boca
de alcancía.

Last Quarter

A SPIDER descending its web, a mature calm; out of the soul is made a shelter.

Indifference, perhaps; life, a philosophism, or at best a chess problem.

The domestic virtues that catch a chill from the slightest draught; the heart in the pipe of dreams.

Rather night than day; cards, a chat, a brew of linden-leaves, coca, slippers and smiles and a mouth of a money-box.

Un poco – poco – de tedio,
la animalidad aterida.
Lo normal (que es la caída
sin remedio).

Infinidad y eternidad

CIERRO los ojos a la Ciencia y la Experiencia
y veo el infinito como una línea recta
que termina en el mismo lugar en que comienza,
pues infinito y línea son la circunferencia.

No hay espacio, ni tiempo, ni más que algo, si hay algo,
ni hay nada que se mueva, como pensaba Heráclito;
yo soy, tú eres y él es esto o aquello, es claro,
pero qué cosa somos no lo sabe ni el diablo.
Lo infinito y lo eterno son fantasmas de aire
de que han hablado muchos sin comprenderlos nadie.
Trataré de explicarlos con prudente lenguaje:
ayer soñé que estaba por emprender un viaje.

A little – little – tedium, numbed animal qualities. The normal thing (which is the inevitable fall).

Infinity and Eternity

I CLOSE my eyes to Science and Experience and I see the infinite as a straight line that finishes exactly where it began, for infinity and line are the circumference.

There is neither time, nor space, nor more than something, if there is something; there is nothing that moves itself, as Heraclitus thought; I am, you are, and he is this or that – that's obvious. But not even the devil knows what we are. The infinite and the eternal are phantoms of air about whom many have spoken, though none have understood. I shall try to explain them in careful language: yesterday I dreamed that I was about to start on a journey.

RICARDO E. MOLINARI (b. 1898)

Una rosa para Stefan George

(*Similis factus sum pellicano solitudinis*)

No es la paciencia de la sangre la que llega a morir,
ni el sueño ni el mármol de Delfos, sino el polvo
que se calienta entre las uñas.
Qué importa morir, que se borren las paredes como un
 río seco;
que no quede una flor en la calle con su borde de luto
 en la frente,
ni el viento sobre las piedras podridas.

Qué haces allí, tronchado sin humedad,
con tu dicha sin aliento, con tu muerte tendida a los pies.
Con tu espuma llena de ceniza. Desdeñoso.

Ya vendrían los hombres con el ruido, con los gestos;
pero el odio seguirá intacto.

A Rose for Stefan George

It is not the patience of the blood that finally dies, nor the dream, nor the marble of Delphi, but the dust that grows hot between the nails. What does it matter to die, [what does it matter] if the walls disappear like a dry river; if not one single flower with a fringe of mourning on its forehead is left in the street; if the wind does not blow over the rotting stones.

What are you doing there, cut off and waterless, with your breathless joy, with your death stretched out at your feet. With your froth full of ash. Disdainful.

Men would then come with their noise, their gestures; but the hate will remain intact.

Todos te habrían estrechado la mano alguna vez,
y tú habrás bebido la cicuta en la soledad,
como un vaso de leche.

Adiós país de nieve, de ventisca agria, sin gentes que digan mal
de ti. Eterno. Desnudo.

La sangre metida en su canal de hielo
– fuego sin aire – Jordán perdido. Si el tiempo tuviera sentido
como el Sol y la Luna presos;
si fuera útil vivir,
si fuera necesario,
qué hermoso espanto: tengo la voluntad avergonzada.

Yo soy menos feliz que tú. Me quedo combatiendo sin honor,
con un haz de ramas en las manos.

Duerme. Dormir para siempre es bueno, junto al mar;
los ríos secos debajo de la tierra con su rosa de sangre muerta.

Everyone would have shaken your hand at some time, and you will have drunk the hemlock in solitude, like a glass of milk.

Farewell, land of snow, of bitter storms, with none who speak ill of you. Eternal. Naked.

Blood filled into its channel of ice – fire without air – lost Jordan. If time made sense like the imprisoned sun and moon; if living were of use, if it were necessary, what a beautiful fright: I have an ashamed will.

I am less happy than you. I am left to fight without honour, with a bunch of twigs in my hands.

Sleep. It is good to sleep for ever, next to the sea; the dry rivers underground with their rose of dead blood.

Duerme, lujo triste, en tu desierto solo.

¡Esta palabra inútil!

Sleep, sad luxury, in your deserted solitude.
This useless word!

JORGE LUIS BORGES (b. 1899)

Amorosa anticipación

Ni la intimidad de tu frente clara como una fiesta
ni la privanza de tu cuerpo, aún misterioso y tácito y de
  niña,
ni la sucesión de tu vida situándose en palabras o aca-
  llamiento
serán favor tan persuasivo de ideas
como el mirar tu sueño implicado
en la vigilia de mis ávidos brazos.
Virgen milagrosamente otra vez por la virtud absolutoria
  del sueño,
quieta y resplandeciente como una dicha en la selección
  del recuerdo,
me darás esa orilla de tu vida que tú misma no tienes.
Arrojado a quietud,
divisaré esa playa última de tu ser
y te veré por vez primera quizás,
como Dios ha de verte,
desbaratada la ficción del Tiempo,
sin el amor, sin mí.

Amorous Anticipation

Neither the intimacy of your forehead as light as a holiday, nor the favour at the court of your body, still mysterious and tacit as that of a young girl, nor the progress of your life placed in words or in quietness will be as persuasive a gift of ideas as watching you sleep tangled in the vigil of my avid arms. Miraculously again a virgin, through the absolving virtue of sleep, still and shining like a joy selected by memory, you will give me that margin of your life that you yourself do not have. Thrown into rest, I will perceive that final shore of your being and I will see you, perhaps for the first time, as God sees you, the fiction of Time broken, without love, without me.

La noche cíclica

A Sylvina Bullrich

LO supieron los arduos alumnos de Pitágoras:
Los astros y los hombres vuelven cíclicamente;
Los átomos fatales repetirán la urgente
Afrodita de oro, los tebanos, las ágoras.

En edades futuras oprimirá el centauro
Con el casco solípedo el pecho del lapita;
Cuando Roma sea polvo, gemirá en la infinita
Noche de su palacio fétido el minotauro.

Volverá toda noche de insomnio: minuciosa.
La mano que esto escribe renacerá del mismo
Vientre. Férreos ejércitos construirán el abismo.
(El filólogo Nietzsche dijo la misma cosa.)

No sé si volveremos en un ciclo segundo
Como vuelven las cifras de una fracción periódica;
Pero sé que una oscura rotación pitagórica
Noche a noche me deja en un lugar del mundo

The Cyclical Night

THE arduous pupils of Pythagoras knew it: stars and men return in cycles: the fatal atoms will repeat the urgent golden Aphrodite, the Thebans, the agoras.

In future times the centaur will oppress the Lapithaean's breast with his soliped hoof; when Rome has come to dust the minotaur will moan in the infinite night of its fetid palace.

Every sleepless night will return, meticulously. The hand that writes this will be born again from the same womb. Iron armies will build the abyss. (The philologist Nietzsche said the same thing.)

I don't know if we will return in a second cycle, as the figures in a periodic fraction return. But I know that an obscure Pythagorean rotation leaves me, night after night, somewhere in the world

Que es de los arrabales. Una esquina remota
Que puede ser del norte, del sur o del oeste,
Pero que tiene siempre una tapia celeste,
Una higuera sombría y una vereda rota.

Ahí está Buenos Aires. El tiempo que a los hombres
Trae el amor o el oro, a mí apenas me deja
Esta rosa apagada, esta vana madeja
De calles que repiten los pretéritos nombres

De mi sangre: Laprida, Cabrera, Soler, Suárez . . .
Nombres en que retumban (ya secretas) las dianas,
Las repúblicas, los caballos y las mañanas,
Las felices victorias, las muertes militares.

Las plazas agravadas por la noche sin dueño
Son los patios profundos de un árido palacio
Y las calles unánimes que engendran el espacio.
Son corredores de vago miedo y de sueño.

Vuelve la noche cóncava que descifró Anaxágoras;
Vuelve a mi carne humana la eternidad constante

Which is in the outskirts. A remote street corner that could be in the north, or in the south, or in the west, but that always has a sky-blue mud-wall, a sombre fig-tree and a broken path.

There is Buenos Aires. Time, that brings love or gold to men, only leaves me this worn-out rose, this useless skein of streets that repeat the past names

Of my ancestors. Laprida, Cabrera, Solar, Suárez . . . names in which resound (now secretly) reveilles, republics, horses and mornings, joyful victories, military deaths.

The squares overwhelmed by the masterless night are the deep patios of an arid palace and the unanimous streets that give birth to space. They are corridors of vague fear and dream.

The concave night that Anaxagoras interpreted returns. The constant eternity returns to my human flesh and the memory – the

Y el recuerdo ¿el proyecto? de un poema incesante:
«Lo supieron los arduos alumnos de Pitágoras . . . »

Poema conjetural

El doctor Francisco Laprida, asesinado el día 22 de setiembre de 1829 por los montoneros de Aldao, piensa antes de morir:

ZUMBAN las balas en la tarde última.
Hay viento y hay cenizas en el viento,
se dispersan el día y la batalla
deforme, y la victoria es de los otros.
Vencen los bárbaros, los gauchos vencen.
Yo, que estudié las leyes y los cánones,
yo, Francisco Narciso de Laprida,
cuya voz declaró la independencia
de estas crueles provincias, derrotado,
de sangre y de sudor manchado el rostro,
sin esperanza ni temor, perdido,
huyo hacia el Sur por arrabales últimos.
Como aquel capitán del Purgatorio
que, huyendo a pie y ensangrentando el llano,
fue cegado y tumbado por la muerte

plan? – of an incessant poem: 'The arduous pupils of Pythagoras knew it . . .'

Conjectural Poem

Doctor Francisco Laprida, murdered on 22 September 1829 by the guerrillas of Aldao, thinks, before he dies:

THE bullets hum on the last evening. It is windy and there are ashes in the wind; the day and the shapeless battle are dispersing and the victory belongs to the others. The barbarians are the victors, victory belongs to the gauchos. I, who studied the laws and the canons, I, Francisco Narciso de Laprida, whose voice declared the independence of these cruel provinces, defeated, my face stained with blood and sweat, without hope or fear, lost, I flee southwards through the last suburbs. Like that captain of [Dante's] *Purgatório* who, escaping on foot and leaving his blood on the plain, was blinded and thrown to

donde un oscuro río pierde el nombre,
así habré de caer. Hoy es el término.
La noche lateral de los pantanos
me acecha y me demora. Oigo los cascos
de mi caliente muerte que me busca.
Yo que anhelé ser otro, ser un hombre
de sentencias, de libros, de dictámenes,
a cielo abierto yaceré entre ciénagas;
pero me endiosa el pecho inexplicable
un júbilo secreto. Al fin me encuentro
con mi destino sudamericano.
A esta ruinosa tarde me llevaba
el laberinto múltiple de pasos
que mis días tejieron desde un día
de la niñez. Al fin he descubierto
la recóndita clave de mis años,
la suerte de Francisco de Laprida,
la letra que faltaba, la perfecta
forma que supo Dios desde el principio.
En el espejo de esta noche alcanzo
mi insospechado rostro eterno. El círculo
se va a cerrar. Yo aguardo que así sea.

the ground by death at that point where an obscure river loses its name; I shall fall in the same manner. Today is the end. The lateral night of the swamps lies in wait for me, delays me. I hear the hooves of my hot death searching for me. I, who dreamed of being someone else, a man of judgements, of books, of opinions, shall lie among bogs under the open sky; but a secret jubilation inexplicably elates my breast. At last I find myself with my South American destiny. The multiple labyrinth of steps that my days have woven since one childhood day has brought me to this ruinous evening. At last I have discovered the recondite key to my years, the fortune of Francisco de Laprida, the missing letter, the perfect form that God knew from the beginning. In the mirror of this night I have caught up with my unsuspected eternal face. The circle is going to close. I am

Pisan mis pies las sombras de las lanzas
que me buscan. Las befas de mi muerte,
los jinetes, las crines, los caballos,
se ciernen sobre mí . . . Ya el primer golpe,
ya el duro hierro que me raja el pecho,
el íntimo cuchillo en la garganta.

waiting for this to happen. The shadows of the lances that seek me are treading on my feet. The tauntings of my death, the riders, the manes, the horses, they hover over me. . . . Now the first blow, now the hard steel that cleaves my breast, the intimate knife in my throat.

ENRIQUE MOLINA (b. 1910)

La vida prenatal

ERA el corazón de mi madre
Aquel tan-tan de las tinieblas
Aquel tambor sobre mi cráneo
En las membranas de la tierra

(La lenta piragua materna
Un ritmo de espumas en viaje
Una seda de grandes aguas
Donde un suave trópico late)

Día y noche su ceremonia
– No había día ni había noche –
Sólo un hondo país de esponjas
Toda una tribu de tambores

El corazón de un sol orgánico
Un ronco sueño de tejidos
Yo era la magia y era el ídolo
En el fondo de las montañas

Life Before Birth

IT was my mother's heart, that boom-boom in the dark regions, that drum above my skull in the membranes of the earth.

(The slow maternal piragua, a rhythm of foam on a journey, silk of high waters where a gentle tropic throbs.)

Day and night its ritual – there was neither day, nor night – only a deep country of sponges, a whole tribe of drums,

The heart of an organic sun, a raucous dream of textures, I was the magic and I was the idol deep in the mountains,

Aquel tambor donde golpeaban
Las galaxias y las mareas
Aquella sangre germinada
Por el vino de la Odisea

Vivir en un huevo de llamas
Mezclando la tierra y el cielo
Vivir en el centro del mundo
Sin rostro ni odio ni tiempo

Crecía antiguo en la dulzura
Con astrales ojos de musgo
Yo era un germen lleno de estrellas
Un poder oscuro y terrible

Tu corazón – ¡oh madre mía! –
Resonaba como el océano
Batía sus alas salvajes
Su insaciable tambor de fuego

Yo te besaba en las entrañas
Yo me dormía entre tus sueños
En un país de rojas plumas
Era tu carne y tu destierro

That drum where galaxies and tides were beating, that blood germinated by the wine of the Odyssey.

To live in an egg of flames, mixing earth and heaven, to live at the centre of the world with no face, nor hate, nor time.

I was growing old wise in sweetness, with starry eyes of moss, I was a seed full of stars, an obscure and terrible power.

Your heart – oh mother! – resounded like the ocean, beat its savage wings, its insatiable drum of fire,

I kissed you in your womb, I fell asleep amidst your dreams, in a country of red feathers I was your flesh and your exile,

El paraíso de tu sangre
La gran promesa de tus brazos
Oía al sol en su corriente:
Tu corazón lleno de pájaros

Aquel tambor de la aventura
Aquel tambor de luna viva
La tierra ardiendo con su grito
Una vida desconocida

Afuera todo era enemigo:
Las uñas las voces el frío
Los días las rosas las uvas
El viento la luz el olvido

The paradise of your blood, the great promise of your arms, I heard the sun in its flow: your heart full of birds,

That drum of adventure, that drum of the living moon, the earth blazing with its cry, an unknown life.

Outside everything was the enemy: the fingernails, the voices, the cold, the days, the roses, the grapes, the wind, the light, the forgetfulness.

EDGAR BAYLEY (b. 1919)

cuestión de tiempo

CUESTIÓN de tiempo quizás
de andar en trenes
de encontrar a la luz del sol
la guerra y la paz
el camino que lleva al hermano
al enemigo
cuestión de tiempo
la música vendrá
un tribunal enjuiciará tu miedo tu pobreza
y otro mañana de distinto modo
al vagabundo que se extravía balbuceando
el idioma que hablarán los hombres
cuestión de tiempo
colonizadores de la riqueza y la claridad
en todos hablará el difícil amor
la transparencia
pero siempre el vértigo
extenderá sombras sobre los senderos
abrirá cielos sobre las voces y el silencio
y hombres solos

A Question of Time

A QUESTION of time perhaps, of travelling on trains, of meeting in the light of the sun war and peace, the road that leads to the brother, to the enemy. A question of time, the music will come, a tribunal will judge your fear, your poverty. And another tomorrow in a different way will judge the vagabond who gets lost, stammering the language that men will speak. A question of time, colonizers of richness and clarity, difficult love will speak in all, the transparency. But always vertigo will stretch out shadows over the paths, will open heavens over the voices and the silence; and men alone,

mujeres solas
hablarán sin amparo
sin encontrar la palabra apropiada
el nombre de la noche

la violencia

LA violencia al sofocar el día
al arrojarte fuera del camino
te hace crecer por dentro un diente helado
violencia reina de una madrugada oscura
olvido entre palabras calcinadas

estoy aquí debo comprender
decir correctamente organizar
no ceder posiciones al tumulto

debo salir cruzar no detenerme
compartir otra vez una alegría
venida del más alto corazón
entre los hombres

debo seguir cavar un nuevo surco
buscar buscar la voz del otro
escuchar extender
la morada y el aire

women alone, will speak without protection, without finding the appropriate word, the name of the night.

Violence

VIOLENCE, on choking the day, on flinging you out of the way, makes an icy tooth grow inside you. Violence, queen of an obscure dawn, oblivion among burnt words.

I am here, I have to understand, to say correctly, to organize, to yield no positions to the tumult.

I have to go out, to cross over, not hold myself back, to share a happiness come from the highest heart of man.

I have to go on, to dig a new groove, to search for the voice of the other, to listen, to stretch out the mansion and the air.

ALBERTO GIRRI (b. 1919)

Mutación

DE la madurez
que la piadosa noche
concede
pasamos a la ligereza;

del fervor
y gozo del silencio,
a la sequedad
del sol en alto.

Y lo que en tinieblas
fue petición a Nuestra Señora
cae
en el remolino del tiempo,
allí
donde siempre se usa mal
lo que se quiere recibir.

Mutation

FROM the maturity that the pitying night concedes, we pass on to lightness;

From the fervour and joy of silence to the dryness of the high sun.

And that which in darkness was a plea to Our Lady falls in the whirlwind of time, there, where what one wanted to receive is always put to bad use.

Sperlonga

Es
una corrupción del latín spelunca,
significa cueva, caverna,
cavidad natural
entre el mar y la montaña,
refugio
de los que traían y llevaban
las guerras, la política,
las religiones extrañas,
las intrigas por celos,
el oprobio
de arrastrar una figura
alta en exceso, un rostro
manchado rabiosamente.
Estaba allí, en la entrada,
como un estandarte,
y a la luz de la luna
lo miré en sus ojos
olvidándome del lado negro,
de Suetonio,
y comprendí
que no era un muerto el que volvía,
sino un destino, su parte
en el drama del mundo condenado,

Sperlonga

It is a corruption of the Latin *spelunca*, meaning a cave, a cavern, a natural cavity between sea and mountain, a refuge for those who dealt in wars, politics, foreign religions, jealous intrigues, the stigma of dragging down an excessively high figure, a rabidly stained face. He was there, at the entrance, like a banner, and in the light of the moon I looked into his eyes, forgetting the dark side of Suetonius, and I understood that the man who was returning was not a corpse, but a fate, his part in the drama of the world condemned, and my

y mi corazón oyó
la voz quejosa del chacal
hablándole a las rocas, el eco
de veinte centurias:
«El enigma
no soy yo, Tiberio, tercer César,
autoridad legítima y universal
y padre infeliz, asesino
del hijo y del adoptivo,
es la tumba
que increpa desde el Este,
abierta por Pilatos, mi vicario,
abierta todavía».
Ay, siquiera un ademán
debí retenerlo,
pero no me moví, amanecía
sobre Sperlonga, la memoria
recomenzaba su fluir
devorando a los sobrevivientes,
y quise ocultarme del tiempo,
de la tenacidad del arqueólogo
que chapotea,
que arranca a las verdes aguas
la cabeza barbada de Ulises,
pedazos de Ganimedes,

heart heard the complaining voice of the jackal talking to the rocks, the echo of twenty centuries: 'The enigma is not I, Tiberius, third Caesar, legitimate and universal authority, unhappy father, murderer of his son and his adopted son; it is the tomb that rebukes from the east, opened by Pilate, my vicar, and open still.' Oh, I should at least have restrained him with a gesture, but I did not move; the dawn was rising over Sperlonga, memory again began to flow, devouring the survivors, and I tried to hide myself from time, from the tenacity of the archaeologist who dabbles and draws from the green water the bearded head of Ulysses, pieces of Ganymede.

y dormité
hasta encontrar en sueños
el fondo de una gruta,
una toga fosforescente,
una inscripción
no descifrada por los buzos.
AVE CRUZ SANCTA.

And I dozed, until in dreams I found the bottom of a cave, a phosphorescent toga, an inscription undeciphered by the divers. AVE CRUZ SANCTA.

RAÚL GUSTAVO AGUIRRE (b. 1927)

El mutilado

OH verano de criaturas efímeras
verano que confías en mis ojos
verano de los juegos puros de los que van a morir

Ya libre de mi cabeza de hierro
de mis pies sigilosos
y de mis manos hábiles

yo entro en tu casa profunda.

Y bien . . .

Y BIEN: las piedras fueron ya lanzadas
al mar. Las piedras, las palabras, los efímeros
tesoros del espectro. En su mansión
prospera una quietud desconocida
y que da miedo: una quietud sin gestos,
ni artilugios ni extrañas ceremonias
para engañar al gran devorador.

The Mutilated Man

OH summer of ephemeral creatures, summer that trusts in my eyes, summer of the pure games of those about to die.

Free now from my iron head, from my stealthy feet, and from my nimble hands

I enter into the depths of your home.

And So . . .

AND SO: the stones were already thrown into the sea. The stones, the words, the ephemeral treasures of the spectre. In its mansion a terrifying unknown quietude flourishes – a quietude without gestures; neither gadgets nor strange rites with which to cheat the

Y no es la muerte esta quietud: silencio,
pero de la voz nula, detención
de un péndulo fallido, libertad
del que estuvo en el sótano. La puerta
permanece entornada. El sol es nuevo.
Y unos ojos que ven miran el mar.

great devourer. And this quietude is not death: silence – but from a null voice, the stopping of a failed pendulum, freedom of he who dwelt in the cellar. The door remains ajar. The sun is new. And some seeing eyes watch the sea.

BOLIVIA

RICARDO JAIMES FREYRE (1868–1933)

Soneto

PEREGRINA paloma imaginaria
que enardeces los últimos amores
alma de luz, de música y de flores,
peregrina paloma imaginaria.

Vuela sobre la roca solitaria
que baña el mar glacial de los dolores;
haya, a tu paso, un haz de resplandores
sobre la adusta roca solitaria.

Vuela sobre la roca solitaria,
peregrina paloma, ala de nieve
como divina hostia, ala tan leve

como un copo de nieve; ala divina,
copo de nieve, lirio, hostia, neblina,
peregrina paloma imaginaria . . .

Sonnet

WANDERING imaginary dove, kindling the last loves, soul of light, of music, and of flowers . . . wandering imaginary dove.

Fly over the solitary rock washed by the icy sea of sorrows; let there be, at your passing, a radiant beam over the gloomy solitary rock.

Soar over the solitary rock, wandering dove, snowy wing like the sacred host, wing as weightless

As a snowflake; divine wing, snowflake, lily, host, mist . . . wandering imaginary dove . . .

El canto del mal

CANTA Lok en la obscura región desolada,
y hay vapores de sangre en el canto de Lok.
El Pastor apacienta su enorme rebaño de hielo,
que obedece – gigantes que tiemblan – la voz del Pastor.
Canta Lok a los vientos helados que pasan,
y hay vapores de sangre en el canto de Lok.

Densa bruma se cierne. Las olas se rompen
en las rocas abruptas, con sordo fragor.
En su dorso sombrío se mece la barca salvaje
del guerrero de rojos cabellos, huraño y feroz.
Canta Lok a las olas rugientes que pasan,
y hay vapores de sangre en el canto de Lok.

Cuando el himno del hierro se eleva al espacio
y a sus ecos responde siniestro clamor,
y en el foso, sagrado y profundo, la víctima busca,
con sus rígidos brazos tendidos, la sombra del Dios,
canta Lok a la pálida muerte que pasa
y hay vapores de sangre en el canto de Lok.

The Song of Evil

LOKI sings in the desolate dark region, and there are mists of blood in Loki's song. The Shepherd pastures his mighty flock of ice which obeys – giants that tremble – the voice of the Shepherd. Loki sings to the icy winds that pass, and there are mists of blood in Loki's song.

Thick fog is hovering. Waves break on the steep rocks with a deafening roar. On their dark back rocks the wild boat of the red-haired warrior, sullen and fierce. Loki sings to the roaring waves that pass, and there are mists of blood in Loki's song.

When the hymn of iron soars into space, its echo answered by evil clamour, and in the deep hallowed pit the victim seeks, with stiff outstretched arms, the shadow of the God, Loki sings to the chalk-white corpse that passes, and there are mists of blood in Loki's song.

BRAZIL

ANTÔNIO GONÇALVES DIAS (1823–64)

Leito de fôlhas verdes

POR que tardas, Jatir, que tanto a custo
À voz do meu amor moves teus passos?
Da noite a viração, movendo as fôlhas,
Já nos cimos do bosque rumoreja.

Eu sob a copa da mangueira altiva
Nosso leito gentil cobri zelosa
Com mimoso tapiz de fôlhas brandas,
Onde o frouxo luar brinca entre flôres.

Do tamarindo a flor abriu-se, há pouco,
Já solta o bogari mais doce aroma!
Como prece de amor, como estas preces,
No silêncio da noite o bosque exala.

Brilha a lua no céu, brilham estrêlas,
Correm perfumes no correr da brisa,
A cujo influxo mágico respira-se
Um quebranto de amor, melhor que a vida!

Bed of Green Leaves

WHY, Jatir, do you dally, and move your feet so much at the expense of my love's voice? Already the night breeze, rustling the leaves, murmurs in the crests of the woods.

Beneath the crown of the lofty mango tree, I carefully covered our pleasant bed with a tender carpet of soft leaves, where the pale moonlight plays amidst flowers.

A short while ago the flower of the tamarind opened – now the jasmine gives a sweeter aroma! Like a prayer of love, like these prayers, the wood breathes in the silence of the night.

The moon shines in the sky, stars shine, perfumes fly with the breeze, in whose magic flow is breathed a gasp of love, better than life!

A flor que desabrocha ao romper d'alva
Um só giro do sol, não mais, vegeta:
Eu sou aquela flor que espero ainda
Doce raio do sol que me dê vida.

Sejam vales ou montes, lago ou terra,
Onde quer que tu vás, ou dia ou noite,
Vai seguindo após ti meu pensamento;
Outro amor nunca tive: és meu, sou tua!

Meus olhos outros olhos nunca viram,
Não sentiram meus lábios outros lábios,
Nem outras mãos, Jatir, que não as tuas
A arazóia na cinta me apertaram.

Do tamarindo a flor jaz entreaberta,
Já solta o bogari mais doce aroma;
Também meu coração, como estas flôres,
Melhor perfume ao pé da noite exala!

The flower which blooms at dawn lives for one course of the sun alone, no more. I am that flower, still awaiting a sweet ray of sun that gives me life.

Be it through valleys or hills, on water or land, wherever you may go, whether day or night, my thoughts go after you; I have never had another love: you are mine, I am yours!

My eyes have never seen other eyes, my lips have never felt other lips, and no hands but yours, Jatir, have pressed my feather skirt about my waist.

The flower of the tamarind lies half-open, now the jasmine gives a sweeter aroma; and my heart, too, like these flowers, breathes a finer perfume near to the night!

Não me escutas, Jatir! nem tardo acodes
À voz do meu amor, que em vão te chama!
Tupã! lá rompe o sol! do leito inútil
À brisa da manhã sacuda as fôlhas!

A uns anos

No segredo da larva delicada
a borboleta mora,
Antes que veja a luz, que estenda as asas,
Que surja fora!

A flor, antes de abrir-se, se recata;
No botão se resume,
Antes que mostre o colorido esmalte,
Que espalhe o seu perfume.

E a flor e a borboleta, após a aurora
Breve – da curta vida,
Encontram nas manhãs da primavera
A luz do sol querida.

You are not listening to me, Jatir! Nor do you respond even too late to my love's voice, calling you in vain! Tupã!* The sun is breaking through! May the morning breeze brush the leaves from the useless bed!

For a Birthday

In the secrecy of the delicate larva lives the butterfly, before it sees the light, stretches its wings, bursts out!

The flower conceals itself before it opens; it condenses itself inside the bud, before it shows its colourful gloss, scatters its perfume.

And the flower and the butterfly, after the swift dawn of a brief life, meet the beloved light of the sun on spring mornings.

---

* Tupã: Indian name for God of Thunder.

De graças cheia, a delicada virgem
  Da vida no verdor,
Semelha a borboleta melindrosa,
  Semelha a linda flor.

Tudo se alegra e ri em torno dela,
  Tudo respira amor,
Que é a virgem formosa semelhante
  À borboleta e à flor.

Mas para estas o sol breve se esconde,
  Passam prestes os dias;
Enquanto a cada sol e nova quadra
  Tu novas graças crias!

Full of graces, the delicate maiden, in the greenness of life, resembles the tender butterfly, resembles the pretty flower.

All is joyous and laughs about her, all breathes love, for the beautiful maiden is like the butterfly and the flower.

But for these the passing sun hides itself, the days go fast; while with every sun and every new season you bring new graces!

OLAVO BILAC (1865–1918)

In extremis

NUNCA morrer assim! Nunca morrer num dia
Assim! de um sol assim!
Tu, desgrenhada e fria,
Fria! postos nos meus os teus olhos molhados,
E apertando nos teus os meus dedos gelados . . .

E um dia assim! de um sol assim! E assim a esfera
Tôda azul, no esplendor do fim da primavera!
Asas, tontas de luz, cortando o firmamento!
Ninhos cantando! Em flor a terra tôda! O vento
Despencando os rosais, sacudindo o arvoredo . . .

E, aqui dentro, o silêncio . . . E êste espanto! e êste mêdo!
Nós dois . . . e, entre nós dois, implacável e forte,
A arredar-me de ti, cada vez mais, a morte . . .

Eu, com o frio a crescer no coração – tão cheio
De ti, mesmo no horror do derradeiro anseio!
Tu, vendo retorcer-se amarguradamente

In Extremis

NEVER to die like this! Never to die on a day like this! in a sun like this! You, dishevelled and cold, cold! Your damp eyes on my eyes, and my icy fingers squeezing yours . . .

And a day like this! in a sun like this! And the whole sphere blue like this in the splendour of the end of spring! Wings, crazy with light, rending the firmament! Children singing! The whole earth in bloom! The wind stripping the rose bushes, rustling the trees . . .

And here inside, silence. . . . And this awe! and this fear! The two of us . . . and between the two of us, implacable and strong, tearing me from you, more and more, death . . .

I, with cold growing in my heart – so full of you, even in the horror of the final longing! You, seeing the bitter twisting of the

A bôca que beijava a tua bôca ardente,
A bôca que foi tua!

E eu morrendo! e eu morrendo,
Vendo-te, e vendo o sol, e vendo o céu, e vendo
Tão bela palpitar nos teus olhos, querida,
A delícia da vida! a delícia da vida!

A um poeta

LONGE do estéril turbilhão da rua,
Beneditino, escreve! No aconchego
Do claustro, na paciência e no sossêgo,
Trabalha, e teima, e lima, e sofre, e sua!

Mas que na forma se disfarce o emprêgo
Do esfôrço; e a trama viva se construa
De tal modo, que a imagem fique nua,
Rica mas sóbria, como um templo grego.

mouth which used to kiss your passionate mouth, of the mouth which was yours!

And I dying! and I dying, seeing you, and seeing the sun, and seeing the sky, and seeing the joy of life sparkle so beautifully in your eyes, my dear! The joy of life!

To a Poet

WRITE, Beneditino, far from the sterile bustle of the street! In the intimacy of the cloister, with patience and calm, work and persist and polish and suffer and sweat!

But let the effort employed be disguised in the form; and the living device contrived in such a way that the image appear bare, rich but sober, like a Greek temple.

Não se mostre na fábrica o suplício
Do mestre. E, natural, o efeito agrade,
Sem lembrar os andaimes do edifício:

Porque a Beleza, gêmea da Verdade,
Arte pura, inimiga do artificio,
É a fôrça e a graça na simplicidade.

Let the construction not reveal the anguish of the master. And, being natural, let the effect be pleasing, without recalling the framework of the building:

For Beauty, twin of Truth, pure Art, the enemy of artifice, is strength and grace in simplicity.

ALPHONSUS DE GUIMARAENS (1870–1921)

Soneto

MÃOS de finada, aquelas mãos de neve,
De tons marfíneos, de ossatura rica,
Pairando no ar, num gesto brando e leve,
Que parece ordenar, mas que suplica.

Erguem-se ao longe como se as eleve
Alguém que ante os altares sacrifica:
Mãos que consagram, mãos que partem breve,
Mas cuja sombra nos meus olhos fica . . .

Mãos de esperança para as almas loucas,
Brumosas mãos que vêm brancas, distantes,
Fechar ao mesmo tempo tantas bôcas . . .

Sinto-as agora, ao luar, descendo juntas,
Grandes, magoadas, pálidas, tacteantes,
Cerrando os olhos das visões defuntas . . .

Sonnet

HANDS of a dead woman, those hands of snow, of ivory hue, of fine bones, pushing out into the air with a slight and delicate movement that seems to be commanding but is imploring.

They rise far away as if someone were lifting them in sacrifice before the altars: hands which consecrate, hands which swiftly part, but whose shadow stays on my eyes . . .

Hands with hope for the wild hearts, misty hands coming white and distant to close so many mouths at once . . .

I feel them now, in the moonlight, descending together, large, bruised, pallid, feeling, closing the eyes of dead visions . . .

Serenada

A Henrique Malta

DA noite pelos ermos
Choram violões.
São como enfermos
Corações.

Dorme a cidade inteira
Em agonia . . .
A lua é uma caveira
Que nos espia.

Todo o céu se recama
De argêntea luz . . .
Uma voz clama
Por Jesus.

A quietude morta
Do luar se espalma . . .
E ao luar em cada porta,
Expira uma alma.

Serenade

GUITARS cry in the wilderness of night. They are like ailing hearts.

The whole town sleeps in agony. . . . The moon is a skull watching over us.

All the sky is laced with silvery light. . . . A voice cries out for Jesus.

The dead stillness of the moonlight spreads low. . . . And in the moonlight at each door a soul expires.

Passam tremendo os velhos . . .
Ide em paz,
Ó evangelhos
Do Aqui-Jaz!

Tôda a triste cidade
É um cemitério . . .
Há um rumor de saudade
E de mistério.

A nuvem guarda o pranto
Que em si contém . . .
Do rio o canto
Chora além.

De sul a norte passa,
Como um segrêdo,
Um hausto de desgraça:
É a voz do mêdo . . .

Há pela paz noturna
Um celestial
Silêncio de urna
Funeral . . .

The old people pass by trembling. . . . Go in peace, you evangelists of the Here-Lies!

All the sad city is a cemetery. . . . There is a murmur of nostalgia and mystery.

The cloud holds back the tears it has in itself. . . . Beyond, weeps the song of the river.

From south to north, like a secret, passes a draught of misfortune: it is the voice of fear . . .

In the peace of the night there is the celestial silence of a funeral urn . . .

Pela infinita mágoa
Que em tudo existe,
Ouço o marulho da água,
Sereno e triste.

Da noite pelos ermos
Choram violões . . .
São como enfermos
Corações,

E em meio da cidade
O rio corre,
Conduzindo a saudade
De alguém que morre . . .

Through the infinite grief that is in everything I hear the rolling of the water, serene and sad.

Guitars cry in the wilderness of night. They are like ailing hearts.

And through the middle of the town runs the river, carrying the memory of someone who is dying . . .

MANUEL BANDEIRA (1886–1968)

O martelo

As rodas rangem na curva dos trilhos
Inexorávelmente.
Mas eu salvei do meu naufrágio
Os elementos mais cotidianos.
O meu quarto resume o passado em tôdas as casas que habitei.

Dentro da noite
No cerne duro da cidade
Me sinto protegido.
Do jardim do convento
Vem o pio da coruja.
Doce como um arrulho de pomba.
Sei que amanhã quando acordar
Ouvirei o martelo do ferreiro
Bater corajoso o seu cântico de certezas.

The Hammer

The wheels grind on the curved track inexorably. But I have saved the most everyday things from my shipwreck. My room takes up the past in all the houses I have lived in.

Deep into night in the hard core of the city, I feel sheltered. From the convent garden comes the cry of the owl. Sweet as the cooing of a dove. I know that tomorrow, when I wake, I shall hear the blacksmith's hammer boldly beating out its canticle of certainties.

Poética

ESTOU farto do lirismo comedido
Do lirismo bem comportado
Do lirismo funcionário público com livro de ponto expediente protocolo e manifestações de aprêço ao sr. diretor

Estou farto do lirismo que pára e vai averiguar no dicionário o cunho vernáculo de um vocábulo

Abaixo os puristas
Tôdas as palavras sobretudo os barbarismos universais
Tôdas as construções sobretudo as sintaxes de exceção
Todos os ritmos sobretudo os inumeráveis

Estou farto do lirismo namorador
Político
Raquítico
Sifilítico
De todo lirismo que capitula ao que quer que seja fora de si mesmo.

Poetics

I'VE had enough of discreet lyricism, well-mannered lyricism, public official lyricism with its clocking-in, protocol and expressions of appreciation to Mr Director Sir.

I've had enough of the lyricism which stops and goes to the dictionary to check the implication of a word in the vernacular.

Down with purists – all words, especially those universal barbarisms, all constructions, especially unusual syntax, all rhythms, especially the uncountable ones.

I've had enough of gallant lyricism, political, rachitic, syphilitic, of all lyricism which submits to whatever is outside itself.

De resto não é lirismo
Será contabilidade tabela de co-senos secretário do amante exemplar com cem modelos de cartas e as diferentes maneiras de agradar à mulheres, etc.

Quero antes o lirismo dos loucos
O lirismo dos bêbedos
O lirismo difícil e pungente dos bêbedos
O lirismo dos clowns de Shakespeare

– Não quero mais saber do lirismo que não é libertação.

Besides, it's not lyricism, it must be accountancy, cosine tables, secretary to the exemplary lover with a hundred standard letters and all the different ways of pleasing women, etc.

I want the lyricism of the mad, the lyricism of the drunk, the difficult and pungent lyricism of the drunk, the lyricism of Shakespeare's clowns,

I don't want to have anything more to do with lyricism which isn't liberation.

MÁRIO DE ANDRADE (1893–1945)

Momento

O MUNDO que se inunda claro em vultos roxos
No cáos profundo em que a tristura
Tange mansinho os ventos aos mulambos.

A gente escapa da vontade.
Se sente prazeres futuros,
Chegar em casa,
Reconhecer-se em naturezas-mortas . . .

Oh, que pra lá da serra caxingam os dinosauros!

Em breve a noite abrirá os corpos,
As embaúbas vão se refazer . . .

A gente escapa da vontade.
Os seres mancham apenas a luz dos olhares,
Se sobrevoam feito músicas escuras.

Moment

THE world overflowing bright with purple shapes in the deep chaos in which sadness gently touches the wind in tatters.

We escape the force of will. One senses future pleasures, arriving home, recognizing oneself in still life . . .

Over the hills the dinosaurs are limping!

Soon the night will open the bodies, the *embaubas** are going to gather themselves together again . . .

We escape the force of will. Creatures scarcely defile the light of the glances, they fly above each other like mysterious music.

---

* *Embauba*: a kind of tree.

E a vida, como viola deshonesta,
Viola a morte do ardor, e se dedilha . . .
Fraca.

O rebanho

OH! minhas alucinações!
Vi os deputados, chapéus altos,
Sob o pálio vesperal, feito de mangas-rosas,
Sairem de mãos dadas do Congresso . . .
Como um possesso num acesso em meus aplausos
Aos salvadores do meu Estado amado! . . .

Desciam, inteligentes, de mãos dadas,
Entre o trepidar dos taxis vascolejantes,
A rua Marechal Deodoro . . .
Oh! minhas alucinações!
Como um possesso num acesso em meus aplausos
Aos herois do meu Estado amado! . . .

And life, like a dishonest viol, violates the death of courage, and plucks its strings . . . weakly.

The Flock

OH! My hallucinations! I saw the deputies, tall hats, under the afternoon canopy, made of red mangoes, coming out hand in hand from the Congress. . . . Like a person possessed by a fit of applause for the saviours of my beloved State! . . .

Intelligent, hand in hand, amidst the trembling of the turbulent taxis, they were coming down Marechal Deodoro Street. . . . Oh! My hallucinations! Like a person possessed by a fit of applause for the heroes of my beloved State! . . .

E as esperanças de ver tudo salvo!
Duas mil reformas, três projetos . . .
Emigram os futuros noturnos . . .
E verde, verde, verde! . . .
Oh! minhas alucinações!
Mas os deputados, chapéus altos,
Mudavam-se pouco a pouco em cabras!

Crescem-lhes os cornos, descem-lhes as barbinhas . . .
E vi que os chapéus altos do meu Estado amado,
Com os triángulos de madeira no pescoço,
Nos verdes esperanças, sob as franjas de ouro da tarde,
Se punham a pastar
Rente do palácio do senhor presidente . . .
Oh! Minhas alucinações!

And the hopes of seeing everything saved! Two thousand reforms, three projects. . . . Nocturnal futures are departing. . . . And green, green, green! . . . Oh! My hallucinations! But the deputies, tall hats, were slowly changing into goats!

They are growing horns, whiskers are falling from their chins. . . . And I saw that the tall hats of my beloved State, with triangles of wood about their necks, their hopes in the green, beneath the golden edges of afternoon, were going to feed close to Mr President's palace. . . . Oh! My hallucinations!

CASSIANO RICARDO (b. 1895)

Paisagem submarina

No antro submarino, onde os pólipos têm
qualquer coisa de humano em seu mistério e são
galhos de sangue aí chorado por alguém
que naufragou depois de haver lutado em vão;

nêsse mundo ignorado, ou nessa escuridão:
que é tôda azul por fora e só monstros contém
é que irei enterrar o meu único bem . . .
Náufrago – devo estar onde os outros estão.

Bem que é meu, ficará guardado onde só eu
o saiba, como alguém que, fugindo a um ladrão,
se tornou o ladrão daquilo que já é seu.

Estarei nêsse caso? Ah! quanta gente que,
pra esconder o seu bem, busca o escuro e não vê
que uma estrêla se vê melhor na escuridão . . .

Submarine Landscape

In the submarine cavern, where the polyps have some human quality in their mystery, and are shoots of blood wept there by someone who was shipwrecked after having fought in vain;

Into that unknown world, or into that darkness which is all blue outside and contains only monsters, I shall go to bury my sole treasure. . . . A shipwreck – I must be where the others are.

This, my treasure, shall lie guarded where only I may know, like someone who, fleeing from a thief, has become thief of what is already his.

Shall I come to that? Ah! how many people, to hide their treasure, seek the dark and do not see that a star is better seen in the darkness . . .

Geografia do sono

BOM tempo aquêle, quando as criaturas
mudavam de alma e ser a qualquer hora.
Agora, nestas horas tão obscuras,
onde a centelha dessa antiga aurora?

Ficou-nos, dêsse tempo, pôsto fora,
em paga destas, de hoje, desventuras,
um só bem, o do sono, em que ainda mora
o sonho que é o licor das vãs procuras.

Por ser eterno é que só Deus não ousa
deixar de ser quem é, ser outra coisa.
Porém, bem haja a borboleta e o eclipse.

Bem haja a criatura que, tristonha,
sem poder ser o anjo do Apocalipse,
passa a ser quem não é, se dorme ou sonha.

Geography of Sleep

THAT was a good time, when creatures changed their soul and being at any time. Now, in these darkest times, where is the sparkle of that earlier dawn?

In recompense for the misfortunes of today, one sole treasure from that time was set aside for us – the treasure of sleep, in which there still dwells the dream that is the liquor of vain quests.

It is because He is eternal that God alone does not venture to cease to be what He is, to become something else. But, let all be well with the butterfly and the eclipse.

Let all be well with the creature who, sad, unable to be the angel of the Apocalypse, becomes what he is not when asleep or dreaming.

JORGE DE LIMA (1893–1953)

Distribuição da poesia

MEL silvestre tirei das plantas,
sal tirei das águas, luz tirei do céu.
Escutai, meus irmãos: poesia tirei de tudo
para oferecer ao Senhor.
Não tirei ouro da terra
nem sangue de meus irmãos.
Estalajadeiros não me incomodeis.
Bufarinheiros e banqueiros
sei fabricar distâncias
para vos recuar.
A vida está malograda,
creio nas mágicas de Deus.
Os galos não cantam,
a manhã não raiou.
Vi os navios irem e voltarem.
Vi os infelizes irem e voltarem.
Vi homens obesos dentro do fogo.
Vi ziguezagues na escuridão.
Capitão-mor, onde é o Congo?
Onde é a Ilha de São Brandão?

Distribution of Poetry

WILD honey I took from the plants, salt I took from the waters, light I took from the sky. Listen, my brothers: poetry I took from everything to offer it to the Lord. I did not take gold from the earth nor blood from my brothers. Do not disturb me, innkeepers. Pedlars and bankers, I can contrive distances to keep you away. Life is thwarted, I believe in the magic illusions of God. The cocks are not crowing, the dawn has not broken. I saw the ships go away and return. I saw the unhappy ones go away and return. I saw obese men in the fire. I saw zigzags in the darkness. Commander, where is the Congo? Where is the isle of São Brandão? Commander, how

Capitão-mor que noite escura!
Uivam molossos na escuridão.
Ó indesejáveis, qual o país,
qual o país que desejais?
Mel silvestre tirei das plantas,
sal tirei das águas, luz tirei do céu.
Só tenho poesia para vos dar.
Abancai-vos, meus irmãos.

from *Canto primeiro*

Fundação da ilha

II

A ILHA ninguém achou
porque todos a sabíamos.
Mesmo nos olhos havia
uma clara geografia.

Mesmo nêsse fim de mar
qualquer ilha se encontrava,
mesmo sem mar e sem fim,
mesmo sem terra e sem mim.

dark the night is! Mastiffs are howling in the darkness. You undesirables, which country do you desire? Wild honey I took from the plants, salt I took from the waters, light I took from the sky. I have only poetry to give you. Be seated, my brothers.

from *First Canto*

The Foundation of the Island

No one found the island for we all know it. Even in our eyes there was a clear geography.

Even at that limit of the sea some island would be found, even with no sea and no limit, even without land and without me.

Mesmo sem naus e sem rumos,
mesmo sem vagas e areias,
há sempre um copo de mar
para um homem navegar.

Nem achada e nem não vista
nem descrita nem viagem,
há aventuras de partidas
porém nunca acontecidas.

Chegados nunca chegamos
eu e a ilha movediça.
Móvel terra, céu incerto,
mundo jamais descoberto.

Indícios de canibais,
sinais de céu e sargaços,
aqui um mundo escondido
geme num búzio perdido.

Rosa-de-ventos na testa,
maré rasa, aljôfre, pérolas,
domingo de pascoelas.
E êsse veleiro sem velas!

Even with no ships and no course, even with no waves and sand, there is always a cup of sea for a man to sail.

No discovery nor sighting, neither recounting nor voyage, there are adventures yet whose departures never happened.

Having arrived, we never arrived, I and the moving island. Shifting land, uncertain sky, world never discovered.

Evidence of cannibals, signs of sky and sargasso, here a hidden world moans in a lost trumpet-shell.

Compass-card at the bridgehead, calm sea, seed-pearl, pearls, Low Sunday. And this sail-less sailing boat.

Afinal: ilha de praias.
Querereis outros achamentos
além dessas ventanias
tão tristes, tão alegrias?

III

E DEPOIS das infensas geografias
e do vento indo e vindo nos rosais
e das pedras dormidas e das ramas
e das aves nos ninhos intencionais
e dos sumos maduros e das chuvas
e das coisas contidas nessas coisas
refletidas nas faces dos espelhos
sete vêzes por sete renegados,
reinventamos o mar com seus colombos,
e columbas revoando sôbre as ondas,
e as ondas envolvendo o peixe, e o peixe
(ó misterioso ser assinalado),
com linguagem dos livros ignorada;
reinventamos o mar para essa ilha
que possui «cabos-não» a ser dobrados
e terras e brasís com boa aguada

At last: an island of beaches. Do you want other discoveries beyond these high winds, so sad, so joyful?

And after the adverse geography and the wind coming and going in the rose-trees and the sleeping stones and the branches and the birds in their would-be nests and the ripe juices and the rains and the things contained in those things reflected in the faces of the mirrors seven times for seven renegades, we reinvented the sea with its columbuses, and doves flying above the waves, and the waves wrapping fish, and fish (O curious distinguished creature), with a language unknown in books; we reinvented the sea for that island which has 'non-capes' to be turned and lands and Brazils with good

para as naves que vão para o oriente.
E demos êsse mar às travessias
a aos mapas-múndi sempre inacabados;
e criamos o convés e o marinheiro
e em tôrno ao marinheiro a lenda esquiva
que êle quer povoar com seus selvagens.
Empreendemos com a ajuda dos acasos
as travessias nunca projetadas,
sem roteiros, sem mapas e astrolábios
e sem carta a El-Rei contando a viagem.
Bastam velas e dados de jogar
e o salitre nas vigas e o agiológio,
e a fé ardendo em claro, nas bandeiras.
O mais: A meia quilha entre os naufrágios
que tão bastantes varram os pavores.
O mais: Êsse farol com o feixe largo
que tão unido varre a embarcação.
Eis o mar: era morto e renasceu.
Eis o mar: era pródigo e o encontrei.
Sua voz? O que voz convalescida!

water for the ships bound for the Orient. And we gave this sea to the crossing and the ever unfinished charts; and we created the deck and the sailor, and around the sailor the elusive legend which he likes to people with his savages. With the help of fortune we undertook crossings never planned, with no log, no maps or astrolabe, and with no letter to the King to tell of the voyage. It is enough to have sails and dice and saltpetre on the beams and the legend and faith burning openly in the flags. Also the half keel between the wrecks which so often may be swept by fear. Also that lighthouse with its broad beam which, so concentrated, sweeps through the boat. Behold the sea: for it was dead and is reborn. Behold the sea: for it was prodigal and I have found it. Its voice? Oh, what relief

Que lamúrias tão fortes nessas gáveas!
Que coqueiros gemendo em suas palmas!
Que chegar de luares e de rêdes!

Contemos uma história. Mas que história?
A história mal-dormida de uma viagem.

there is in its voice! How strong the lamentation in those topsails! How the cocoa-palms whine! What an arrival of moonlight and nets!

Let us tell a story. But which story? The ill-slept story of a voyage.

CECÍLIA MEIRELES (1901–64)

Ária

NA noite profunda,
deixa-me existir
como os loucos em nuvens
como os cegos em flores.
Na profunda noite,
deixa-me chorar
sôbre os rios convulsos.
Na noite profunda,
deixa-me cair
entre os céus impotentes.
Na profunda noite,
deixa-me morrer
como um pássaro inábil.
Na noite profunda.

Quem nos vai recordar
na noite profunda?
Pensamento tão gasto,
amor sem milagre
na profunda noite.
Os amigos se extinguem.

Aria

IN the deep night let me exist like the mad in clouds, like the blind in flowers. In the deep night let me weep on the convulsive rivers. In the deep night let me fall amidst the impotent skies. In the deep night let me die like a feckless bird. In the deep night.

Who shall remember us in the deep night? Thoughts so spent, wonderless love in the deep night. Friends flicker out.

Deixa-me sofrer
na profunda noite.
Ó mãos separadas
que ninguém reconhece
na profunda noite

Na noite profunda,
deixa para sempre,
deixa agonizar
solitário meu rosto,
na noite profunda,
na profunda noite
que a memória levar.

Presença

NÃO mais a pessoa: o interstício do tempo
habitado por ela,
outrora, quando a presença era visível e esquecível.

A memória padece
nêsse lugar, que pertencia a algum destino,
pelas coisas estranhas
e no entanto banais que representam a existência.

Let me suffer in the deep night. Oh parted hands that no one recognizes in the deep night.

In the deep night let forever, let my face be in solitary agony, in the deep night, in the deep night which might carry the memory away.

Presence

NO longer the person; the interstice of time occupied by her, before, when her presence was visible and forgettable.

The memory suffers on in that place, which belonged to some destiny, through the strange yet banal things which make up existence.

Custa a cerrar o oceano
de onde aflorava a imagem desnuda e desprezada.
Inùtilmente a levam . . .
que a solidão respira, anuncia seu nome,
seu rosto inviolado.
E a secreta evidência
perturba os que vão morrer, agora que a notaram,
e alucina seus olhos
com a tentação raramente possível da efígie eterna.

It is hard to close the ocean from which arose the bare, scorned image. It is useless for them to take her away . . . for the solitude breathes, announces her name, her unblemished face. And the secret evidence troubles those who are going to die, now that they have seen it, and it deludes their eyes with the temptation, scarcely possible, of the eternal effigy.

CARLOS DRUMMOND DE ANDRADE

(b. 1902)

Aurora

O POETA ia bêbedo no bonde.
O dia nascia atrás dos quintais.
As pensões alegres dormiam tristíssimas.
As casas também iam bêbedas.

Tudo era irreparável.
Ninguém sabia que o mundo ia acabar
(apenas uma criança percebeu mas ficou calada),
que o mundo ia acabar às 7 e 45.

Últimos pensamentos! últimos telegramas!
José, que colocava pronomes,
Helena, que amava os homens,
Sebastião, que se arruinava,
Artur, que não dizia nada,
embarcam para a eternidade.

O poeta está bêbedo, mas
escuta um apêlo na aurora:

Dawn

THE poet was riding, drunken, in the tram. The day was breaking beyond the gardens. The joyful *pensions* were sleeping full of sadness. The houses moving by were drunk, as well.

Everything was irreparable. No one knew that the world would come to an end (only one child noticed, but he kept quiet), that the world would come to an end at 7.45.

Final thoughts! Final telegrams! José, who placed pronouns in the right place, Helena, who loved men,

Sebastian, who would go bankrupt, Arthur, who never said anything, are all embarking for eternity.

The poet is drunk, but he hears a cry at dawn: Shall we all go

Vamos todos dançar
entre o bonde e a árvore?

Entre o bonde e a árvore
dançai, meus irmãos!
Embora sem música
dançai, meus irmãos!

Os filhos estão nascendo
com tamanha espontaneidade.
Como é maravilhoso o amor
(o amor e outros produtos).
Dançai, meus irmãos!
a morte virá depois
como um sacramento.

Procura da poesia

NÃO faças versos sôbre acontecimentos.
Não há criação nem morte perante a poesia.
Diante dela, a vida é um sol estático,
não aquece nem ilumina.
As afinidades, os aniversários, os incidentes pessoais não
contam.

and dance between the tram and the tree?

Between the tram and the tree, dance, my brothers! Dance, my brothers, even though without music!

Children are being born so spontaneously. What a wonderful thing love is (love and other products). Dance, my brothers! Death will come later, like a sacrament.

In Search of Poetry

DON'T write poetry about events. There's neither creation nor death in poetry. Faced with it life is a static sun which neither warms nor brightens. Affinities, birthdays, personal incidents don't

Não faças poesia com o corpo,
êsse excelente, completo e confortável corpo, tão infenso á efusão lírica.
Tua gôta de bile, tua careta de gôzo ou de dor no escuro
são indiferentes.
Nem me reveles teus sentimentos,
que se prevalecem do equívoco e tentam a longa viagem.
O que pensas e sentes, isso ainda não é poesia.
Não cantes tua cidade, deixa-a em paz.
O canto não é o movimento das máquinas nem o segrêdo das casas.
Não é música ouvida de passagem; rumor do mar nas ruas junto à linha de espuma.
O canto não é a natureza
nem os homens em sociedade.
Para êle, chuva e noite, fadiga e esperança nada significam.
A poesia (não tires poesia das coisas)
elide sujeito e objeto.

Não dramatizes, não invoques,
não indagues. Não percas tempo em mentir.
Não te aborreças.
Teu iate de marfim, teu sapato de diamante,

count. Don't write poetry with your body, that fine, well-made, comfortable body, so hostile to lyrical effusions.

Your drop of bile, your grimace of pleasure or grief in the darkness, are indifferent. And do not reveal your feelings to me, for they take advantage of misunderstandings, and try for a long trip. Whatever you think or feel, it is still not poetry. Do not sing the praises of your city, leave it in peace. The song is neither the movement of machines nor the secret of houses. It is not music heard in passing; the murmur of the sea in the streets beside the line of foam. The song is neither nature nor man in society. For it, rain and night, fatigue and hope have no meaning. Poetry (don't draw poetry from things) elides subject and object.

Don't dramatize, don't invoke, don't investigate. Don't lose time in lying. Don't be exasperated. Your ivory yacht, your diamond

vossas mazurcas e abusões, vossos esqueletos de família
desaparacem na curva do tempo, é algo imprestável.

Não recomponhas
tua sepultada e merencória infancia.
Não osciles entre o espelho e a
memória em dissipação.
Que se dissipou, não era poesia.
Que se partiu, cristal não era.

Penetra surdamente no reino das palavras.
Lá estão os poemas que esperam ser escritos.
Estão paralisados, mas não há desespêro,
há calma e frescura na superfície intacta.
Ei-los sós e mudos, em estado de dicionário.

Convive com teus poemas, antes de escrevê-los.
Tem paciência, se obscuros. Calma, se te provocam.
Espera que cada um se realize e consume
com seu poder de palavra
e seu poder de silêncio.

shoe, your mazurkas and superstitions, your family skeletons disappear in the curve of time, they are useless.

Don't recompose your buried and gloomy childhood. Don't oscillate between the mirror and your fading memory. If it faded, it wasn't poetry. If it broke, it wasn't glass.

Explore quietly into the realm of words. That's where the poems are waiting to be written. They are paralysed, but there is no despair, there is calm and freshness in the unbroken surface. There they are, alone and silent, in dictionary form.

Live with your poems before you write them. Be patient if they are obscure. Be calm if they provoke you. Wait for each to be realized and consumed in the power of its words and the power of its silence.

Não forces o poema a desprender-se do limbo.
Não colhas no chão o poema que se perdeu.
Não adules o poema. Aceita-o
como êle aceitará sua forma definitiva e concentrada
no espaço.

Chega mais perto e contempla as palavras.
Cada uma
tem mil faces secretas sob a face neutra
e te pergunta, sem interêsse pela resposta,
pobre ou terrível, que lhe deres:
Trouxeste a chave?

Repara:
êrmas de melodia e conceito,
elas se refugiaram na noite, as palavras.
Ainda úmidas e impregnadas de sono,
rolam num rio difícil e se transformam em desprêzo.

Don't force the poem to tear itself from the limbo. Don't pick up a lost poem from the floor. Don't flatter the poem. Accept it as it will accept its form, definitive and concentrated in space.

Draw closer and look at the words. Each one has a thousand secret faces beneath its blank face, and is asking you, with no interest in the reply you may give – poor or terrible: Did you bring the key?

Look: barren of melody and concept, those words took refuge in the night. Still damp and impregnated with sleep, they roll in a difficult river and turn into scorn.

MURILO MENDES (b. 1902)

Poema barroco

Os cavalos da aurora derrubando os pianos
Avançam furiosamente pelas portas da noite.
Dormem na penumbra antigos anjos com os pés feridos,
Dormem relógios e cristais de outras épocas, esqueletos
de atrizes.

O poeta calça nuvens ornadas de cabeças gregas
E ajoelha-se ante a imagem de Nossa Senhora das
Vitórias
Enquanto os primeiros ruídos de carrocinhas de leiteiros
Atravessam o céu de açucenas e bronze.

Preciso conhecer meu sistema de artérias
E saber até que ponto me sinto limitado
Pelos sonhos a galope, pelas últimas notícias de massacres,
Pelo caminhar das constelações, pela coreografia dos
pássaros,

Baroque Poem

THE horses of dawn advance wildly through the portals of night, overturning the pianos. In the half-light sleep angels of old with wounded feet, sleep clocks and crystal of other eras, skeletons of actresses.

The poet puts on clouds ornate with Greek heads and kneels before the figure of Our Lady of the Victories, while the first sounds of milk-floats cross the sky of lilies and bronze.

I need to know my arterial system and know how far I feel limited by breakneck dreams, by the latest news of massacres, by the movement of the constellations, by bird choreography, by the

Pelo labirinto da esperança pela respiração das plantas
E pelos vagidos da criança recém-parida na maternidade
ao fundo.

Preciso conhecer os porões da minha miséria,
Tocar fogo nas ervas que crescem pelo corpo acima
Ameaçando tapar meus olhos meus ouvidos
E amordaçar a indefesa e nua castidade.

É então que viro a bela imagem azul-vermelha:
Apresentando-me o outro lado coberto de punhais
Nossa Senhora das Derrotas, coroada de goivos,
Aponta seu coração e também pede auxílio.

Algo

A Maria de Saudade

O QUE raras vêzes a forma
Revela.
O que, sem evidência, vive.
O que a violeta sonha.
O que o cristal contém
Na sua primeira infância.

labyrinth of hope, by the respiration of plants and by the cries of the newborn child in the maternity home at the end.

I need to know the cellar of my misery, to set fire to the weeds which are growing up my body, threatening to block my eyes and choke my bare defenceless chastity.

And then, I turn the beautiful blue-red figure: revealing to me the other side, covered with daggers, Our Lady of the Defeats, crowned with gillyflowers, points to her heart and also asks for help.

Something

WHAT form rarely reveals. What, without evidence, lives. What the violet dreams. What glass contains in its early infancy.

Idéias rosas

MINHAS idéias abstratas,
De tanto as tocar, tornaram-se concretas:
São rosas familiares
Que o tempo traz ao alcance da mão,
Rosas que assistem a inauguração de eras novas
No meu pensamento,
No pensamento do mundo em mim e nos outros;
De eras novas, mas ainda assim
Que o tempo conheceu, conhece e conhecerá.
Rosas! Rosas!
Quem me dera que houvesse
Rosas abstratas para mim.

Rose Ideas

MY abstract ideas, that I have touched so often, have become concrete: they are familiar roses which time brings within reach, roses which are there at the inauguration of new eras in my thinking, in what the world thinks about me and others; of new eras, but nevertheless which time has known, knows and shall know. Roses! Roses! If only there were abstract roses for me.

AUGUSTO FREDERICO SCHMIDT
(1906–65)

O caminho do frio

Foi um fruto que caiu da árvore,
Foi alguém que passou na estrada,
Foi um pássaro,
Foi a história de uma viagem que pousou em mim,
Foi uma hora de ausência em que voltei a mim mesmo.

E senti que ressurgiste com tuas mãos pequenas
Com teus olhos que não tinham côr certa;
Estávamos assentados no alto muro de pedra.
No sítio em que as águas se dividem.
E me indicavas o início do caminho do frio dizendo:
« – É lá, onde se alinham aquelas árvores
Magras e feias, que começa o caminho do frio.»

The Road of the Cold

It was a fruit that fell from a tree, it was someone going by on the road, it was a bird, it was the story of a journey which alighted on me, it was an hour of absence when I came back to myself.

And I felt you rise again with your tiny hands, with your eyes of no certain colour; we were seated on the high stone wall. At the place where the waters divide. And you were pointing out to me the beginning of the road of the cold, saying: 'There, where that line of ugly, bare trees is, that's where the road of the cold begins.'

Canto matinal

O CANTO matinal é amplo,
Lúcido, sereno;
Espelha a emoção
Do mundo despertando;
Eleva-se da terra aos céus
Agradecendo a Deus o nascer do sol,
E a revelação da paisagem
Mal a aurora desfolhou as suas flôres sôbre nossas cabeças
E a claridade, que se firmara aos poucos,
Oferece-nos os primeiros frutos da manhã,
Ainda molhados de orvalho.
Ao ouvir o canto matinal,
Sopra repentinamente no meu ser
O amor dêste reino terrestre,
Ressuscitando as esperanças e renovando a face das coisas . . .

Morning Song

THE morning song is full, lucid, serene; it mirrors the emotion of the world awakening: it rises from the earth to the heavens thanking God for the sunrise, and the revelation of the countryside when dawn has scarcely stripped its flowers over our heads, and the brightness, having grown stronger little by little, offers us the first fruits of morning, still wet with dew. On hearing the morning song, there flutters suddenly within me the love of this terrestrial realm, giving new life to hopes and renewing the face of things . . .

Luciana

E NUM instante vi a eternidade.
Vi o frágil perene, a flor que nasce
e o vento agita mas não destrói jamais.
Vi o mistério, o fruto claro
Que a luz tocou de leve
e para sempre fêz maduro
e fixou de maneira imperecível.
Era pura e julgava-se sensível ao mal.
Era inocente e pensava conter malícia e engano.
No seu sorriso pousava o sal da graça.
No seu corpo guardava-se o segrêdo
do sêres intocáveis pela morte.

Luciana

AND for a moment I saw eternity. I saw the fragile perennial, the flower that is born and that the wind blows but never destroys. I saw the mystery, the bright fruit which the sun lightly touched and made ripe forever and caught imperishably. She was pure and thought herself sensible to evil. She was innocent and thought she had malice and deceit in her. In her smile was charm itself. In her body was held the secret of those beings death cannot touch.

VINÍCIUS DE MORAES (b. 1913)

from *A última elegia*

Ô ROOFS of Chelsea!
Encantados roofs, multicolores, briques, bridges, brumas
Da aurora em Chelsea! ô melancholy!
«I wish, I wish I were asleep . . . » but the morning
Rises, o perfume da madrugada em Londres
Makes me fluid . . . darling, acorda, escuta
Amanheceu, não durmas . . . o bálsamo do sono
Fechou-te as pálpebras de azul . . . Victoria & Albert
resplende
Para o teu despertar; ô darling, vem amar
A luz de Chelsea! não ouves o rouxinol cantar em Central
Park?
Não ouves resvalar no rio, sob os chorões, o leve batel
Que Bilac deitou à correnteza para eu te passear? não
sentes
O vento brando e macio nos mahoganies? the leaves of
brown
Came tumbling down, remember?

from *Final Elegy*

O ROOFS of Chelsea! Enchanted roofs, multicoloured, bricks, bridges, mists of daybreak in Chelsea! O melancholy! 'I wish, I wish I were asleep . . .' but the morning rises, O perfume of the early morning in London, makes me fluid . . . darling, wake up, listen, it's morning, don't sleep . . . sleep's balsam has closed your blue eyelids . . . the Victoria and Albert is resplendent for your awakening: O darling, come love the light of Chelsea! Can't you hear the nightingale singing in Central Park? Can't you hear the little boat, which Bilac cast into the current for me to take you out in, gliding along the river beneath the willows? Can't you feel the gentle, soft wind in the mahoganies? The leaves of brown came

«Escrevi dez canções . . .
. . . escrevi um soneto . . .
. . . escrevi uma elegia . . . »
Ô darling, acorda, give me thy eyes of brown, vamos fugir
Para a Inglaterra?
« . . . escrevi um soneto . . .
. . . escrevi uma carta . . . »
Ô darling, vamos fugir para a Inglaterra?
. . . «que irão pensar
Os quatro cavaleiros do Apocalipse . . . »
. . . escrevi uma ode . . . »
Ô darling!
O PAVEMENTS!
O roofs of Chelsea!
Encantados roofs, noble pavements, cheerful pubs, delicatessen
Crumpets, a glass of bitter, cap and gown . . . – don't cry don't cry!
Nothing is lost, I'll come again, next week, I promise thee . . .
Be still, don't cry . . .
. . . don't cry . . .
. . .don't cry . . .
RESOUND

tumbling down, remember? 'I wrote ten songs . . . I wrote one sonnet . . . I wrote an elegy . . .' O darling, wake up, give me thy eyes of brown, shall we run away to England? 'I wrote a sonnet . . . I wrote a letter . . .' O darling, shall we run away to England? . . . 'What will the four horsemen of the Apocalypse think . . .' ' . . . I wrote an ode . . .' O darling! O PAVEMENTS! O roofs of Chelsea! Enchanted roofs, noble pavements, cheerful pubs, delicatessen crumpets, a glass of bitter, cap and gown . . . – don't cry, don't cry! Nothing is lost, I'll come again, next week, I promise thee. . . . Be still, don't cry . . . don't cry . . . don't cry . . . RESOUND

Ye pavements!
 – até que a morte nos separe –
 ô brisas do Tamisa, farfalhai!
Ô telhados de Chelsea,
 amanhecei!

O verbo no infinito

SER criado, gerar-se, transformar
O amor em carne e a carne em amor; nascer
Respirar, e chorar, e adormecer
E se nutrir para poder chorar

Para poder nutrir-se; a despertar
Um dia à luz a ver, ao mundo e ouvir
E começar a amar e então sorrir
E então sorrir para poder chorar.

E crescer, e saber, e ser, e haver
E perder, e sofrer, e ter horror
De ser e amar, e se sentir maldito

E esquecer tudo ao vir um nôvo amor
E viver êsse amor até morrer
E ir conjugar o verbo no infinito . . .

ye pavements! – till death us do part – O breezes of the Thames, rustle! O roofs of Chelsea, wake up!

The Verb in the Infinite

To be created, to beget oneself, to transform love into flesh and flesh into love; to be born, to breathe, and cry, and doze. To nourish oneself to be able to cry

To be able to nourish oneself. And, one day, to wake up to see the light, the world and hear and begin to love and then smile and then smile to be able to cry.

And grow, and know, and be, and have, and lose, and suffer, and dread to be and love, and feel oneself cursed

And forget everything when seeing a new love and live that love until one dies and go to conjugate the verb in the infinite . . .

JOÃO CABRAL DE MELO NETO (b. 1920)

A palavra sêda

A ATMOSFERA que te envolve
atinge tais atmosferas
que transforma muitas coisas
que te concernem, ou cercam.

E como as coisas, palavras
impossíveis de poema:
exemplo, a palavra ouro,
e até êste poema, sêda.

É certo que tua pessoa
não faz dormir, mas desperta;
nem é sedante, palavra
derivada da de sêda.

E é certo que a superfície
de tua pessoa externa,
de tua pele e de tudo
isso que em ti se tateia,

The Word Silk

THE atmosphere that envelops you touches such atmospheres that it transforms many things which concern or surround you.

And like the things, the impossible words of a poem; example, the word gold, and up till this poem, silk.

It is certain that your person does not induce sleep but awakens; nor is it sedative, a word derived from the one for silk,

And it is certain that the surface of your exterior person, of your skin and of all those things which are groping inside you,

nada tem da superfície
luxuosa, falsa, acadêmica,
de uma superfície quando
se diz que ela é «como sêda».

Mas em ti, em algum ponto,
talvez fora de ti mesma,
talvez mesmo no ambiente
que retesas quando chegas,

há algo de muscular,
de animal, carnal, pantera,
de felino, da substância
felina, ou sua maneira,

de animal, de animalmente,
de cru, de cruel, de crueza,
que sob a palavra gasta
persiste na coisa sêda.

Has nothing of the opulent, false, academic surface, of a surface one would say is 'like silk'.

But in you, at some point, perhaps outside yourself, perhaps right in the atmosphere which you stiffen when you arrive,

There is something muscular, animal, carnal, panther-like, feline, feline in substance, or in manner,

Animal, of the way an animal acts, crude, cruel, of cruelty, which beneath the worn-out word persists in the thing silk.

A bailarina

A BAILARINA feita
de borracha e pássaro
dança no pavimento
anterior do sonho.

A três horas de sono,
mais além dos sonhos,
nas secretas câmaras
que a morte revela.

Entre monstros feitos
a tinta de escrever,
a bailarina feita
de borracha e pássaro.

Da diária e lenta
borracha que mastigo.
Do inseto ou pássaro
que não sei caçar

The Dancer

THE dancer made of rubber and bird dances in the foreground of the dream.

At three hours of sleep, beyond the dreams, in the secret chambers death reveals.

Among monsters made in writing-ink, the dancer made of rubber and bird.

Of the daily and slow rubber I chew. Of the insect or bird I can't catch.

CHILE

VICENTE HUIDOBRO (1893–1948)

En la tumba de un poeta

RUISEÑOR que cansado de la tierra
Alzaste el vuelo al alto firmamento,
A la mansión donde la luz se encierra
Oye benigno mi dolido acento.
Y tú, Señor, escucha esta plegaria
Que triste y solitaria
En alas del amor elevo al cielo
Y dale pronto el eternal consuelo.
Sufrió mucho, Señor; su vida entera
Fue un eterno pesar.
Sólo de Ti la dicha ansioso espera,
No le hagas aguardar.
Y tú, errabundo, eterno caminante,
Detente ante la tumba del poeta,
Detente un solo instante,
Y derrama una lágrima secreta,
Una sentida lágrima por él
Que riegue acaso su inmortal laurel.

On the Tomb of a Poet

NIGHTINGALE that, tired of the earth, took wing to the lofty firmament, to the mansion to which light retires, hear benignly my hurt voice. And you, Lord, listen to this plea that, sad and solitary, on wings of love I raise to heaven, and grant him soon eternal consolation. He suffered much, Lord: his whole life was a never-ending sorrow. Only from You comes the eagerly hoped-for happiness. Do not make him wait for it. And you, eternal wandering traveller, stop before the tomb of the poet; stop one single instant and shed a secret tear, a heartfelt tear for him, that perhaps will water his immortal laurel.

Nipona

Ven
Flor rara
De aquel edén
Que llaman Yoshiwara.
Ven, muñequita japonesa
Que vagaremos juntos nuestro anhelo
Cabe el maravilloso estanque de turquesa
Bajo un cielo que extienda el palio de ónix de su velo.
Deja que bese
Tu rostro oblicuo
Que se estremece
Por un inicuo
Brutal deseo.
¡Oh! Déjame así
Mientras te veo
Como un biscuit.
Son tus ojos dos gotas ovaladas y enervantes
Es tu rostro amarillo y algo marfileño
Y tienes los encantos lancinantes
De un ficticio y raro ensueño
Mira albas y olorosas
Sobre el plaqué
Las rosas
Té.

Nipponese

COME, rare flower from that eden they call Yoshiwara. Come, little Japanese doll, let us roam our yearning together. The marvellous pool of turquoise remains, under a sky that extends the onyx canopy of its veil. Let me kiss your slanted countenance made to tremble by evil, brutal desire. Oh, let me, while I see you as a biscuit. Your eyes are two oval and enervating drops. Your face is yellow and somewhat ivory. And you have the piercing charms of a fictitious and uncommon dream. See, white and scented on the veneer – roses. Tea.

Alerta

Media noche
En el jardín
Cada sombra es un arroyo

Aquel ruido que se acerca no es un coche

Sobre el cielo de París
Otto von Zeppelín

Las sirenas cantan
Entre las olas negras
Y este clarín que llama ahora
No es el clarín de la Victoria
Cien aeroplanos
Vuelan en torno de la luna

Apaga tu pipa

Los obuses estallan como rosas maduras
Y las bombas agujerean los días
Canciones cortadas
tiemblan entre las ramas

The Alert

MIDNIGHT. In the garden. Each shadow is a stream. That noise approaching is no car. In the sky above Paris – Otto von Zeppelin. Sirens sing among the black waves. And this trumpet that calls now is not the trumpet of victory. One hundred aeroplanes wing round the moon.

Put Out Your Pipe

SHELLS burst like ripe roses and bombs puncture the days. Cut-off songs tremble among the branches.

El viento contorsiona las calles

COMO APAGAR LA ESTRELLA DEL ESTANQUE

Emigrante a América

ESTRELLAS eléctricas
Se encienden en el viento
Y algunos signos astrológicos
han caído al mar

Ese emigrante que canta
Partirá mañana

Vivir

Buscar

Atado al barco
como a un horóscopo
Veinte días sobre el mar

Bajo las aguas
Nadan los pulpos vegetales

The wind twists the streets.
HOW TO EXTINGUISH THE STAR IN THE POOL.

Emigrant to America

ELECTRIC stars catch fire in the wind. And some astrological signs have fallen into the sea. That singing emigrant will leave tomorrow. To live. To search. Bound to the boat as to a horoscope, twenty days at sea. Beneath the water float vegetable octopuses. Past the

Detrás del horizonte abierto
        El otro puerto

Entre el boscaje
Las rosas deshojadas
                        iluminan las calles

Affiche

DANS tes cheveux il y a une musique
Sous l'étoile quotidienne ma guitare unique

Ta chevelure pleuvait sur la campagne

Celui qui a perdu le chemin
À l'autre rive tombera dans l'espace

            Astre natal
            Cet oiseau dans la gorge me fait mal
            Et ma vie
            Derrière moi reste endormie

En bas du soir
Une voix qui crie
ÊTRE AVEUGLE À MIDI

open horizon, the other port. In the foliage, blown roses brighten the streets.

Poster

THERE is a music in your hair. Under the daily star, my sole guitar.
The locks of your hair wept over the countryside.
He who has lost the way will tumble into space at the other bank.
Birth star, this bird in my throat is hurting me and my life stays sleeping behind.
In the depth of evening a voice that cries TO BE BLIND AT NOON.

Je regarde mon toit
Douce mer pleine d'aventures
Et le collier de tes larmes
Rouillé dans ma poitrine

Fumée du vide
Chevelure fidèle de mon navire

Ces fils qui montent à l'horizon
Sont les cordes oubliées de mon violon

Balada de lo que no vuelve

VENÍA hacia mí por la sonrisa
Por el camino de su gracia
Y cambiaba las horas del día
El cielo de la noche se convertía en el cielo del amanecer
El mar era un árbol frondoso lleno de pájaros
Las flores daban campanadas de alegría
Y mi corazón se ponía a perfumar enloquecido

Van andando los días a lo largo del año
¿En dónde estás?

I look at my roof. Sweet sea full of adventures. And the necklace of your tears has mouldered in my breast.

Smoke of emptiness. Faithful ringlets of my ship.

These threads that climb to the horizon are the forgotten strings of my violin.

Ballad of That Which Does Not Return

SHE came towards me through her smile, through the path of her grace, and changed the hours of the day. The night sky changed to the sky of dawn. The sea was a leafy tree full of birds. Flowers gave chimes of happiness, and my heart began to perfume wildly.

The days go walking along the year. Where are you? My glance

Me crece la mirada
Se me alargan las manos
En vano la soledad abre sus puertas
Y el silencio se llena de tus pasos de antaño
Me crece el corazón
Se me alargan los ojos
Y quisiera pedir otros ojos
Para ponerlos allí donde terminan los míos
¿En dónde estás ahora?
Qué sitio del mundo se está haciendo tibio con tu presencia
Me crece el corazón como una esponja
O como esos corales que van a formar islas.

Es inútil mirar los astros
O interrogar las piedras encanecidas
Es inútil mirar ese árbol que te dijo adiós el último
Y te saludará el primero a tu regreso
Eres substancia de lejanía
Y no hay remedio
Andan los días en tu busca
A qué seguir por todas partes la huella de sus pasos
El tiempo canta dulcemente

grows, my hands lengthen. Solitude opens its doors in vain, and silence is filled with your former steps. My heart swells, my eyes reach out, and I would like to ask for other eyes to put there where mine end. Where are you now? What place in the world is warmed by your presence? My heart swells like a sponge, or like coral that joins to form islands.

It is futile to look at the heavens, or to question the greying stones. It is useless to look at that tree – the last to bid you farewell, the first which will greet your return. You are the substance of remoteness and there is no cure. The days are looking for you. Why follow the track of your step everywhere? Time sings sweetly while

Mientras la herida cierra los párpados para dormirse
Me crece el corazón
Hasta romper sus horizontes
Hasta saltar por encima de los árboles
Y estrellarse en el cielo
La noche sabe qué corazón tiene más amargura

Sigo las flores y me pierdo en el tiempo
De soledad en soledad
Sigo las olas y me pierdo en la noche
De soledad en soledad
Tú has escondido la luz en alguna parte
¿En dónde?, ¿en dónde?
Andan los días en tu busca

Los días llagados coronados de espinas
Se caen se levantan
Y van goteando sangre
Te buscan los caminos de la tierra
De soledad en soledad
Me crece terriblemente el corazón
Nada vuelve
Todo es otra cosa

the wound shuts its eyelids to sleep. My heart swells until it breaks its bounds, until it leaps the trees and is shattered* in the sky. The night knows which heart has the more sorrow.

I follow the flowers and am lost in the time of solitude upon solitude. I follow the waves and am lost in the night of solitude upon solitude. You have hidden the light somewhere. But where? But where? The days are searching for you.

The wounded days, crowned with thorns, fall and rise and go dripping blood. The roads of the earth look for you, solitude upon solitude. My heart swells terribly. Nothing returns. All is some-

---

* *Estrellarse* might mean here 'to shatter' or 'to become stars'. Huidobro plays with the ambiguity.

Nada vuelve nada vuelve
Se van las flores y las hierbas
El perfume apenas llega como una campanada de otra provincia
Vienen otras miradas y otras voces
Viene otra agua en el río
Vienen otras hojas de repente en el bosque
Todo es otra cosa
Nada vuelve
Se fueron los caminos
Se fueron los minutos y las horas
Se alejó el río para siempre
Como los cometas que tanto admiramos

Desbordará mi corazón sobre la tierra
Y el universo será mi corazón

thing else. Nothing returns. Nothing returns. The flowers and grass leave. Their perfume hardly reaches me, like a bell chiming in another province. Other glances come, and other voices. Other water comes in the rivers. Other leaves come suddenly in the forest. All is something else. Nothing returns. The roads went. The minutes and hours went. The river went away for ever, like those comets we admire so much.

My heart will overflow on to the earth. And the universe will be my heart.

Altazor

Prefacio

NACÍ a los treinta y tres años, el día de la muerte de Cristo; nací en el Equinoccio, bajo las hortensias y los aeroplanos del calor.

Tenía yo un profundo mirar de pichón, de túnel y de automóvil sentimental. Lanzaba suspiros de acróbata.

Mi padre era ciego y sus manos eran más admirables que la noche.

Amo la noche, sombrero de todos los días.

La noche, la noche del día, del día al día siguiente.

Mi madre hablaba como la aurora y como los dirigibles que van a caer. Tenía cabellos color de bandera y ojos llenos de navíos lejanos.

Una tarde cogí mi paracaídas y dije: «Entre una estrella y dos golondrinas.» He aquí la muerte que se acerca como la tierra al globo que cae.

Altazor

Preface*

I WAS born thirty-three years old, on the day of Christ's death; I was born in the Equinox, under the hydrangeas and aeroplanes of heat.

I had the profound stare of a fledgling, of a tunnel, and of a sentimental car. I heaved sighs like an acrobat.

My father was blind, and his hands were more admirable than the night.

I love the night, the sombrero of every day.

The night, the night of day, of day following after day.

My mother spoke like the dawn, and like airships about to fall. I had hair the colour of flags and eyes full of distant ships.

One afternoon I took my parachute and said: 'Between one star and two swallows.' Here is death drawing closer like the earth to a falling balloon.

---

* Translated by John Hill.

Mi madre bordaba lágrimas desiertas en los primeros arcos iris.

Y ahora mi paracaídas cae de sueño en sueño por los espacios de la muerte.

El primer día encontré un pájaro desconocido que me dijo: «Si yo fuese dromedario no tendría sed. ¿Qué hora es?» Bebió las gotas de rocío de mis cabellos, me lanzó tres miradas y media y se alejó diciendo: «Adiós», con su pañuelo soberbio.

Hacia las dos, aquel día, encontré un precioso aeroplano, lleno de escamas y caracoles. Buscaba un rincón del cielo donde guarecerse de la lluvia.

Allá lejos, todos los barcos anclados, en la tinta de la aurora. De pronto, comenzaron a desprenderse, uno a uno, arrastrando como pabellón jirones de aurora incontestable.

Junto con marcharse los últimos, la aurora desapareció tras algunas olas desmesuradamente infladas.

Entonces oí hablar al Creador, sin nombre, que es un simple hueco en el vacío, hermoso como un ombligo:

My mother embroidered deserted tears on the first rainbows.

And now my parachute falls from dream to dream through the spaces of death.

The first day I met an unfamiliar bird who told me: 'If I were a dromedary I wouldn't be thirsty. What time is it?' It drank the dewdrops from my hair, cast me three and a half glances and went away saying 'Adiós', with its superb handkerchief.

About two o'clock, that day, I found a precious aeroplane, full of scales and snail-shells. It was looking for a corner in the sky to shelter from the rain.

Far away, all the ships anchored in the ink of dawn. Suddenly, they started to break away, one by one, dragging like flags the tatters of an incontestable dawn.

As the last ones went, the dawn disappeared behind some extremely over-inflated waves.

Then I heard the voice of the Creator, nameless, who is a simple cavity in the vacuum, beautiful as a navel:

«Hice un gran ruido y este ruido formó el océano y las olas del océano.

«Este ruido irá siempre pegado a las olas del mar y las olas del mar irán siempre pegadas a él, como los sellos en las tarjetas postales.

«Después tejí un largo bramante de rayos luminosos para coser los días uno a uno; los días que tienen un oriente legítimo o reconstituido, pero indiscutible.

«Después tracé la geografía de la tierra y las líneas de la mano.

«Después bebí un poco de coñac (a causa de la hidrografía).

«Después creé la boca y los labios de la boca, para aprisionar las sonrisas equívocas, y los dientes de la boca, para vigilar las groserías que no vienen a la boca.

«Creé la lengua de la boca que los hombres desviaron de su rol, haciéndola aprender a hablar . . . , a ella, ella, la bella nadadora, desviada para siempre de su rol acuático y puramente acariciador.»

'I made a great noise, and this noise made the ocean and the waves of the ocean.

'This noise will go forever bound to the waves of the sea, and the waves of the sea will go forever bound to it, like stamps on postcards.

'Afterwards I wove a long hempen cloth of luminous rays, to stitch the days together; the days which hold a legitimate or reconstituted orient, but indisputable.

'Afterwards I drew the geography of the earth, and the lines of the hand.

'Afterwards I drank a little cognac (because of hydrography).

'Afterwards I created the mouth and the lips of the mouth, to imprison the equivocal smiles, and the teeth of the mouth, to guard the vulgarities which do not come to the mouth.

'I created the tongue of the mouth, which men diverted from its role, making her learn to speak . . . her, the lovely swimmer, forever misled from her aquatic, purely caressing role.'

Mi paracaídas empezó a caer vertiginosamente. Tal es la fuerza de atracción de la muerte y del sepulcro abierto.

Podéis creerlo, la tumba tiene más poder que los ojos de la amada. La tumba abierta con todos sus imanes. Y esto te lo digo a ti, a ti que cuando sonríes haces pensar en el comienzo del mundo.

Mi paracaídas se enredó en una estrella apagada que seguía su órbita concienzudamente, como si ignorara la inutilidad de sus esfuerzos.

Y aprovechando este reposo bien ganado, comencé a llenar con profundos pensamientos las casillas de mi tablero:

«Los verdaderos poemas son incendios. La poesía se propaga por todas partes, iluminando sus consumaciones con estremecimientos de placer o de agonía.

«Se debe escribir en una lengua que no sea materna.

«Los cuarto puntos cardinales son tres: el sur y el norte.

«Un poema es una cosa que será.

My parachute began to fall vertiginously. Such is the force of attraction of death and of the opened sepulchre.

You can take it from me, the tomb is stronger than the eyes of the beloved. The tomb opened with all its magnets. And this I say to you, to you, that when you smile you recall the beginning of the world.

My parachute got tangled up in a quenched star, which was conscientiously following its orbit, as if it didn't know the uselessness of its efforts.

And taking advantage of this well-earned rest I started to fill up the squares of my chess-board with profound thoughts:

'True poems are fires. Poetry propagates itself everywhere, illuminating its consummations with shudders of pleasure or agony.

'It must be written in a language other than the mother-tongue.

'The four cardinal points are three: north and south.

'A poem is a thing which will be.

«Un poema es una cosa que nunca es, pero que debiera ser.

«Un poema es una cosa que nunca ha sido, que nunca podrá ser.

«Huye del sublime externo si no quieres morir aplastado por el viento.

«Si yo no hiciera al menos una locura por año, me volvería loco.»

Tomo mi paracaídas, y del borde de mi estrella en marcha me lanzo a la atmósfera del último suspiro.

Ruedo interminablemente sobre las rocas de los sueños, ruedo entre las nubes de la muerte.

Encuentro a la Virgen sentada en una rosa, y me dice:

«Mira mis manos: son transparentes como las bombillas eléctricas. ¿Ves los filamentos de donde corre la sangre de mi luz intacta?

«Mira mi aureola. Tiene algunas saltaduras, lo que prueba mi ancianidad.

«Soy la Virgen, la Virgen sin mancha de tinta humana, la única que no lo sea a medias, y soy la capitana de las otras once mil que estaban en verdad demasiado restauradas.

'A poem is a thing which never is, but ought to be.

'A poem is a thing which never has been, which never could be.

'Run away from the externally sublime, if you don't want to get crushed to death by the wind.

'If I didn't do at least one crazy thing a year I'd go crazy.'

I take my parachute, and from the edge of my moving star I launch myself into the atmosphere of the last sigh.

I roll interminably over the rocks of dreams, I roll between the clouds of death.

I find the Virgin sitting on a rose, and she says to me:

'Look at my hands: they are transparent as electric light bulbs. Do you see the filaments whence flows the blood of my intact light?

'Look at my halo. It has a few cracks, which prove how old I am.

'I am the Virgin, with no blot of humanity, the only [Virgin] not a half[-Virgin], and I am the captain of the other eleven thousand who really were over-restored.

«Hablo una lengua que llena los corazones según la ley de las nubes comunicantes.

«Digo siempre adiós, y me quedo.

«Ámame, hijo mío, pues adoro tu poesía y te enseñaré proezas aéreas.

«Tengo tanta necesidad de ternura, besa mis cabellos, los he lavado esta mañana en las nubes del alba y ahora quiero dormirme sobre el colchón de la neblina intermitente.

«Mis miradas son un alambre en el horizonte para el descanso de las golondrinas.

«Ámame.»

Me puse de rodillas en el espacio circular y la Virgen se elevó y vino a sentarse en mi paracaídas.

Me dormí y recité entonces mis más hermosos poemas.

Las llamas de mi poesía secaron los cabellos de la Virgen, que me dijo gracias y se alejó, sentada sobre su rosa blanda.

Y heme aquí, solo, como el pequeño huérfano de los naufragios anónimos.

'I speak a language which fills hearts according to the laws of clouds like communicating vessels.

'I always say *adiós*, and stay.

'Love me, my son, for I adore your poetry, and I'll teach you aerial feats.

'I have such a great need for tenderness, kiss my hair, I washed it this morning in the clouds of dawn, and now I want to go to sleep on the mattress of intermittent mist.

'My looks are a wire on the horizon where swallows may rest.

'Love me.'

I knelt in the round space, and the Virgin stood up and came and sat on my parachute.

I slept and then said my most beautiful poems.

The flames of my poetry dried the hair of the Virgin, who said thanks and went away sitting on her soft rose.

And here I am alone like the little orphan of the anonymous shipwrecks.

Ah, qué hermoso . . . , qué hermoso.

Veo las montañas, los ríos, las selvas, el mar, los barcos, las flores y los caracoles.

Veo la noche y el día y el eje en que se juntan.

Ah, ah, soy Altazor, el gran poeta, sin caballo que coma alpiste, ni caliente su garganta con claro de luna, sino con mi pequeño paracaídas como un quitasol sobre los planetas.

De cada gota del sudor de mi frente hice nacer astros, que os dejo la tarea de atizar como a botellas de vino.

Lo veo todo, tengo mi cerebro forjado en lenguas de profeta.

La montaña es el suspiro de Dios, ascendiendo en termómetro hinchado hasta tocar los pies de la amada.

Aquel que todo lo ha visto, que conoce todos los secretos sin ser Walt Whitman, pues jamás he tenido una barba blanca como las bellas enfermeras y los arroyos helados.

Aquel que oye durante la noche los martillos de los monederos falsos, que son solamente astrónomos activos.

Ah, how beautiful, how beautiful.

I see mountains, rivers, woods, the sea, ships, flowers and shells.

I see night and day and the axis where they meet.

Ah, ah, I am Altazor, the great poet without a horse to eat birdseed, nor to warm its throat with moonlight, but with my little parachute, like a parasol on the planets.

I give birth to stars from each drop of sweat on my forehead, and I leave you to poke them up as if they were bottles of wine.

I see everything: I have my brain wrought in the tongues of prophets.

The mountain is the sigh of God, climbing the swelling thermometer until it touches the feet of the beloved.

[I am] he who has seen it all, who knows all the secrets without being Walt Whitman, for I have never had a beard as white as lovely nurses and frozen brooks.

He who hears at night the hammers of counterfeiters, who are only active astronomers.

Aquel que bebe el vaso caliente de la sabiduría después del diluvio obedeciendo a las palomas y que conoce la ruta de la fatiga, la estela hirviente que dejan los barcos.

Aquel que conoce los almacenes de recuerdos y de bellas estaciones olvidadas.

Él, el pastor de aeroplanos, el conductor de las noches extraviadas y de los ponientes amaestrados hacia los polos únicos.

Su queja es semejante a una red parpadeante de aerolitos sin testigo.

El día se levanta en su corazón y él baja los párpados para hacer la noche del reposo agrícola.

Lava sus manos en la mirada de Dios, y peina su cabellera como la luz y la cosecha de esas flacas espigas de la lluvia satisfecha.

Los gritos se alejan como un rebaño sobre las lomas cuando las estrellas duermen después de una noche de trabajo continuo.

El hermoso cazador frente al bebedero celeste para los pájaros sin corazón.

He who drinks the hot glass of wisdom after the deluge, obeying the doves, and who knows the route of fatigue, the boiling wakes of ships.

He who knows the depot of memories and lovely forgotten seasons.

He, shepherd of aeroplanes, the leader of stray nights and tamed sunsets towards the only poles.

His dirge is like a net blinking with meteorites, and there is no witness.

The day rises in his heart and he lowers his eyelids to make the night of agrarian repose.

He washes his hands in the look of God, and combs his hair like light, and the harvest of those thin ears of corn of satisfied rain.

The shouts go away like a herd on the hills when the stars are asleep after a night of continual work.

The beautiful hunter before the celestial trough for the heartless birds.

Sé triste tal cual las gacelas ante el infinito y los meteoros, tal cual los desiertos sin mirajes.

Hasta la llegada de una boca hinchada de besos para la vendimia del destierro.

Sé triste, pues ella te espera en un rincón de este año que pasa.

Está quizá al extremo de tu canción próxima y será bella como la cascada en libertad y rica como la línea ecuatorial.

Sé triste, más triste que la rosa, la bella jaula de nuestras miradas y de las abejas sin experiencia.

La vida es un viaje en paracaídas y no lo que tú quieres creer.

Vamos cayendo, cayendo de nuestro cenit a nuestro nadir, y dejamos el aire manchado de sangre para que se envenenen los que vengan mañana a respirarlo.

Adentro de ti mismo, fuera de ti mismo, caerás del cenit al nadir porque ése es tu destino, tu miserable destino. Y mientras de más alto caigas, más alto será el rebote, más larga tu duración en la memoria de la piedra.

Be sad, like the gazelle before the infinite and the meteors, like deserts without mirages.

Until the arrival of a mouth swollen with kisses for the vintage of banishment.

Be sad, for she waits for you in a corner of this year which is passing.

Maybe she is at the end of your next song and will be as lovely as the waterfall at liberty, and as rich as the equatorial line.

Be sad, sadder than the rose, the beautiful cage of our glances and of the inexperienced bees.

Life is a trip in a parachute, and not what you want to believe.

We are falling, falling from our zenith to our nadir, and we leave the air stained with blood to poison those who will come to breathe it tomorrow.

Within yourself, outside yourself, you will fall from zenith to nadir for that is your destiny, your miserable destiny. And the greater your fall, the greater your bounce, the longer your duration in the memory of stone.

Hemos saltado del vientre de nuestra madre o del borde de una estrella y vamos cayendo.

Ah mi paracaídas, la única rosa perfumada de la atmósfera, la rosa de la muerte, despeñada entre los astros de la muerte.

¿Habéis oído? Ese es el ruido siniestro de los pechos cerrados.

Abre la puerta de tu alma y sal a respirar al lado afuera. Puedes abrir con un suspiro la puerta que haya cerrado el huracán.

Hombre, he ahí tu paracaídas, maravilloso como el vértigo.

Poeta, he ahí tu paracaídas, maravilloso como el imán del abismo.

Mago, he ahí tu paracaídas que una palabra tuya puede convertir en un parasubidas maravilloso como el relámpago que quisiera cegar al creador.

¿Qué esperas?

We have jumped from our mother's womb or from the edge of a star, and we go on falling.

Ah, my parachute, the unique and perfumed rose of the atmosphere, the rose of death, flung headlong between the stars of death.

Have you heard? That is the sinister noise of closed breasts.

Open the door of your soul, and come out to breathe on the outside. You can open with a breath the door which the hurricane would have slammed.

Man, here is your parachute, marvellous like vertigo.

Poet, here is your parachute, marvellous like the magnet of the abyss.

Magician, here is your parachute which with a word you can turn into a marvellous para-rise, marvellous as lightning which seeks to blind the creator.

What do you expect?

Mas he ahí el secreto del Tenebroso que olvidó sonreír.

Y el paracaídas aguarda amarrado a la puerta como el caballo de la fuga interminable.

But here is the secret of the Shadowy One who forgot to smile.

And the parachute waits tied to the door like the horse of the interminable flight.

GABRIELA MISTRAL (1889–1957)

La extranjera

A Francis de Miomandre

HABLA con dejo de sus mares bárbaros,
con no sé qué algas y no sé qué arenas;
reza oración a dios sin bulto y peso,
envejecida como si muriera.
Ese huerto nuestro que nos hizo extraño,
ha puesto cactus y zarpadas hierbas.
Alienta del resuello del desierto
y ha amado con pasión de que blanquea,
que nunca cuenta y que si nos contase
sería como el mapa de otra estrella.
Vivirá entre nosotros ochenta años,
pero siempre será como si llega,
hablando lengua que jadea y gime
y que le entienden sólo bestezuelas.
Y va a morirse en medio de nosotros,
en una noche en la que más padezca,
con sólo su destino por almohada,
de una muerte callada y *extranjera.*

Foreigner

SHE speaks of her barbarous seas with a strange accent; her seas with I don't know what kinds of seaweeds and sands. She raises a prayer to God without form or weight, looking old, as though she were dying. That orchard of ours that she made strange has grown cactus and scratching grasses. She is nourished by the breath of the desert, and has loved with a passion that made her grey, that she never speaks of, and that would be like the map of another star if she were to tell us of it. She will live eighty years among us, always seeming to have just arrived; speaking a tongue that pants and moans, understood only by small animals. And she will die among us, on a night during which she suffers more, with only her destiny as a pillow, stricken with a quiet and *foreign* death.

La medianoche

FINA, la medianoche.
Oigo los nudos del rosal:
la savia empuja subiendo a la rosa.

Oigo
las rayas quemadas del tigre
real: no le dejan dormir.

Oigo
la estrofa de uno,
y le crece en la noche
como la duna.

Oigo
a mi madre dormida
con dos alientos.
(Duermo yo en ella,
de cinco años.)

Oigo el Ródano
que baja y que me lleva como un padre
ciego de espuma ciega.

Midnight

IT is delicate, midnight. I hear the knots of the rose-bush, the pushing sap rising to the rose.

I hear the scorched stripes of the regal tiger: they do not let him sleep.

I hear a canto of one, and it swells in the night like a sand dune.

I hear my mother sleeping with two breaths. I have slept in her for five years.

I hear the Rhone that descends and carries me like a father, blind with blind foam.

Y después nada oigo
sino que voy cayendo
en los muros de Arlés,
llenos de sol . . .

And afterwards I hear nothing, but keep falling on the walls of Arles, full of sunlight . . .

PABLO NERUDA (b. 1904)

Walking Around

SUCEDE que me canso de ser hombre.
Sucede que entro en las sastrerías y en los cines
marchito, impenetrable, como un cisne de fieltro
navegando en un agua de origen y ceniza.

El olor de las peluquerías me hace llorar a gritos.
Sólo quiero un descanso de piedras o de lana,
sólo quiero no ver establecimientos ni jardines,
ni mercaderías, ni anteojos, ni ascensores.

Sucede que me canso de mis pies y mis uñas
y mi pelo y mi sombra.
Sucede que me canso de ser hombre.

Sin embargo sería delicioso
asustar a un notario con un lirio cortado
o dar muerte a una monja con un golpe de oreja.
Sería bello

Walking Around

IT happens that I'm tired of being a man. It happens that, withered, inpenetrable, like a swan made of felt, navigating in a water of origin and ash, I enter tailors' shops and cinemas.

The smell of hairdressers' shops makes me cry and weep. I only want a rest from stones or wool. I only want not to see establishments or gardens, goods, spectacles or lifts.

It happens that I'm tired of my feet and my nails and my hair and my shadow. It happens that I'm tired of being a man.

Nonetheless, it would be delicious to frighten a notary with a cut lily, or to kill a nun by a blow with the ear. It would be beautiful to

ir por las calles con un cuchillo verde
y dando gritos hasta morir de frío.

No quiero seguir siendo raíz en las tinieblas,
vacilante, extendido, tiritando de sueño,
hacia abajo, en las tapias mojadas de la tierra,
absorbiendo y pensando, comiendo cada día.

No quiero para mí tantas desgracias.
No quiero continuar de raíz y de tumba,
de subterráneo solo, de bodega con muertos,
aterido, muriéndome de pena.

Por eso el día lunes arde como el petróleo
cuando me ve llegar con mi cara de cárcel,
y aúlla en su transcurso como una rueda herida,
y da pasos de sangre caliente hacia la noche.

Y me empuja a ciertos rincones, a ciertas casas
    húmedas,
a hospitales donde los huesos salen por la ventana,

go through the streets with a green knife shouting until I died of cold.

I don't want to continue to be a root in utter darkness, vacillating, stretched out, shivering with sleep, turned down on to the damp walls of the earth, absorbing and thinking, eating every day.

For me, I don't want all these disasters. I don't want to go on as a root or a tomb; as a solitary tunnel, as a cellar of corpses, stiff with cold, dying of misery.

That's why Monday blazes like petrol when it sees me arrive with my prison face, and howls in its passing like a wounded wheel and makes steps of warm blood into the night.

And pushes me into certain corners, towards certain damp houses, into hospitals where bones fly out of the window, into

a ciertas zapaterías con olor a vinagre,
a calles espantosas como grietas.

Hay pájaros de color de azufre y horribles intestinos
colgando de las puertas de las casas que odio,
hay dentaduras olvidadas en una cafetera,
hay espejos
que debieran haber llorado de vergüenza y espanto,
hay paraguas en todas partes, y venenos, y ombligos.

Yo paseo con calma, con ojos, con zapatos,
con furia, con olvido,
paso, cruzo oficinas y tiendas de ortopedia,
y patios donde hay ropas colgadas de un alambre:
calzoncillos, toallas y camisas que lloran
lentas lágrimas sucias.

certain cobblers' shops smelling of vinegar, into streets terrifying as crevices.

Hanging from the doors of houses I hate are birds the colour of sulphur, and disgusting intestines. There are dentures forgotten in a coffeepot, mirrors that must surely have wept with shame and fear. And everywhere there are umbrellas, and poisons, and navels.

I pass calmly, with eyes, shoes, rage and forgetfulness. I pass, crossing offices and orthopaedic shops, courtyards with clothes hanging from wires; underpants, towels and shirts that weep slow, dirty tears.

Bruselas

DE TODO LO QUE HE HECHO, DE TODO
LO QUE HE PERDIDO,
de todo lo que he ganado sobresaltadamente,
en hierro amargo, en hojas, puedo ofrecer un poco.

Un sabor asustado, un río que las plumas
de las quemantes águilas van cubriendo, un sulfúrico
retroceso de pétalos.
No me perdona ya la sal entera
ni el pan continuo, ni la pequeña iglesia devorada
por la lluvia marina, ni el carbón mordido
por la espuma secreta.

He buscado y hallado, pesadamente,
bajo la tierra, entre los cuerpos temibles,
como un diente de pálida madera
llegando y yendo bajo el ácido duro,
junto a los materiales
de la agonía, entre luna y cuchillos,
muriendo de nocturno.
Ahora, en medio

Brussels

OF ALL I HAVE DONE, OF ALL I HAVE LOST, of all I have won unexpectedly, in bitter iron, in leaves; I can offer a little.

A fearsome taste, a river that the feathers of the flaming eagles keep covering, a sulphuric recoil of petals. Not the whole salt nor the unceasing bread, not the tiny church devoured by sea rain nor the coal gnawed by the secret foam can pardon me.

I have sought and found, weightily, under the ground, among fearful bodies, like a tooth of pale wood arriving and leaving under the hard acid, next to the materials of agony, between moon and knives, dying nightly. Now, in the midst of disregarded speed,

de la velocidad desestimada, al lado
de los muros sin hilos,
en el fondo cortado por los términos,
aquí estoy con aquello que pierde estrellas,
vegetalmente, solo.

Alturas de Macchu Picchu

DEL aire al aire, como una red vacía,
iba yo entre las calles y la atmósfera, llegando y despi-
 diendo,
en el advenimiento del otoño la moneda extendida
de las hojas, y entre la primavera y las espigas,
lo que el más grande amor, como dentro de un guante
que cae, nos entrega como una larga luna.

(Días de fulgor vivo en la intemperie
de los cuerpos: aceros convertidos
al silencio del ácido:
noches deshilachadas hasta la última harina:
estambres agredidos de la patria nupcial.)

beside walls without seams, in the depth cut by boundaries, I am here with that which loses stars, vegetally, alone.

The Heights of Macchu Picchu

FROM air to air, I went through the streets and the atmosphere like an empty net, arriving and leaving at the advent of autumn, the spread coinage of the leaves, and, between spring and the ears of corn, that which the greatest love, as in a falling glove, delivers up to us like a lengthened moon.

(Days of live brilliance in the rough weather of bodies: steels changed to the silence of acid: nights unravelled to the final flour: assaulted stamens of the nuptial land.)

Alguien que me esperó entre los violines
encontró un mundo como una torre enterrada
hundiendo su espiral más abajo de todas
las hojas de color de ronco azufre:
más abajo, en el oro de la geología,
como una espada envuelta en meteoros,
hundí la mano turbulenta y dulce
en lo más genital de lo terrestre.

Puse la frente entre las olas profundas,
descendí como gota entre la paz sulfúrica,
y, como un ciego, regresé al jazmín
de la gastada primavera humana.

II

Si la flor a la flor entrega el alto germen
y la roca mantiene su flor diseminada
en su golpeado traje de diamante y arena,
el hombre arruga el pétalo de la luz que recoge
en los determinados manantiales marinos
y taladra el metal palpitante en sus manos.

Someone who awaited me among the violins met with a world like a buried tower, sinking its spiral beneath all the leaves the colour of harsh sulphur: and lower still, in the gold of geology, like a sword sheathed in meteors, I sank my turbulent and gentle hand into the deepest genitals of terrestrial things.

Leaning my forehead through unfathomed waves, I submerged, one drop within the peace of sulphur, and, like a blind man, I returned to the jasmine of our worn-out human spring.

If flower gives up its precious seed to flower, and rock keeps its bloom scattered in a bruised garment of diamond and sand, then man crumples the petal of light he gleans from the fixed sources of the sea and pierces the metal throbbing in his hands. And soon, on

Y pronto, entre la ropa y el humo, sobre la mesa hundida
como una barajada cantidad, queda el alma:
cuarzo y desvelo, lágrimas en el océano
como estanques de frío: pero aún
mátala y agonízala con papel y con odio,
sumérgela en la alfombra cotidiana, desgárrala
entre las vestiduras hostiles del alambre.

No: por los corredores, aire, mar o caminos,
quién guarda sin puñal (como las encarnadas
amapolas) su sangre? La cólera ha extenuado
la triste mercancía del vendedor de seres,
y, mientras en la altura del ciruelo, el rocío
desde mil años deja su carta transparente
sobre la misma rama que lo espera, oh corazón, oh frente
  triturada
entre las cavidades del otoño:

Cuántas veces en las calles de invierno de una ciudad o en
un autobús o un barco en el crepúsculo, o en la soledad
más espesa, la de la noche de fiesta, bajo el sonido
de sombras y campanas, en la misma gruta del placer
  humano,

the sunken table, the soul remains, like a shuffled quantity, among the clothes and smoke: quartz and sleeplessness, tears in the ocean like pools of cold: but even then, kill it, and quicken its death with paper and hate, suffocate it in the carpet of habit, rend it in the hostile garments of wire.

No: who (like the scarlet poppies), through the corridors, air, sea or highway, guards his blood without a dagger? Anger has exhausted the sad wares of the dealer in creatures, whilst in the plum-tree's summit the dew has left for a thousand years its transparent map on the branch that awaits it: oh heart, oh brow crushed among the cavities of autumn:

How many times in wintry city streets, or in a bus, or a boat at dusk, or in the denser solitude of festive nights, under the sounds of shadows and bells, in the very cave of human delight, have I

me quise detener a buscar la eterna veta insondable
que antes toqué en la piedra o en el relámpago que el
beso desprendía.

(Lo que en el cereal como una historia amarilla
de pequeños pechos preñados va repitiendo un número
que sin cesar es ternura en las capas germinales,
y que, idéntica siempre, se desgrana en marfil
y lo que en el agua es patria transparente, campana
desde la nieve aislada hasta las olas sangrientas.)

No pude asir sino un racimo de rostros o de máscaras
precipitadas, como anillos de oro vacío,
como ropas dispersas hijas de un otoño rabioso
que hiciera temblar el miserable árbol de las razas asus-
tadas.

No tuve sitio donde descansar la mano
y que, corriente como agua de manantial encadenado,
o firme como grumo de antracita o cristal,
hubiera devuelto el calor o el frío de mi mano extendida.
Qué era el hombre? En qué parte de su conversación
abierta

wanted to linger and search for the eternal unfathomable vein I'd touched before in a stone or in the lightning released by a kiss.

(That which in wheat, like a yellow story of small swollen breasts, keeps repeating a number that is ceaselessly tender in the fecund layers, and that, ever identical, sheds its grains in ivory: and that which in water is the translucent homeland, a bell from isolated snows down to bloody waves.)

I could only seize a cluster of faces or fallen masks, like rings of hollow gold, like scattered clothes, daughters of a rabid autumn that shook the wretched trees of frightened races.

I had no place to rest my hand, no place which, running like chained spring water or firm as a nugget of anthracite or crystal, would have returned the heat or cold of my open hand. What was man? In what part of his open conversation, among shops and

entre los almacenes y los silbidos, en cuál de sus movimientos metálicos
vivía lo indestructible, lo imperecedero, la vida?

III

El ser como el maíz se desgranaba en el inacabable
granero de los hechos perdidos, de los acontecimientos
miserables, del uno al siete, al ocho,
y no una muerte, sino muchas muertes llegaba a cada uno:
cada día una muerte pequeña, polvo, gusano, lámpara
que se apaga en el lodo del suburbio, una pequeña muerte de alas gruesas
entraba en cada hombre como una corta lanza
y era el hombre asediado del pan o del cuchillo,
el ganadero: el hijo de los puertos, o el capitán oscuro del arado,
o el roedor de las calles espesas:

todos desfallecieron esperando su muerte, su corta muerte diaria:

whistles, in which of his metallic movements lived the indestructible, the imperishable, life?

Being, like maize, shed its grains in the endless granary of lost deeds, wretched events, from one to seven, to eight. And not one death, but many deaths, came to everyone: each day a little death, dust, maggot, lamp that extinguishes itself in the mire of suburbia, a little death with fat wings entered into each man like a short spear, and man was besieged by bread or knife; the cattle-raiser, the son of the ports; or the dark captain of the plough, or a rodent of dense streets:

All grew weak awaiting their death, their short daily death; and

y su quebranto aciago de cada día era
como una copa negra que bebían temblando.

IV

La poderosa muerte me invitó muchas veces:
era como la sal invisible en las olas,
y lo que su invisible sabor diseminaba
era como mitades de hundimientos y altura
o vastas construcciones de viento y ventisquero.

Yo al férreo filo vine, a la angostura
del aire, a la mortaja de agricultura y piedra,
al estelar vacío de los pasos finales
y a la vertiginosa carretera espiral:
pero, ancho mar, oh muerte!, de ola en ola no vienes,
sino como un galope de claridad nocturna
o como los totales números de la noche.

Nunca llegaste a hurgar en el bolsillo, no era
posible tu visita sin vestimenta roja:
sin auroral alfombra de cercado silencio:
sin altos o enterrados patrimonios de lágrimas.

their ominous suffering each day was like a black cup which they drank trembling.

Many times mighty death invited me: it was as salt invisible in the waves, and what its invisible savour was scattering was as halves of downfalls and heights, or vast constructions of wind and snowdrift.

I came to the iron's edge, to the narrow passage of air, to the shroud of husbandry and stone, to the interstellar void of final steps and to the dizzy spiral highway: but, wide sea, oh death!, you do not come from wave to wave, but as a gallop of nocturnal clarity or the absolute numbers of the night.

You never came to meddle in our pockets, your visit was not possible without a scarlet garment, without a dawn carpet of enclosed silence, without a heritage of tears, enshrined or interred.

No pude amar en cada ser un árbol
con su pequeño otoño a cuestas (la muerte de mil hojas),
todas las falsas muertes y las resurrecciones
sin tierra, sin abismo:
quise nadar en las más anchas vidas,
en las más sueltas desembocaduras,
y cuando poco a poco el hombre fue negándome
y fue cerrando paso y puerta para que no tocaran
mis manos manantiales su inexistencia herida,
entonces fui por calle y calle y río y río,
y ciudad y ciudad y cama y cama,
y atravesó el desierto mi máscara salobre,
y en las últimas casas humilladas, sin lámpara, sin fuego,
sin pan, sin piedra, sin silencio, solo,
rodé muriendo de mi propia muerte.

V

No eres tú, muerte grave, ave de plumas férreas,
la que el pobre heredero de las habitaciones
llevaba entre alimentos apresurados, bajo la piel vacía:

I could not love within each being a tree with its small autumn on its shoulders (the death of a thousand leaves), all those false deaths and resurrections, without earth, without depths; I wished to swim in the widest lives, in the most freely flowing estuaries. And when, little by little, man came denying me, shutting his path and door so that my life-bringing hands could not touch his wounded inexistence – then I went through street after street, river after river, city after city, bed after bed. And my brackish mask crossed the desert and in the last degraded dwellings, without lamp, fire, bread, stone or silence, alone, I wandered, dying of my own death.

It was not you, grave death, iron-plumed bird, that the poor heir to the dwellings carried among gulped food under the empty skin:

era algo, un pobre pétalo de cuerda exterminada:
un átomo del pecho que no vino al combate
o el áspero rocío que no cayó en la frente.
Era lo que no pudo renacer, un pedazo
de la pequeña muerte sin paz ni territorio:
un hueso, una campana que morían en él.
Yo levanté las vendas del yodo, hundí las manos
en los pobres dolores que mataban la muerte,
y no encontré en la herida sino una racha fría
que entraba por los vagos intersticios del alma.

VI

Entonces en la escala de la tierra he subido
entre la atroz maraña de las selvas perdidas
hasta ti, Macchu Picchu.
Alta ciudad de piedras escalares,
por fin morada del que lo terrestre
no escondió en las dormidas vestiduras.
En ti, como dos líneas paralelas,
la cuna del relámpago y del hombre
se mecían en un viento de espinas.

rather it was a rotten thread of old rope, an atom of breast that never came to the fight, or the harsh dew that never fell on the forehead. It was what could not be reborn, a fragment of little death with neither peace nor territory: a bone, a church bell that died within itself. I took off the iodine bandages, plunged my hands into the poor pains that were killing death, and met nothing in the wound save an icy draught that entered through the loose interstices of the soul.

Then I climbed the ladder of the earth, through the savage tangle of lost jungles to you, Macchu Picchu. Tall city of stepped stone, finally the abode of him whom earth had not hidden within her sleeping garments. In you, as two parallel lines, the cradles of both lightning and man swayed in a wind of thorns.

Madre de piedra, espuma de los cóndores.

Alto arrecife de la aurora humana.

Pala perdida en la primera arena.

Ésta fue la morada, éste es el sitio:
aquí los anchos granos del maíz ascendieron
y bajaron de nuevo como granizo rojo.

Aquí la hebra dorada salió de la vicuña
a vestir los amores, los túmulos, las madres,
el rey, las oraciones, los guerreros.

Aquí los pies del hombre descansaron de noche
junto a los pies del águila en las altas guaridas
carniceras, y en la aurora
pisaron con los pies del trueno la niebla enrarecida,
y tocaron las tierras y las piedras
hasta reconocerlas en la noche o la muerte.

Miro las vestiduras y las manos,
el vestigio del agua en la oquedad sonora,
la pared suavizada por el tacto de un rostro

Mother of stone, foam of the condors.

High reef of human dawn.

Spade buried in the primordial sand.

This was the dwelling, this is the place: here the fat grains of maize sprang high, and fell again like red hail.

Here the golden fibre was stripped from the vicuña to clothe the loves, the tombs, the mothers, the king, the prayers, the warriors.

Here at night men's feet rested next to eagles' claws in the high bloody lairs, and in the dawn they trod the rarefied mist with thundering steps and touched the earth and stones until they recognized them in the night, or in death.

I gaze at clothes and hands, at the trace of water in the echoing hollow, at the wall worn smooth by the touch of a face that watched

que miró con mis ojos las lámparas terrestres,
que aceitó con mis manos las desaparecidas
maderas: porque todo, ropaje, piel, vasijas,
palabras, vino, panes,
se fue, cayó a la tierra.

Y el aire entró con dedos
de azahar sobre todos los dormidos:
mil años de aire, meses, semanas de aire,
de viento azul, de cordillera férrea,
que fueron como suaves huracanes de pasos
lustrando el solitario recinto de la piedra.

VII

Muertos de un solo abismo, sombras de una hondonada,
la profunda, es así como al tamaño
de vuestra magnitud
vino la verdadera, la más abrasadora
muerte y desde las rocas taladradas,
desde los capiteles escarlatas,
desde los acueductos escalares
os desplomásteis como en un otoño
en una sola muerte.

earth's lanterns with my eyes, that oiled the vanished timbers with my hands: for everything, clothing, skin, pots, words, wine, bread, has gone, has fallen to earth.

And the air entered with fingers of orange-blossom over all who slept: a thousand years of air, months, weeks of air, of blue wind, of iron mountain ranges, that were as gentle hurricanes of footsteps polishing the solitary precinct of the stone.

Dead of a sole abyss, shades of one gully – the deep one – that is how to the dimensions of your magnitude came the true, the most scorching death, and from the perforated rocks, the scarlet cornices and tiered aqueducts you tumbled, like in an autumn, into a single

Hoy el aire vacío ya no llora,
ya no conoce vuestros pies de arcilla,
ya olvidó vuestros cántaros que filtraban el cielo
cuando lo derramaban los cuchillos del rayo,
y el árbol poderoso fue comido
por la niebla, y cortado por la racha.
Él sostuvo una mano que cayó de repente
desde la altura hasta el final del tiempo.
Ya no sois, manos de araña, débiles
hebras, tela enmarañada:
cuanto fuistes cayó: costumbres, sílabas
raídas, máscaras de luz deslumbradora.

Pero una permanencia de piedra y de palabra:
la ciudad como un vaso se levantó en las manos
de todos, vivos, muertos, callados, sostenidos
de tanta muerte, un muro, de tanta vida un golpe
de pétalos de piedra: la rosa permanente, la morada:
este arrecife andino de colonias glaciales.

Cuando la mano de color de arcilla
se convirtió en arcilla, y cuando los pequeños párpados
se cerraron
llenos de ásperos muros, poblados de castillos,

death. Today the empty air no longer weeps, nor knows your feet of clay: already it has forgotten your ewers that filtered the sky when knives of lightning scattered it and the powerful tree was devoured by mist and cut down by a blast [of wind]. It held up a hand that fell suddenly from the heights to the end of time. You are no more, spider hands, weak threads, tangled web: all that you were dropped away: customs, tattered syllables, dazzling masks of light.

But a permanence of stone and word: the city like a cup was raised by every hand, living, dead, silent, sustained by so much death, a wall, of so much life, a blow of stone petals: the everlasting rose, the abode: this Andean reef of glacial colonies.

When the clay-coloured hand became truly clay, and when the tiny eyelids closed, filled with rough walls, peopled with castles;

y cuando todo el hombre se enredó en su agujero,
quedó la exactitud enarbolada:
el alto sitio de la aurora humana:
la más alta vasija que contuvo el silencio:
una vida de piedra después de tantas vidas.

VIII

Sube conmigo, amor americano.

Besa conmigo las piedras secretas.
La plata torrencial del Urubamba
hace volar el polen a su copa amarilla.
Vuela el vacío de la enredadera,
la planta pétrea, la guirnalda dura
sobre el silencio del cajón serrano.

Ven, minúscula vida, entre las alas
de la tierra, mientras – cristal y frío, aire golpeado
apartando esmeraldas combatidas,
oh, agua salvaje, bajas de la nieve.

and when men were all jumbled in their pit, unfurled precision remained; the high place of human dawn: the tallest vessel that contained the silence: a life of stone after so many lives.

Climb with me, American love.

Kiss with me the secret stones. The torrential silver of the Urubamba makes pollen fly to its golden cup. The hollow of the creeper, the petrified plant, the rigid garland, soar over the silence of the mountain coffer.

Come, tiny life, between the wings of the earth, whilst you, oh savage water – crystal and cold, beaten air, parting embattled emeralds – descend from the snow.

Amor, amor, hasta la noche abrupta,
desde el sonoro pedernal andino,
hacia la aurora de rodillas rojas,
contempla el hijo ciego de la nieve.

Oh, Wilkamayu de sonoros hilos,
cuando rompes tus truenos lineales
en blanca espuma, como herida nieve,
cuando tu vendaval acantilado
canta y castiga despertando al cielo,
qué idioma traes a la oreja apenas
desarraigada de tu espuma andina?

Quién apresó el relámpago del frío
y lo dejó en la altura encadenado,
repartido en sus lágrimas glaciales,
sacudido en sus rápidas espadas,
golpeando sus estambres aguerridos,
conducido en su cama de guerrero,
sobresaltado en su final de roca?

Qué dicen tus destellos acosados?
Tu secreto relámpago rebelde
antes viajó poblado de palabras?

Love, love, until the sudden night; contemplate the blind son of the snow from the sonorous Andean flint towards the red knees of dawn.

Oh Wilkamayu of sonorous fibres, when you break your lineal thunders in white foam, like wounded snow, when your bluff gale sings and chastises, awakening heaven, what language do you bring to an ear hardly uprooted from your Andean foam?

Who seized the lightning of cold and left it bound to the heights, shared out among its frozen tears, shaken on its swift swords, pounding its veteran fabric, guided to its warrior's bed, startled in its rocky end?

What do your harried flashes say? Did your secret rebel lightning once travel peopled by words? Who goes shattering frozen

Quién va rompiendo sílabas heladas,
idiomas negros, estandartes de oro,
bocas profundas, gritos sometidos,
en tus delgadas aguas arteriales?

Quién va cortando párpados florales
que vienen a mirar desde la tierra?
Quién precipita los racimos muertos
que bajan en tus manos de cascada
a desgranar su noche desgranada
en el carbón de la geología?

Quién despeña la rama de los vínculos?
Quién otra vez sepulta los adioses?

Amor, amor, no toques la frontera,
ni adores la cabeza sumergida:
deja que el tiempo cumpla su estatura
en su salón de manantiales rotos,
y, entre el agua veloz y las murallas,
recoge el aire del desfiladero,
las paralelas láminas del viento,
el canal ciego de las cordilleras,

syllables, black languages, golden banners, bottomless mouths and subjugated cries in your meagre arterial waters?

Who wanders slicing floral eyelids that come from earth to watch? Who hurls the dead seed clusters that fall from your cascading hands to scatter their flailed night in the coal of geology?

Who precipitates the branch of these bonds? Who, once more, has buried the farewells?

Love, love, neither touch the border, nor worship the sunken head: let time fulfil its stature in its hall of broken sources, and between the swift water and the ramparts gather the air from the gorge, the parallel sheets of wind, the blind canal of mountain

el áspero saludo del rocío,
y sube, flor a flor, por la espesura,
pisando la serpiente despeñada.

En la escarpada zona, piedra y bosque,
polvo de estrellas verdes, selva clara,
Mantur estalla como un lago vivo
o como un nuevo piso del silencio.

Ven a mi propio ser, al alba mía,
hasta las soledades coronadas.
El reino muerto vive todavía.

Y en el Reloj la sombra sanguinaria
del cóndor cruza como una nave negra.

IX

Águila sideral, viña de bruma.
Bastión perdido, cimitarra ciega.
Cinturón estrellado, pan solemne.
Escala torrencial, párpado inmenso.
Túnica triangular, polen de piedra.
Lámpara de granito, pan de piedra.

ranges, the harsh greeting of the dew; and climb, flower after flower, through the thickness, trampling the cast-down serpent.

In this jagged zone – stone and forest, dust of green stars, bright jungle – Mantur bursts out like a living lake, or a new level of silence.

Come to my very being, to my own dawn, up to the crowned solitudes. The dead kingdom lives still.

And on the Clock the bloody shadow of the condor crosses like a black ship.

Sidereal eagle, vineyard of mist. Lost bastion, blind scimitar. Star-strewn belt, sacred bread. Torrential stairway, giant eyelid. Triangular tunic, pollen of stone. Granite lamp, bread of stone. Mineral

Serpiente mineral, rosa de piedra.
Nave enterrada, manantial de piedra.
Caballo de la luna, luz de piedra.
Escuadra equinoccial, vapor de piedra.
Geometría final, libro de piedra.
Témpano entre las ráfagas labrado.
Madrépora del tiempo sumergido.
Muralla por los dedos suavizada.
Techumbre por las plumas combatida.
Ramos de espejo, bases de tormenta.
Tronos volcados por la enredadera.
Régimen de la garra encarnizada.
Vendaval sostenido en la vertiente.
Inmóvil catarata de turquesa.
Campana patriarcal de los dormidos.
Argolla de las nieves dominadas.
Hierro acostado sobre sus estatuas.
Inaccesible temporal cerrado.
Manos de puma, roca sanguinaria.
Torre sombrera, discusión de nieve.
Noche elevada en dedos y raíces.
Ventana de las nieblas, paloma endurecida.
Planta nocturna, estatua de los truenos.
Cordillera esencial, techo marino.

snake, rose of stone. Buried ship, source of stone. Horse of the moon, light of stone. Equinoctial quadrant, vapour of stone. Ultimate geometry, book of stone. Iceberg carved among the gusts. Coral of sunken time. Ramparts smoothed by fingers. Roof fought by feathers. Clusters of mirror, foundations of tempest. Thrones overturned by the climbing vine. Regime of the bloody talon. Gale held on the slope. Immobile turquoise cataract. Patriarchal bell of those who sleep. Collar of the subjugated snows. Iron stretched out over its statues. Closed and inaccessible storm. Puma paws, bloodthirsty stone. Shadowed tower, snow's argument. Night raised upon fingers and roots. Window of mists, obdurate dove. Nocturnal plant, statue of thunderclaps. Essential cordillera, marine roof.

Arquitectura de águilas perdidas.
Cuerda del cielo, abeja de la altura.
Nivel sangriento, estrella construída.
Burbuja mineral, luna de cuarzo.
Serpiente andina, frente de amaranto.
Cúpula del silencio, patria pura.
Novia del mar, árbol de catedrales.
Ramo de sal, cerezo de alas negras.
Dentadura nevada, trueno frío.
Luna arañada, piedra amenazante.
Cabellera del frío, acción del aire.
Volcán de manos, catarata oscura.
Ola de plata, dirección del tiempo.

X

Piedra en la piedra, el hombre, dónde estuvo?
Aire en el aire, el hombre, dónde estuvo?
Tiempo en el tiempo, el hombre, dónde estuvo?
Fuiste también el pedacito roto
del hombre inconcluso, de águila vacía
que por las calles de hoy, que por las huellas,
que por las hojas del otoño muerto

Architecture of lost eagles. Rope of the sky, bee of the summit. Bloody level, built star. Mineral bubble, moon of quartz. Andean serpent, brow of amaranth. Dome of silence, pure fatherland. Bride of the sea, tree of cathedrals. Cluster of salt, black-winged cherry-tree. Teeth of snow, icy thunder. Scratched moon, menacing stone. Icy head of hair, action of air. Volcano of hands, gloomy cataract. Wave of silver, destination of time.

Stone within stone, and where was man? Air within air, and where was man? Time within time, and where was man? Were you also the broken fragment of incomplete man, of the hollow eagle that goes pounding the soul into the tomb through the streets of today, through tracks, through the leaves of dead autumn? Poor hand,

va machacando el alma hasta la tumba?
La pobre mano, el pie, la pobre vida . . .
Los días de la luz deshilachada
en ti, como la lluvia
sobre las banderillas de la fiesta,
dieron pétalo a pétalo de su alimento oscuro
en la boca vacía?
                    Hambre, coral del hombre,
hambre, planta secreta, raíz de los leñadores,
hambre, subió tu raya de arrecife
hasta estas altas torres desprendidas?

Yo te interrogo, sal de los caminos,
muéstrame la cuchara, déjame, arquitectura,
roer con un palito los estambres de piedra,
subir todos los escalones del aire hasta el vacío,
rascar la entraña hasta tocar el hombre.

Macchu Picchu, pusiste
piedras en la piedra, y en la base, harapo?
Carbón sobre carbón, y en el fondo la lágrima?
Fuego en el oro, y en él, temblando el rojo
goterón de la sangre?

[poor] foot, poor life. . . . Days of frayed light, in you, like rain over the festive *banderillas*, did they give the empty mouth their dark nourishment petal by petal? Hunger, coral of man, hunger, secret plant, root of the woodcutters, hunger – did your line of reefs climb to these loosed towers?

I ask you, salt of the roads; show me the trowel. Permit me, architecture, to wear away the stone stamens with a small stick, to climb all the rungs of air to emptiness, to scrape the vitals until I touch man.

Macchu Picchu, did you place stone within stone and rag in the foundation? Coal upon coal, and a tear at the bottom? Fire within gold and within it, trembling, the red raindrop of the blood? Return

Devuélveme el esclavo que enterraste!
Sacude de las tierras el pan duro
del miserable, muéstrame los vestidos
del siervo y su ventana.
Dime cómo durmió cuando vivía.
Dime si fue su sueño
ronco, entreabierto, como un hoyo negro
hecho por la fatiga sobre el muro.
El muro, el muro! Si sobre su sueño
gravitó cada piso de piedra, y si cayó bajo ella
como bajo una luna, con el sueño!
Antigua América, novia sumergida,
también tus dedos,
al salir de la selva hacia el alto vacío de los dioses,
bajo los estandartes nupciales de la luz y el decoro,
mezclándose al trueno de los tambores y de las lanzas,
también, también tus dedos,
los que la rosa abstracta y la línea del frío, los
que el pecho sangriento del nuevo cereal trasladaron
hasta la tela de materia radiante, hasta las duras cavidades,
también, también, América enterrada, guardaste en lo
más bajo,
en el amargo intestino, como un águila, el hambre?

me the slave you buried! Shake off from these lands the hard bread of the poor. Show me the garments, and the window, of the serf. Tell me how he slept while he was living. Tell me if his sleep was raucous, gaping; like a black hole worn into the wall by fatigue. The wall! The wall! If each floor of stone weighed on his sleep, and if he fell beneath it, as beneath a moon, with that dream! Ancient America, submerged bride, your fingers also, when leaving the jungle for the empty height of the gods, under the nuptial banners of light and reverence, mixing with the thunder of drums and lances, also, your fingers also, those that the abstract rose and the line of cold, those that the bloody breast of the new corn changed into the fabric of radiant matter, into the hard cavities, also, also, buried America, did you keep hunger in the greatest depth, in the bitter gut, like an eagle?

XI

A través del confuso esplendor,
a través de la noche de piedra, déjame hundir la mano
y deja que en mí palpite, como un ave mil años prisionera,
el viejo corazón del olvidado!
Déjame olvidar hoy esta dicha, que es más ancha que el
mar,
porque el hombre es más ancho que el mar y que sus
islas,
y hay que caer en él como en un pozo para salir del fondo
con un ramo de agua secreta y de verdades sumergidas.
Déjame olvidar, ancha piedra, la proporción poderosa,
la trascendente medida, las piedras del panal,
y de la escuadra déjame hoy resbalar
la mano sobre la hipotenusa de áspera sangre y cilicio.
Cuando, como una herradura de élitros rojos, el cóndor
furibundo
me golpea las sienes en el orden del vuelo
y el huracán de plumas carniceras barre el polvo sombrío
de las escalinatas diagonales, no veo a la bestia veloz,
no veo el ciego ciclo de sus garras,
veo el antiguo ser, servidor, el dormido

Through the confused splendour, through the night of stone, let me plunge my hand, and let the old heart of the forgotten one beat in me like a bird imprisoned for a thousand years. Let me forget this happiness today, wider than the sea, for man is wider than the sea and its islands, and must be fallen into as into a well, to rise from the depths with a branch of secret water and submerged truths. Let me forget, spacious stone, the powerful proportion, the transcendental measure, the honeycombed stones, and today let me slide my hand from the set-square down the hypotenuse of rasping blood and sackcloth. When, like a horseshoe of red wing-cases, the raging condor smites my brow in the order of flight, and the hurricane of carnivorous feathers sweeps the gloomy dust from the diagonal stairways, I do not see the swift beast, I do not see the blind cycle of his claws; I see the ancient being, the servant, the

en los campos, veo un cuerpo, mil cuerpos, un hombre,
mil mujeres,
bajo la racha negra, negros de lluvia y noche,
con la piedra pesada de la estatua:
Juan Cortapiedras, hijo de Wiracocha,
Juan Comefrío, hijo de estrella verde,
Juan Piesdescalzos, nieto de la turquesa,
sube a nacer conmigo, hermano.

XII

Sube a nacer conmigo, hermano.

Dame la mano desde la profunda
zona de tu dolor diseminado.
No volverás del fondo de las rocas.
No volverás del tiempo subterráneo.
No volverá tu voz endurecida.
No volverán tus ojos taladrados.

sleeper in the fields; I see a body, a thousand bodies, a man, a thousand women under the black gust, black with rain and night, with the heavy stone of the statue. Juan Cortapiedras, son of Wiracocha. Juan Comefrío, son of the green star. Juan Piesdescalzos,* grandson of the turquoise; rise to birth with me, brother.

Rise to birth with me, brother. Give me your hand out of the deep zone of your scattered sorrow. You will not return from the depth of the rocks. You will not return from subterranean time. Your hardened voice will not return. Your perforated eyes will not return. Look at me from the depths of the earth, tiller, weaver, silent shep-

---

* Cortapiedras: stonecutter
Comefrío: cold-eater
Piesdescalzos: bare-footed.

Mírame desde el fondo de la tierra,
labrador, tejedor, pastor callado:
domador de guanacos tutelares:
albañil del andamio desafiado:
aguador de las lágrimas andinas:
joyero de los dedos machacados:
agricultor temblando en la semilla:
alfarero en tu greda derramado:
traed a la copa de esta nueva vida
vuestros viejos dolores enterrados.
Mostradme vuestra sangre y vuestro surco,
decidme: aquí fui castigado,
porque la joya no brilló o la tierra
no entregó a tiempo la piedra o el grano:
señaladme la piedra en que caísteis
y la madera en que os crucificaron,
encendedme los viejos pedernales,
las viejas lámparas, los látigos pegados
a través de los siglos en las llagas
y las hachas de brillo ensangrentado.
Yo vengo a hablar por vuestra boca muerta.

herd, trainer of tutelary *guanacos*:* stonemason of the challenged scaffolding, water-bearer of Andean tears: jeweller with pounded fingers: husbandman trembling among the grain: potter spilled out among your clay – bring your old buried sorrows to the cup of this new life. Show me your blood and your furrow. Tell me: here I was punished because a jewel didn't shine, or the earth did not yield stone, or grain, in time. Show me the stone you fell on and the wood on which they crucified you. Light the old flints, the old lamps, the whips glued across the centuries to the wounds, and the axes of gory lustre. I come to speak through your dead mouth.

* *guanaco:* a kind of wild llama.

A través de la tierra juntad todos
los silenciosos labios derramados
y desde el fondo habladme toda esta larga noche,
como si yo estuviera con vosotros anclado,
contadme todo, cadena a cadena,
eslabón a eslabón, y paso a paso,
afilad los cuchillos que guardásteis,
ponedlos en mi pecho y en mi mano,
como un río de rayos amarillos,
como un río de tigres enterrados,
y dejadme llorar, horas, días, años,
edades ciegas, siglos estelares.

Dadme el silencio, el agua, la esperanza.

Dadme la lucha, el hierro, los volcanes.

Apegadme los cuerpos como imanes.

Acudid a mis venas y a mi boca.

Hablad por mis palabras y mi sangre.

Throughout the earth join all the scattered silent lips, and out of the depths speak to me all this long night as though I were anchored to you. Tell me everything, chain by chain, link by link, step by step; sharpen the knives you hoard, thrust them into my breast, into my hand, like a river of yellow rays, like a river of buried tigers and let me weep hours, days, years, blind ages, stellar centuries.

Give me silence, water, hope.
Give me the struggle, the iron, the volcanoes.
Let bodies cling to me like magnets.
Come to my veins and my mouth.
Speak through my words and my blood.

NICANOR PARRA (b. 1914)

La montaña rusa

DURANTE medio siglo
la poesía fue
el paraíso del tonto solemne.
Hasta que vine yo
y me instalé con mi montaña rusa.

Suban, si les parece.
Claro que yo no respondo si bajan
echando sangre por boca y narices.

Soliloquio del Individuo

Yo soy el Individuo.
Primero viví en una roca
(Allí grabé algunas figuras).
Luego busqué un lugar más apropriado.
Yo soy el Individuo.
Primero tuve que procurarme alimentos,
Buscar peces, pájaros, buscar leña,
(Ya me preocuparía de los demás asuntos).

The Roller-Coaster

FOR half a century poetry was the paradise of the solemn fool. Until I came along and established myself with my roller-coaster.

Come on – climb up if you want. Obviously it's not my affair if you get off, spouting blood from [your] mouth and nostrils.

*Soliloquy of the Individual**

I AM the Individual. First I lived in a rock (there I scratched some figures). Afterwards I looked for a more appropriate place. I am the Individual. First of all I had to get myself some food, to look for fish, birds, to look for wood (I'd worry about other things in good

* Translated by John Hill.

Hacer una fogata,
Leña, leña, dónde encontrar un poco de leña,
Algo de leña para hacer una fogata,
Yo soy el Individuo.
Al mismo tiempo me pregunté,
Fuí a un abismo lleno de aire;
Me respondió una voz:
Yo soy el Individuo.
Después traté de cambiarme a otra roca,
Allí también grabé figuras,
Grabé un río, búfalos,
Yo soy el Individuo.
Pero no. Me aburrí de las cosas que hacía,
El fuego me molestaba,
Quería ver más,
Yo soy el Individuo.
Bajé a un valle regado por un río,
Allí encontré lo que necesitaba,
Encontré un pueblo salvaje,
Una tribu,
Yo soy el Individuo.
Vi que allí se hacían algunas cosas,
Figuras grababan en las rocas,
Hacían fuego, ¡también hacían fuego!

time), to make a fire, wood, wood, where to get hold of a bit of wood, some wood to build a fire, I am the Individual. At the same time I asked myself, I went to an abyss full of air; a voice replied to me: I am the Individual. Afterwards I tried to move to another rock, and there too I scratched figures, I scratched a river, buffaloes, I am the Individual. But no; I got bored with the things I was doing, I got sick of the fire, I wanted to see more, I am the Individual. I went down to a valley watered by a river, there I found what I needed, I found a primitive people, a tribe, I am the Individual. I saw that different things went on there, they were scratching figures on the rocks, they were making fire, they too were making fire! I am

Yo soy el Individuo.
Me preguntaron que de dónde venía.
Contesté que sí, que no tenía planes determinados,
Contesté que no, que de ahí en adelante.
Bien.
Tomé entonces un trozo de piedra que encontré en un río
Y empecé a trabajar con ella,
Empecé a pulirla,
De ella hice una parte de mi propia vida.
Pero esto es demasiado largo.
Corté unos árboles para navegar,
Buscaba peces,
Buscaba diferentes cosas,
(Yo soy el Individuo).
Hasta que me empecé a aburrir nuevamente.
Las tempestades aburren,
Los truenos, los relámpagos,
Yo soy el Individuo.
Bien. Me puse a pensar un poco.
Preguntas estúpidas se me venían a la cabeza,
Falsos problemas.
Entonces empecé a vagar por unos bosques.
Llegué a un árbol y a otro árbol,
Llegué a una fuente,
A una fosa en que se veían algunas ratas:

the Individual. They asked me where I came from. Sometimes I said yes, that I'd not fixed plans, sometimes I said no, that from there on. O.K. Then I took a piece of stone that I'd found in a river, and started to work on it, started to polish it, out of it I made a piece of my own life. But this is too long. I cut down a few trees to go sailing. I went after fish, I went after different things (I am the Individual). Until I started to get bored all over again. Storms bored me, and thunder, lightning, I am the Individual. O.K. I had a little think, silly questions came into my head, imaginary problems. Then I started wandering through some forests, I came to a tree and to another tree, I came to a fountain, to a ditch, in which I could

Aquí vengo yo, dije entonces,
¿Habéis visto por aquí una tribu,
Un pueblo salvaje que hace fuego?
De este modo me desplacé hacia el oeste
Acompañado por otros seres,
O más bien solo.
Para ver hay que creer, me decían,
Yo soy el Individuo.
Formas veía en la obscuridad,
Nubes tal vez,
Tal vez veía nubes, veía relámpagos,
A todo esto habían pasado ya varios días,
Yo me sentía morir;
Inventé unas máquinas,
Construí relojes,
Armas, vehículos,
Yo soy el Individuo.
Apenas tenía tiempo para enterrar a mis muertos,
Apenas tenía tiempo para sembrar,
Yo soy el Individuo.
Años más tarde concebí unas cosas,
Unas formas,
Crucé las fronteras
Y permanecí fijo en una especie de nicho,
En una barca que navegó cuarenta días,
Cuarenta noches,

see some rats: here I come I said then, have you seen a tribe anywhere about, a primitive people who make fire? In this way I wandered to the west, along with others, or rather on my own. To see, one must believe, they told me, I am the Individual. I saw shapes in the darkness, clouds perhaps, maybe I saw clouds, I saw flashes of lightning, meanwhile several days had already passed, I felt myself dying: I invented a few machines, I made clocks, weapons, vehicles, I am the Individual. I hardly had time to bury my dead, I hardly had time to sow, I am the Individual. A few years later, I thought of a few things, a few shapes, I crossed frontiers, and stood fixed in a kind of niche, in a ship which sailed for forty days, forty nights,

Yo soy el Individuo.
Luego vinieron unas sequías,
Vinieron unas guerras,
Tipos de color entraron al valle,
Pero yo debía seguir adelante,
Debía producir.
Produje ciencia, verdades inmutables,
Produje tanagras,
Dí a luz libros de miles de páginas,
Se me hinchó la cara,
Construí un fonógrafo,
La máquina de coser,
Empezaron a aparecer los primeros automóviles,
Yo soy el Individuo.
Alguien segregaba planetas,
¡Árboles segregaba!
Pero yo segregaba herramientas,
Muebles, útiles de escritorio;
Yo soy el Individuo.
Se construyeron también ciudades,
Rutas,
Instituciones religiosas pasaron de moda,
Buscaban dicha, buscaban felicidad,
Yo soy el Individuo.

I am the Individual. Then droughts came, wars came, coloured fellows came into the valley, I had to go ahead, I had to produce. I produced science, immutable truths, I produced *tanagras*,* I gave birth to thousand-page books, my face swelled up, I built a gramophone, the sewing-machine, the first cars started to appear, I am the Individual. Someone secreted planets, secreted trees! But I secreted tools, furniture, office equipment, I am the Individual. Cities were also built, roads, religious institutions went out of fashion, they looked for happiness, they looked for joy, I am the Individual.

---

* *tanagra*: terracotta statuette.

Después me dediqué mejor a viajar,
A practicar, a practicar idiomas,
Idiomas,
Yo soy el Individuo.
Miré por una cerradura,
Sí, miré, qué digo, miré,
Para salir de la duda miré,
Detrás de unas cortinas,
Yo soy el Individuo.
Bien.
Mejor es tal vez que vuelva a ese valle,
A esa roca que me sirvió de hogar,
Y empiece a grabar de nuevo,
De atrás para adelante grabar
El mundo al revés.
Pero no: la vida no tiene sentido.

Desorden en el cielo

UN cura sin saber cómo
Llegó a las puertas del cielo,
Tocó la aldaba de bronce,
A abrirle vino San Pedro:

Afterwards I devoted myself to travel, to practice, to the practice of languages, languages, I am the Individual. I peeped through a keyhole, yes, I peeped, as I say, I peeped to rid myself of doubt, behind some curtains, I am the Individual. O.K. Maybe it's better for me to go back to that valley, to that rock which was my home and start to scratch [the rock] again, to scratch from end to beginning the world in reverse. But no; life doesn't make sense.

Disorder in Heaven

A PRIEST, without knowing how, arrived at the gates of heaven and struck the knocker of bronze: Saint Peter came to open. 'If you

«Si no me dejas entrar
Te corto los crisantemos».
Con voz respondióle el santo
Que se parecía al trueno:
«Retírate de mi vista
Caballo de mal agüero,
Cristo Jesús no se compra
Con mandas ni con dinero
Y no se llega a sus pies
Con dichos de marinero.
Aquí no se necesita
Del brillo de tu esqueleto
Para amenizar el baile
De Dios y de sus adeptos.
Viviste entre los humanos
Del miedo de los enfermos
Vendiendo medallas falsas
Y cruces de cementerio.
Mientras los demás mordían
Un mísero pan de afrecho
Tú te llenabas la panza
De carne y de huevos frescos.
La araña de la lujuria
Se multiplicó en tu cuerpo
Paraguas chorreando sangre
¡Murciélago del infierno!»

don't let me in I'll cut down your chrysanthemums.' With a voice like thunder the saint answered him: 'Get out of my sight, horse of ill-omen. Christ is not bought with bequests, or money, and you don't reach his feet using the language of sailors. We don't need the splendour of your skeleton here, to brighten up the dance of God and his followers. You lived among humanity, off the fear of ill people, selling false medals and graveyard crosses. Whilst others were biting on a miserable crust of bran, you filled your belly with meat and fresh eggs. The spider of lechery bred in your body, umbrellas dripping blood. Bat of Hell!'

Después resonó un portazo,
Un rayo iluminó el cielo,
Temblaron los corredores
Y el ánima sin respeto
Del fraile rodó de espaldas
Al hoyo de los infiernos.

Afterwards a door slammed. A beam of light lit up the sky. The corridors trembled, and the disrespectful soul of the friar rolled backwards into the pit of hell.

ENRIQUE LIHN (b. 1929)

Recuerdos de matrimonio

BUSCÁBAMOS un subsuelo donde vivir,
cualquier lugar que no fuera una casa de huéspedes. El paraíso perdido
tomaba ahora su verdadero aspecto: unos de esos pequeños departamentos
que se arriendan por un precio todavía razonable;
pero a las seis de la mañana: «Ayer, no más, lo tomó un matrimonio joven».
Mientras íbamos y veníamos en la oscuridad en direcciones capciosas.
El hombre es un lobo para el hombre y el lobo una dueña de casa de pensión con los dientes cariados, húmeda en las axilas, dudosamente viuda.
Y allí donde el periódico nos invitaba a vivir se alzaba un abismo de tres pisos:
un nuevo foco de corrupción conyugal.

Mientras íbamos y veníamos en la oscuridad, más distantes el uno del otro a cada paso

Memories of Marriage

WE were searching for a basement to live in: any place that wasn't a boarding house. Paradise lost was already taking on its true aspect – one of those small apartments that are still leased at a reasonable price – but at six in the morning: 'Only yesterday a young married couple took it.' In the darkness, meanwhile, we came and went in deceiving directions. Man is a wolf to man and the wolf is a landlady with rotten teeth, sweaty armpits . . . doubtfully a widow. And there where the newspaper invited us to live, a three-storied abyss rose up: a new source of conjugal corruption.

While we came and went in the darkness, further away from each other at every step, they were already there, establishing their

ellos ya estaban allí, estableciendo su nido sobre una base sólida,
ganándose la simpatía del conserje, tan hosco con los extraños
como ansioso de inspirarles gratitud filial.
«No se les habrá escapado nada. Seguramente el nuevo ascensorista recibió una propina».
«La pareja ideal». A la hora justa. En el momento oportuno.
De ellos, los invisibles, sólo alcanzábamos a sentir su futura presencia en un cuarto vacío:
nuestras sombras tomadas de la mano entre los primeros brotes del sol en el parquet,
un remanso de blanca luz nupcial.

«Pueden verlo, si quieren,
pero han llegado tarde».
Se nos hacía tarde.
Se hacía tarde en todo.
Para siempre.

nest on a solid base, winning the sympathy of the caretaker, so surly with strangers, as though anxious to inspire in them filial gratitude. 'Nothing will have escaped their notice.... Certainly the new lift-attendant received a tip.' 'The ideal couple.' At the right time. At the opportune moment. Of them, the invisibles, we could only sense their future presence in an empty room: our shadows, hand in hand among the first signs of sun on the parquet, a still pool of white nuptial light.

'You can see it, if you want to, but you've come too late.' It was getting late for us. It was getting late for everything. For ever.

COLOMBIA

GREGORIO GUTIÉRREZ GONZÁLEZ
(1826–72)

Memoria sobre el cultivo del maíz en Antioquía

Capítulo I

De los terrenos propios para el cultivo y manera de hacerse los barbechos, que decimos rozas

BUSCANDO en donde comenzar la roza,
de un bosque primitivo la espesura
treinta peones y un patrón por jefe
van recorriendo en silenciosa turba.

Vestidos todos de calzón de manta
y de camisa de coleta cruda
aquél a la rodilla, ésta a los codos,
dejan sus formas de titán desnudas.

El sombrero de caña, con el ala
prendida de la copa con la aguja,

*Report on the Cultivation of Maize in Antioquía**

Part 1

Concerning lands suitable for cultivation, and the way of establishing the ploughlands called rozas.

LOOKING for where to begin the *roza*, thirty peons, a silent crowd, the owner in charge, move up and down through the thickness of a primeval forest.

All dressed in cotton trousers and hempen shirts, one to the knees, the other to the elbows, they have the appearance of naked Titans.

The sombrero, made of reeds, the brim pinned to the crown with

* Antioquía is a region of Colombia. This poem was presented as a formal report to a scientific congress.

deja mirar el bronceado rostro,
que la bondad y la franqueza anuncia.

Atado por detrás con la correa
que el pantalón sujeta a la cintura,
con el recado de sacar candela,
llevan repleto su carriel de nutria.

Envainado y pendiente del costado
va su cuchillo de afilada punta;
y, en fin, al hombro, con marcial despejo,
el calabazo que en el sol relumbra.

Al fin eligen un tendón de tierra
que dos quebradas serpeando cruzan,
en el declive de una cuesta amena
poco cargada de maderas duras.

Y dan principio a socolar el monte
los peones formados en columna;
a seis varas distante uno del otro
marchan de frente con presteza suma.

a needle, leaves bare the bronzed features, which declare goodness and candour.

Slung behind them, on the string which anchors the trousers to the waist, along with the tinder-box and flint-stone, they have full bags of food, made from nutria-skin.

Sheathed, and hanging from the side, goes the sharpened knife, and finally, on the shoulder, with martial smartness, the machete, glinting in the sunlight.

At last they choose a strip of land crossed by two winding streams, on the incline of a pleasant slope, not too thickly covered with tough trees.

And the peons, formed into a column, make a start at clearing the undergrowth; six yards apart, they advance with greatest speed.

Voleando el calabazo a un lado y otro,
que relámpagos forma en la espesura,
los débiles arbustos, los helechos
y los bejucos por doquiera truncan,

Las matambas, los chusques, los carrizos
que forman un toldo de verdura,
todo deshecho y arrollado cede
del calabazo a la encorvada punta.

Con el rostro encendido, jadeantes,
los unos a los otros se estimulan;
ir por delante alegres quieren todos,
romper la fila cada cual procura.

Cantando a todo pecho la guavina,
canción sabrosa, dejativa y ruda,
ruda cual las montañas antioqueñas,
donde tiene su imperio y fue su cuna,

no miran en su ardor a la culebra
que entre las hojas se desliza en fuga,

The machete swinging from side to side, and flashing in the density [of the wood], they cut down everywhere the fragile shrubs, the ferns, and the creepers,

The sedges, rushes and reeds, which form a canopy of verdure; everything, destroyed and crushed flat, yields to the curved blade of the machete.

Their faces burning, panting, they encourage each other; all want to go ahead, and joyful, each one tries to break the line.

[They are] singing the *guavina* at the tops of their voices, a spicy song, lazy and earthy, earthy as the mountains of Antioquía, its empire and cradle.

In their ardour, they do not see the snake, which slithers away

y presurosa en su sesgada marcha,
cinta de azogue, abrillantada ondula;

ni de monos observan las manadas
que por las ramas juguetones cruzan;
ni se paran a ver de aves alegres
las mil bandadas de pintadas plumas;

ni ven los saltos de la inquieta ardilla,
ni las nubes de insectos que pululan,
ni los verdes lagartos que huyen listos,
ni el enjambre de abejas que susurra.

Concluye la socola. De malezas
queda la tierra vegetal desnuda.
Los árboles elevan sus cañones
hasta perderse en prodigiosa altura,

semejantes de un templo a los pilares
que sostiene su toldo de verdura;
varales largos de ese palio inmenso,
de esa bóveda verde altas columnas.

in flight among the leaves, and, rapid in its oblique movement, shimmeringly undulates, [like] a belt of quicksilver;

Nor do they see the tribes of monkeys which playfully jump around in the branches; nor do they stop to look at the happy birds, the thousand flocks of painted plumes;

Nor do they see the leaps of the restless squirrel, nor the clouds of humming insects, nor the green lizards, smartly running away, nor the swarm of buzzing bees.

The clearing is finished. The vegetal land is stripped of undergrowth. The trees lift up their trunks till they are lost in prodigious height,

Resembling the pillars of a temple, propping up a canopy of green; the tall poles of that immense state-canopy, the high columns of that green vault.

El viento, en su follaje entretejido,
con voz ahogada y fúnebre susurra,
como un eco lejano de otro tiempo,
como un vago recuerdo de ventura.

Los árboles sacuden sus bejucos,
cual destrenzada cabellera rubia
donde tienen guardados los aromas
con que el ambiente, en su vaivén, perfuman.

De sus copas galanas se desprende
una constante, embalsamada lluvia
de frescas flores, de marchitas hojas,
verdes botones y amarillas frutas.

Muestra el cachimbo su follaje rojo,
cual canastillo que una ninfa pura
en la fiesta del Corpus lleva ufana
entre la Virgen, inocente turba.

El guacayán con su amarilla copa
luce a lo lejos en la selva oscura,

The wind, in the intertwined foliage, whispers with a muffled funereal voice, like a distant echo of olden times, like a vague intimation of a happy destiny.

The trees shake their creepers like a head of blonde unplaited hair, where they keep guarded the aromas which, in their swinging movement, perfume the atmosphere.

From their elegant crowns falls a constant, embalming rain of fresh flowers, withered leaves, green buds, and yellow fruit.

The ceiba-tree displays its russet leaves, an innocent crowd, like a basket which a pure nymph joyfully and proudly carries along by the Virgin, on the feast of Corpus Christi.

The *guacayán* tree, with its yellow crown, shines in the distance,

cual luce entre las nubes una estrella,
cual grano de oro que la jagua oculta.

El azuceno, el floro azul, el caunce
y el yaramo, en el monte se dibujan
como piedras preciosas que recaman
el manto azul que con la brisa ondula.

Y sobre ellos gallardo se levanta,
meciendo sus racimos en la altura,
recta y flexible la altanera palma,
que aire mejor entre las nubes busca.

Ved otra vez a los robustos peones
que el mismo bosque secular circunda:
divididos están en dos partidas,
y un capitán dirige cada una.

Su alegre charla, sus sonoras risas,
no se oye ya, ni su canción se escucha;
de una grave atención cuidado serio
se halla pintado en sus facciones rudas.

in the dark wood, as a star shines amongst the clouds, as a speck of gold which the silt of the pan hides.

The cinchona, the [blue-flowering] *floro azul*, the [yellow-flowering] *caunce*, and the [white-flowering] *yaramo* are displayed amongst the bushes like precious stones, encrusted on a blue mantle, which waves with the breeze.

And above them, proudly graceful, cradling its clusters in the heights, rises, straight and flexible, the haughty palm, which seeks for better air amongst the clouds.

Look again at the robust peons, which the same ancient wood surrounds; they are divided into two groups, and a captain leads each one.

Their joyful chattering, their sonorous laughter are no longer heard, nor is their song; a grave attention and the greatest care are pictured on their rough features.

En lugar del ligero calabazo
la hacha afilada con su mano empuñan;
miran atentos el cañón del árbol,
su comba ven, su inclinación calculan.

Y a dos manos el hacha levantando,
con golpe igual y precisión segura,
y redoblando golpes sobre golpes,
causan los ecos de la selva augusta.

Anchas astillas y cortezas leves
rápidamente por el aire cruzan;
a cada golpe el árbol se estremece,
tiemblan sus hojas, y vacila . . . , y duda . . .

Tembloroso un momento cabecea,
cruje en su corte, y en graciosa curva
empieza a descender, y rechinando
sus ramas enlazadas se apeñuscan;

y silbando al caer, cortando el viento,
despedazado por los aires zumba . . .

Instead of the light machete, they hold the sharpened axes in their hands; they stare, intent, at the trunk of the tree, they study its swell, and calculate its lean.

And, lifting the axe in both hands, with even strokes and sure precision, redoubling blow after blow, they make the august jungle resound.

Broad splinters and thin bits of bark rapidly fly through the air; at each blow the tree shudders, its leaves tremble, and hesitate . . . , and doubt . . .

Quivering, for a moment it totters, creaks where it is cut, and in a gracious curve, begins to fall, and, crackling, its matted branches cling together;

And whistling as it falls, cutting the wind, shattered, it hums

Sobre el tronco el peón apoya el hacha
y el trueno, al lejos, repetir escucha.

Las tres partidas observad. A un tiempo
para echar una galga se apresuran:
en tres faldas distintas, el redoble
se oye del hacha en variedad confusa.

En una fila de árboles picando
sin hacerlos caer, está la turba,
y arriba de ellos, para echarlo encima,
el más copudo por madrino buscan.

Y recostando andamios en su tronco
para cortarlo a regular altura,
sobre las bambas, y al andamio trepan
cuatro peones con destreza suma.

through the air. . . . The peon rests his axe on the trunk, and listens to the echo of the thunder in the distance.

Behold the three groups. All as one they hasten to put a rolling-platform underneath; on three different sections [of the tree] the beat of the axe is heard in a confused melée.

The crowd is in a row of trees, cutting them, but not felling them, and they look above them for the one with the heaviest crown, which they will use as *madrino** in order to knock the other trees down.

And resting scaffolding against its trunk, in order to cut it at the proper height, above the protuberances of the lower bole, four peons climb on to the scaffolding with utmost dexterity.

---

*The *madrino* is the biggest tree in any one group, which is felled across a row of trees previously half sawn through, so bringing them down with it.

Y en rededor del corpulento tronco
sus hachas baten y a compás sepultan,
y repiten hachazos sobre hachazos
sin descansar, aunque en sudor se inundan.

Y vencido, por fin, cruje el madrino,
y el otro más allá: todos a una,
las ramas extendidas enlazando,
con otras ramas enredadas pugnan;

y abrazando al caer los de adelante,
se atropellan, se enredan y se empujan,
y así arrollados en revuelta tromba
en trueno sordo, aterrador retumban . . .

El viento azota el destrozado monte,
leves cortezas por el aire cruzan,
tiembla la tierra, y el estruendo ronco
se va a perder en las lejanas grutas.

And all round its swelling trunk rhythmically their axes beat and bury themselves, and they repeat axe-blow after axe-blow without stopping, although bathed in perspiration.

And conquered at last, the *madrino* cracks, and another [tree] further up; all as one the stretched, tangled branches battle with other branches matted with them;

And embracing the trees in the row as they fall, they crush each other, twist together, and push each other, and thus hurled in a spinning whirlwind, they fearfully boom in muffled thunder . . .

The wind slashes the destroyed undergrowth, light bits of bark shoot through the air, the earth trembles, and the thunderous noise goes and is lost in the distant cliffs.

Todo queda en silencio. Acaba el día,
todo en redor desolación anuncia;
cual hostia santa que se eleva al cielo,
se alza callada la modesta luna.

Troncos tendidos, destrozadas ramas
y un campo extenso desolado alumbra,
donde se ven como fantasmas negros
los viejos troncos, centinelas mudos.

Everything falls silent. The day dies, everything around announces desolation; the modest moon silently rises, like the sacred host which is lifted to heaven.

It shines on prone trunks, shattered branches, and a field of wide desolation, where are seen, like black phantoms, the old trunks, the silent sentries.

JOSÉ ASUNCIÓN SILVA (1865–96)

Nocturno

UNA noche,
Una noche toda llena de murmullos, de perfumes
Y de músicas de alas:
Una noche
En que ardían en la sombra nupcial y húmeda
Las luciérnagas fantásticas,
A mi lado, lentamente, contra mí ceñida toda,
Muda y pálida,
Como si un presentimiento de amarguras infinitas
Hasta el más secreto fondo de las fibras te agitara,
Por la senda florecida que atraviesa la llanura
Caminabas;
Y la Luna llena,
Por los cielos azulosos, infinitos y profundos,
Esparcía su luz blanca;
Y tu sombra,
Esbelta y ágil,
Fina y lánguida,
Y mi sombra
Por los rayos de la Luna proyectadas,
Sobre las arenas tristes

Nocturne

A NIGHT, a night quite full of murmurs, of perfumes, and the music of wings: a night when the fantastic glow-worms burn in the nuptial, humid darkness, and, along the flowery path which crosses the field, you walked, silent and pale, pressed up against me, as if a presentiment of infinite bitterness was troubling the most secret depths of your heart; and the full moon scattered her white light through the bluish, infinite and profound skies; and your shadow, agile and graceful, delicate and languid, and my shadow, projected by the moonbeams across the sad sands of the path,

De la senda se juntaban,
Y eran una,
Y eran una
Y eran una sola sombra larga,
Y eran una sola sombra larga,
Y eran una sola sombra larga . . .

Esta noche
Solo; el alma
Llena de las infinitas amarguras y agonías
De tu muerte,
Separado di ti misma por el tiempo,
Por la tumba y la distancia,
Por el infinito negro
Donde nuestra voz no alcanza,
Mudo y solo
Por la senda caminaba . . .
Y se oían los ladridos de los perros a la Luna,
A la Luna pálida,
Y el chillido
De las ranas . . .
Sentí frío. Era el frío que tenían en tu alcoba
Tus mejillas y tus sienes y tus manos adoradas,
Entre las blancuras níveas
De las mortuorias sábanas.

joined and were one, and were one, and were one single long shadow, and were one single long shadow, and were one single long shadow . . .

Tonight, alone; the soul full of the infinite bitterness and agonies of your death, separated from you yourself by time, by the tomb and distance, by the black infinitude where our voice will not carry, dumb and alone I walked along the path, and the barking of dogs to the moon, to the pallid moon, was heard, and the croaking of the frogs . . . I felt chill. It was the chill which, in your bedroom, was held in your cheeks, in your brows, and your beloved hands, amongst the snowy whitenesses of your burial-sheets. It was the

Era el frío del sepulcro, era el hielo de la muerte,
Era el frío de la nada . . .
Y mi sombra
Por los rayos de la Luna proyectada,
Iba sola,
Iba sola,
Iba sola por la estepa solitaria;
Y tu sombra esbelta y ágil,
Fina y lánguida,
Como en esa noche tibia de la muerta primavera,
Como en esa noche llena de murmullos, de perfumes
Y de músicas de alas,
Se acercó y marchó con ella,
Se acercó y marchó con ella,
Se acercó y marchó con ella . . .
¡Oh las sombras enlazadas!
¡Oh las sombras de los cuerpos que se juntan
Con las sombras de las almas!
¡Oh las sombras que se buscan
En las noches de tristezas y de lágrimas! . . .

chill of the sepulchre, it was the ice of death, it was the chill of nothingness . . . And my shadow, projected by the moonbeams, passed on alone, passed on alone, passed on alone through the solitary plain, and your shadow, agile and graceful, delicate and languid, as on that warm night of that dead spring, as on that night full of murmurs, perfumes, and the music of wings, came up to and walked with mine, came up to and walked with mine, came up to and walked with mine. . . . Oh, the embraces of shadows! Oh, the shadows of the bodies which join the shadows of the souls! Oh the shadows which seek each other in the nights of sorrows and tears!

Avant-propos

PRESCRIBEN los facultativos
cuando el estómago se estraga,
al paciente, pobre dispéptico,
dieta sin grasas.

Le prohiben las cosas dulces,
le aconsejan la carne asada
y le hacen tomar como tónico
gotas amargas.

¡Pobre estómago literario
que lo trivial fatiga y cansa,
no sigas leyendo poemas
llenos de lágrimas!

Deja las comidas que llenan,
historias, leyendas y dramas
y todas las sensiblerías
semi-románticas.

Avant-propos

DOCTORS prescribe to the patient, poor dyspeptic, a fat-free diet for the upset stomach.

They forbid sweet things, advise roast meat, and make him take bitter drops as a tonic.

Poor literary stomach, tired and bored by the trivial, don't go on reading poems full of tears!

Give up indigestible meals, histories, legends, and dramas, and all the semi-romantic lachrymose novelettes.

Y para completar el régimen
que fortifica y que levanta,
ensaya una dosis de estas
gotas amargas.

Realidad

NATURALEZA es una dondequiera
en Japón o en Gonesa, – las distancias
suprime y son lo mismo Triptolemo
y Dombasle, la toga y las enaguas.

Lavallière con su Luis, entra la regia
carroza blasonada,
es tan feroz cual la chipriota Venus
en el capullo de la concha blanca.

¡Oh mis hijos! ¡Oh hermanos! ¡Oh poetas!
Decid si existe el hecho, la palabra.
Sed espíritus puros, y haced siempre,
no hay nada bajo para nobles almas.

And to complete the diet, which fortifies and builds you up, try a dose of these bitter drops.

Reality

NATURE is an anywhere in Japan or in Gonesse – it conquers distances, and Triptolemus and Dombasle are the same, the toga and the petticoats.

Lavallière enters the regal and emblazoned coach with her Louis, and is as fierce as the Cyprian Venus in the cup of her white shell.

Oh my children! Oh brothers! Oh poets! Say if the fact, the word exists. Be pure spirits, and always act, let there be nothing low for noble souls.

En Poestum se convierte en hipo triste
la risa de Sileno, a Priapo canta
Horacio y cruza Bottom, el grotesco,
de Shakespeare por el drama.

¡No tiene la verdad límites, hijo!
Del gran Pan, dios bestial, la hirsuta barba
y los cuernos torcidos se columbran
del ideal tras de la frente pálida.

Sus dos mesas

De soltera

EN los tallados frascos guardados los olores
de las esencias diáfanas, dignas de alguna hurí;
un vaso raro y frágil do expiran unas flores;
el iris de un diamante; la sangre de un rubí
cuyas facetas tiemblan con vivos resplandores
entre el lujoso estuche de seda carmesí,
y frente del espejo la epístola de amores
que al irse para el baile dejó olvidada allí . . .

In Paestum the laughter of Silenus is turned into a sad hiccough, Horace sings to Priapus, and grotesque Bottom travels through Shakespeare's drama.

Truth has no limits, child! Through the shaggy beard and twisted horns of great Pan, the beast-God, may be glimpsed the pallid forehead of the ideal.

Her Two Tables

When Single

IN the carved flasks [are] guarded the perfumes of pellucid essences fit for some houri; a rare and fragile vase where flowers expire; the rainbow of a diamond; the blood of a ruby whose facets tremble with vivid reflections in the sumptuous vanity-case of crimson silk, and in front of the looking-glass a love-letter she left forgotten there when she went to the dance . . .

De casada

UN biberón que guarda mezclados dos terceras
partes de leche hervida y una de agua de cal,
la vela que reclama las despaviladeras
desde la palmatoria verdosa de metal;
en rotulado frasco, cerca de las tijeras,
doscientos gramos de una loción medicinal;
un libro de oraciones, dos cucharas dulceras,
un reverbero viejo y un chupo y un pañal.

El mal del siglo

El paciente

DOCTOR, un desaliento de la vida
que en lo íntimo de mí se arraiga y nace,
el mal del siglo . . . el mismo mal de Werther,
de Rolla, de Manfredo y Leopardi.
Un cansancio de todo, un absoluto

When Married

A FEEDING bottle which holds two-thirds boiled milk, and one-third *agua de cal*,* a candle which needs the snuffers, by a greenish metal candlestick; in a labelled bottle, near the scissors, two hundred grammes of medicinal lotion; a prayer-book, two glass spoons, an old hand-mirror, and a dummy and a nappy.

Mal-de-siècle

The Patient

DOCTOR, a despair for life, which is rooted and born in my innermost spirit, the *mal-de-siècle* . . . the same illness of Werther, Rolla, Manfred, and Leopardi. Weariness with everything, an absolute

**agua de cal*: prepared of water and lime in a ratio of 100 : 1.

desprecio por lo humano . . . un incesante
renegar de lo vil de la existencia
digno de mi maestro Schopenhauer;
un malestar profundo que se aumenta
con todas las torturas del análisis . . .

El médico

– ESO es cuestión de régimen: camine
de mañanita; duerma largo; báñese;
beba bien; coma bien; cuídese mucho:
¡Lo que usted tiene es hambre! . . .

contempt for everything human . . . an incessant abhorrence of the vileness of existence worthy of my master Schopenhauer, a profound malaise which grows greater with all the ortures of analysis . . .

The Doctor

IT'S a question of regimen; go for a walk first thing in the morning; get plenty of sleep; go swimming; have a lot to drink; eat well; look after yourself; what's wrong with you is that you are hungry! . . .

GUILLERMO VALENCIA (1873–1943)

A Erasmo de Rotterdam

PINTÓ Hans Holbein, dice la envejecida tela
que a cierta ciudad muerta me fuí a buscar un día,
por ver ¡oh, padre Erasmo!, la búdica ironía
que de tu boca fluye, que tu desdén revela.

Si tú del polvo alzaste la derribada Escuela
porque a regir tornase la helénica armonía,
¿cómo en la mustia boca de la melancolía
tus labios aprendieron ese reir que hiela?

Enfermo que en mí fijas tus ojos de fantasma:
el frío de tu estéril desilusión me pasma;
atas mi ser y domas, ascética figura

que vas entre los mártires de mi martirologio,
y vuela con tu nombre la voz de mi eucologio,
¡oh, cuerdo que tu elogio le diste a la locura!

To Erasmus of Rotterdam

HANS HOLBEIN painted it, says the aged canvas which I went to look for one day in a certain dying city, to see, Oh father Erasmus!, the Buddhist irony which flows from your mouth, revealing your disdain.

If you raised from the dust the shattered School, so that the Hellenic harmony should again return to rule how in the withered mouth of melancholy did your lips learn that chilling laughter?

Diseased, you fix your phantom eyes upon me; the cold of your sterile disillusionment stuns me; you bind and tame my being, ascetic figure,

You who are numbered among the martyrs of my martyrology, and the voice of my euchologion arises with your name. Oh!, you judicious man, who could make a praise of folly.

PORFIRIO BARBA JACOB (1883–1942)

La Reina

EN nada creo, en nada . . . Como noche iracunda
llena del huracán, así es mi «Nada».
En su fuente profunda
mi estirpe fue de hieles abrevada.

Solloza en mi razón un soplo frío
que antiguo brío hiela en la inacción.
¡Desprecio de mí mismo: estoy llagado!
¡Desprecio de mí mismo: has gangrenado
mi corazón!

Ni un albo amor, ni un odio me estremece,
forma ciega en negrura ilimitada;
y a ritmo y ritmo en el corazón parece
decir muriendo: «Nada . . . nada . . . »

Mi Musa fue de dioses engañada.

The Queen

I BELIEVE in nothing, in nothing. . . . My 'Nothing' is like a furious night, full of the hurricane. In its profound depths my lineage was watered by gall.

A cold gust of wind, which freezes ancient vigour to inaction, weeps in my reason. Self-despising, I am wounded! Self-despising, you have put gangrene in my heart.

Neither a white love nor a hatred makes me tremble, a blind form in limitless blackness; and in rhythm after rhythm in my heart there seems to be said in death-agony, 'Nothing . . . nothing . . . '

My Muse was deceived by the Gods.

Al aura errante, al lampo del lucero,
al tremulante amor de un joven marinero,
en la noche de caudas opalinas pregunto:
« ¿Qué enigma está en vosotros?» Y responde
– por mi carne de cirios alumbrada –
mi Musa en sus laureles desolada:
– Nada . . .

¡Oh Reina, rencorosa y enlutada!

Of the wandering breeze, of the lamp of the morning star, of the trembling love of a young sailor, in the night with its bishop's robes of opal, I ask 'What enigma lies in you?' And my Muse – through my flesh, illumined by tapers – answers, desolate in her laurels, 'Nothing . . .'

Oh Queen, rancorous, and in mourning!

LEÓN DE GREIFF (b. 1895)

Relato de Sergio Stepansky

¡Juego mi vida!
¡Bien poco valía!
La llevo perdida sin remedio.
– Erik Sjordsson

JUEGO mi vida, cambio mi vida.
De todos modos
la llevo perdida . . .

Y la juego o la cambio por el más infantil espejismo,
la dono en usufructo, o la regalo . . .

La juego contra uno o contra todos,
la juego contra el cero o contra un infinito,
la juego en una alcoba, en el ágora, en el garito,
en una encrucijada, en una barricada, en un motín;
la juego definitivamente, desde el principio hasta el fin,
a todo lo ancho y a todo lo hondo
en la periferia, en el medio,
y en el sub-fondo . . .

The Story of Sergio Stepansky

I gamble my life!
It wasn't worth anything.
I've lost it irretrievably.

I GAMBLE my life, I barter my life. Anyway, it's lost to me.

And I gamble it, or barter it for the most infantile mirage, I let somebody else profit by it, or I give it away.

I gamble it against one or against all, I gamble it against nought or against infinity, I gamble it in a bedroom, in the market-place, in the betting-shop, at a crossroads, at a barricade, in a mutiny; I definitively gamble with it, from start to finish, to all heights and to all depths, in the periphery, in the centre, and in the underneath . . .

Juego mi vida, cambio mi vida;
la llevo perdida
sin remedio.

Y la juego, o la cambio por el más infantil espejismo;
la dono en usufructo, o la regalo . . .
o la trueco por una sonrisa y cuatro besos:
todo, todo me da lo mismo:
lo eximio y lo ruin, lo trivial, lo perfecto, lo malo . . .

Todo, todo me da lo mismo:
todo me cabe en el diminuto, hórrido abismo
donde se anudan serpentinos mis sesos.

Cambio mi vida por lámparas viejas
o por los dados con los que se jugó la túnica inconsútil:
por lo más anodino, por lo más obvio, por lo más fútil:
por los colgajos que se guindan en las orejas
la simiesca mulata,
la terracota nubia,
la pálida morena, la amarilla oriental, o la hiperbórea
rubia:
cambio mi vida por un anillo de hojalata

I gamble my life, I barter my life. It's lost to me, irretrievably.

And I gamble it, or barter it for the most infantile mirage, I let somebody else profit by it, or I give it away . . . or I barter it for a smile and four kisses; it's all, all the same to me: the best and the worst, the trivial, the perfect, the evil . . .

It's all, all the same to me; there's room for everything in the diminutive, awful abyss where my serpentine brains are knotted together.

I barter my life for old oil-lamps, for the dice which were cast for the diaphanous tunic: for the most anodyne, for the most obvious, for the most futile: for the gaudy pendants which are hung in the ears of the simian mulatto woman, the terracotta Nubian, the pale brown woman, the yellow Oriental, the auburn Hyperborean: I barter my life for a tin-plate ring, for Sigmund's

o por la espada de Sigmundo,
o por el mundo
que tenía en los dedos Carlomagno: para echar a rodar
  la bola . . .

  Cambio mi vida por la cándida aureola
del idiota o del santo;
                                la cambio por el collar
que le pintaron al gordo Capeto;
o por la ducha rígida que le llovió en la nuca
a Carlos de Inglaterra;
                                la cambio por un romance, la
    cambio por un soneto;
por once gatos de Angora,
por una copla, por una saeta,
por un cantar;
por una baraja incompleta;
por una faca, por una pipa, por una sambuca . . .

  o por esa muñeca que llora
por cualquier poeta.

sword, for the world Charlemagne held in his fingers: to set the ball rolling . . .

I barter my life for the white halo of the idiot or the saint; I barter it for the chain of office which the fat Capetian had painted; or for the rigid shower which rained on Charles of England's neck; I barter it for a romance, I barter it for a sonnet, for eleven Persian cats, for a little lyric, for an arrow, for a song; for an incomplete pack of cards; for a knife, for a pipe, for a *sambuca** . . .

Or for that doll which cries over some poet or other.

**sambuca*: an old stringed instrument.

Cambio mi vida – al fiado – por una fábrica de crepúsculos
(con arreboles):
por un gorila de Borneo;
por dos panteras de Sumatra;
por las perlas que se bebió la cetrina Cleopatra
o por su naricilla que está en algún Museo;
cambio mi vida por lámparas viejas,
o por la escala de Jacob, o por su plato de lentejas . . .

o por dos huequecillos minúsculos
– en las sienes – , ¡por donde se me fugue, en gríseas podres,
toda la hartura, todo el fastidio, todo el horror que almaceno en mis odres! . . .

Juego mi vida, cambio mi vida.
De todos modos
la llevo perdida . . .

I barter my life – on credit – for a twilight-factory (with rosy tints); for a gorilla from Borneo; for two Sumatran panthers; for the pearls tawny Cleopatra drank, or for her little nose, which lies in some museum; I barter my life for old oil-lamps, or for Jacob's ladder, or for his mess of pottage . . .

Or for two tiny little pin-holes – in the temples – through which all the satiety, all the sulkiness, all the horror I store in my glands will trickle away from me in grey suppurations . . .

I gamble my life, I barter my life, anyway, it is lost to me . . .

ÁLVARO MUTIS (b. 1923)

Una palabra

CUANDO de repente en mitad de la vida llega una palabra
jamás antes pronunciada,
una densa marea nos recoge en sus brazos y comienza el
largo viaje entre la magia recién iniciada,
que se levanta como un grito en un inmenso hangar aban-
donado donde el musgo cobija las paredes,
entre el óxido de olvidadas criaturas que habitan un mun-
do en ruinas, una palabra basta,
una palabra y se inicia la danza pausada que nos lleva por
entre un espeso polvo de ciudades,
hasta los vitrales de una oscura casa de salud, a patios
donde florece el hollín y anidan densas sombras,
húmedas sombras, que dan vida a cansadas mujeres.
Ninguna verdad reside en estos rincones y, sin embargo
allí sorprende el mudo pavor
que llena la vida con su aliento de vinagre – rancio vinagre
que corre por la mojada despensa de una humilde casa
de placer.
Y tampoco es esto todo.

A Word

WHEN suddenly in the midst of life comes a word never pronounced before, a dense tide gathers us up in its arms, and there begins the long journey into newly-initiated magic, which rises like a scream in an immense abandoned hangar, where moss clothes the walls, amidst the oxide of forgotten creatures which inhabit a world in ruins. A word is enough, a word, and there begins [again] the arrested dance which carries us through a thick dust of cities, up to the stained glass of a dark hospital, with patios where soot flowers and dense shadows nest, damp shadows which give life to weary women. Not one truth resides in these corners, and yet there is the surprise of that dumb fear which fills life with its vinegary breath – stale vinegar which runs through the wet pantry of a humble brothel. Neither is this enough. There are also the

Hay también las conquistas de calurosas regiones, donde
los insectos vigilan la copulación de los guardianes del
sembrado
que pierden la voz entre los cañaduzales sin límite surca-
dos por rápidas acequias
y opacos reptiles de blanca y rica piel.
¡Oh el desvelo de los vigilantes que golpean sin descanso
sonoras latas de petróleo
para espantar los acuciosos insectos que envía la noche
como una promesa de vigilia!
Camino del mar pronto se olvidan estas cosas.
Y si una mujer espera con sus blancos y espesos muslos
abiertos como las ramas de un florido písamo cente-
nario,
entonces el poema llega a su fin, no tiene ya sentido su
monótono treno
de fuente turbia y siempre renovada por el cansado cuerpo
de viciosos gimnastas.
Sólo una palabra.
Una palabra y se inicia la danza
de una fértil miseria.

conquests of hot regions, where insects keep watch over the copulation of the guardians of the corn-fields who lose their voices amongst the limitless sugar plantations crossed by fast-running canals and opaque reptiles with a white rich skin. Oh, the sleeplessness of the watchers who beat without rest the sonorous petrol-cans to drive away the assailing insects sent by the night like a promise of vigil! On the way to the sea these things are soon forgotten. And if a woman waits, her thick white thighs open like the branches of a hundred-year-old ceiba-tree in flower, then the poem draws to a close, already not making sense with its monotonous lamentation of a turbid fountain, and always renewed by the weary bodies of licentious gymnasts.

Only a word. A word, and the dance of fertile misery begins.

CUBA

JOSÉ MARTÍ (1853–95)

Sed de belleza

SOLO, estoy solo: viene el verso amigo,
Como el esposo diligente acude
De la erizada tórtola al reclamo.
Cual de los altos montes en deshielo
Por breñas y por valles en copiosos
Hilos las nieves desatadas bajan –
Así por mis entrañas oprimidas,
Un balsámico amor y una celeste avaricia,
Celeste de hermosura se derraman.
Tal desde el vasto azul, sobre la tierra,
Cual si de alma virgen la sombría
Humanidad sangrienta perfumasen,
Su luz benigna las estrellas vierten
Esposas del silencio! – y de las flores
Tal el aroma vago se levanta.
Dadme lo sumo y lo perfecto: dadme
Un dibujo de Angelo: una espada
Con puño de Cellini, más hermosa
Que las techumbres de marfil calado
Que se place en labrar Naturaleza.

Thirst for Beauty

ALONE, I am alone; the friendly verse comes, as the spouse diligently answers to the call of the bristling dove. As, in time of thaw, the unbound snows descend from the high mountains and through the crags and valleys in copious streams, so through my oppressed vitals pour out a balmy love and a celestial avarice, celestial in its beauty. Thus from the vast azure above the earth, as if so sombre bloodstained humanity were perfumed by the virgin spirit, their benign light shed by the stars, the brides of silence! – and from flowers thus is wafted a wandering scent. Give me the greatest, and the perfect; give me a sketch by Michelangelo, a sword hilted by Cellini, more lovely than the roofs of openwork ivory Nature

El cráneo augusto dadme donde ardieron
El universo Hamlet y la furia
Tempestuosa del moro: – la manceba
India que a orillas del ameno río
Que del viejo Chitchen los muros baña
A la sombra de un plátano pomposo
Y sus propios cabellos, el esbelto
Cuerpo bruñido y nítido enjugaba.
Dadme mi cielo azul . . . , dadme la pura,
La inefable, la plácida, la eterna
Alma de mármol que al soberbio Louvre
Dió, cual su espuma y flor, Milo famosa.

Copa con alas

UNA copa con alas ¿quién la ha visto
Antes que yo? Yo ayer la ví. Subía
Con lenta majestad, como quien vierte
Oleo sagrado; y a sus dulces bordes
Mis regalados labios apretaba.
Ni una gota siquiera, ni una gota
Del bálsamo perdí que hubo en tu beso!

amuses herself by working. Give me a great brain, in which will burn Hamlet, that universe, and the tempestuous madness of the Moor: the Indian concubine, who dries her elegant, lustrous, brown body by the banks of the pleasant river, which bathes the walls of old Chitchen, in the shade of a pompous banana-tree and of her own hair. Give me my blue sky . . . give me the pure, the ineffable, the peaceful, eternal soul of marble, which renowned Milo gave, as its foam and flower, to the proud Louvre.

Winged Goblet

A WINGED goblet – who has seen it before me? I saw it yesterday. It arose with slow majesty, like a man pouring sacred oil, and to its sweet sides I pressed my feasting lips. Not one single drop, not one drop of balm did I lose which was in your kiss.

Tu cabeza de negra cabellera
¿Te acuerdas? con mi mano requería,
Porque de mí tus labios generosos
No se apartaran. Blanca como el beso
Que a ti me transfundía, era la suave
Atmósfera en redor; la vida entera
Sentí que a mí abrazándote, abrazaba!
Perdí el mundo de vista, y sus ruídos
Y su envidiosa y bárbara batalla!
Una copa en los aires ascendía
Y yo, en brazos no vistos reclinado
Tras ella, asido de sus dulces bordes,
Por el espacio azul me remontaba!

Oh, amor, oh inmenso, oh acabado artista!
En rueda o riel funde el herrero el hierro;
Una flor o mujer o águila o ángel
En oro o plata el joyador cincela;
Tú sólo, sólo tú, sabes el modo
De reducir el Universo a un beso!

Your head, with its long black hair (do you remember?), I caressed with my hand, so that your generous lips would not leave me. White as the kiss which transfixed me into you was the gentle atmosphere around. I felt that I embraced my whole life when I embraced you. The world was lost to my sight, and its clamours, its envious and barbarous battle. A goblet ascended into the air, and I, reclining behind it in unseen arms, clinging to its sweet sides, ascended through the azure space.

O love, O the immense, the consummated artist! Into wheel or rail the smith beats out the iron; the engraver chases, in gold or silver, a flower, a woman, an eagle or an angel; you alone, only you, know the way to condense the universe into a kiss!

JULIÁN DEL CASAL (1863–93)

Pax animae

No me habléis más de dichas terrenales
que no ansío gustar. Está ya muerto
mi corazón, y en su recinto abierto
sólo entrarán los cuervos sepulcrales.

Del pasado no llevo las señales
y a veces de que existo no estoy cierto,
porque es la vida para mí un desierto
poblado de figuras espectrales.

No veo más que un astro oscurecido
por brumas de crepúsculo lluvioso,
y, entre el silencio de sopor profundo,

tan sólo llega a percibir mi oído
algo extraño y confuso y misterioso
que me arrastra muy lejos de este mundo.

Pax Animae

SPEAK to me no more of earthly pleasures which I do not wish to savour. My heart is already dead, and only the ravens of death will enter its opened chambers.

I have no traces of the past upon me, and sometimes I am not sure of whether I exist, since to me life is a desert peopled with spectral figures.

I see only a planet darkened by the mists of drizzling twilight, and, in the silence of profound drowsiness,

My ears only discern something strange, indistinct, mysterious, which drags me very far from this world.

Tardes de lluvia

BATE la lluvia la vidriera
y las rejas de los balcones,
donde tupida enredadera
cuelga sus floridos festones.

Bajo las hojas de los álamos
que estremecen los vientos frescos,
piar se escucha entre sus tálamos
a los gorriones picarescos.

Abrillántanse los laureles,
y en la arena de los jardines
sangran corolas de claveles,
nievan pétalos de jazmines.

Al último fulgor del día
que aún el espacio gris clarea,
abre su botón la peonía,
cierra su cáliz la ninfea.

Afternoons of Rain

THE rain beats the window-pane and the railings of the balcony, where overgrown creepers hang their flowering garlands.

Beneath the leaves of the aspens, shuddering in the cold winds, the chirp of knavish sparrows is heard among the cavities of the trunks.

The laurels glisten, and in the sand of the gardens the corollas of the carnations are bleeding, the petals of jasmine are snowing.

At the last glimmer of day, which still lightens the grey space, the peony opens her bud, the water-lily closes her calyx.

Cual los esquifes en la rada
y reprimiendo sus arranques,
duermen los cisnes en bandada
a la margen de los estanques.

Parpadean las rojas llamas
de los faroles encendidos,
y se difunden por las ramas
acres olores de los nidos.

Lejos convoca la campana,
dando sus toques funerales,
a que levante el alma humana
las oraciones vesperales.

Todo parece que agoniza
y que se envuelve lo creado
en un sudario de ceniza
nor la llovizna adiamantado.

Yo creo oir lejanas voces
que, surgiendo de lo infinito,
inícianme en extraños goces
fuera del mundo en que me agito.

Controlling their hasty movements, a flock of swans sleeps by the sides of the pools, like skiffs in harbour.

The red flames of the lighted lanterns are blinking, and the acrid smells of the nests drift through the branches.

Far away the bell calls, in funereal peals, lifting the human soul to evening prayers.

Everything seems in its death agony, and as if the created world were wrapped in a winding-sheet of ashes, diamonded by the raindrops.

I think I hear distant voices, surging from infinitude, initiating me into strange appetites, outside the world in which I fret.

Veo pupilas que en las brumas
dirígenme tiernas miradas,
como si de mis ansias sumas
ya se encontrasen apiadadas.

Y, a la muerte de estos crepúsculos,
siento, sumido en mortal calma,
vagos dolores en los músculos,
hondas tristezas en el alma.

I see eyes casting tender glances to me through the mist, as if they were already pitying my deepest anguish.

And, on the death oi this twilight, I feel, drowned in mortal calm, vague pains in the muscles, deep sorrows in the soul.

NICOLÁS GUILLÉN (b. 1902)

Caminando

CAMINANDO, caminando,
¡caminando!

Voy sin rumbo caminando,
caminando;
voy sin plata caminando,
caminando.

Está lejos quien me busca,
caminando;
quien me espera está más lejos,
caminando;
y ya empeñé mi guitarra,
caminando.

Ay,
las piernas se ponen duras,
caminando;
los ojos ven desde lejos,
caminando;
la mano agarra y no suelta,
caminando.

Marching

MARCHING, marching, marching.

I'm marching in no direction; I'm marching with no money.

He who looks for me is far away, marching; he who waits for me is further, marching; and I've already pawned my guitar, marching.

Ay, the legs become stiff, marching; the eyes see from afar, marching; the hand grips, and will not let go, marching.

Al que yo coja y lo apriete,
caminando,
ése la paga por todos,
caminando;
a ése le parto el pescuezo,
caminando,
y aunque me pida perdón,
me lo como y me lo bebo,
me lo bebo y me lo como,
caminando,
caminando,
caminando . . .

No sé por qué piensas tú

No sé por qué piensas tú,
soldado, que te odio yo,
si somos la misma cosa
yo.
tú.

Tú eres pobre, lo soy yo;
soy de abajo, lo eres tú;
¿de dónde has sacado tú,
soldado, que te odio yo?

The one I grip and squeeze, marching, he will pay for them all, marching, I will break his neck, marching, and though he begs for mercy, I'll eat him and drink him, I'll drink him and eat him, marching, marching, marching.

I Don't Know Why You Think

I DON'T know why you think, soldier, that I hate you, since we are the same, I, you.

You are poor, so am I; I am low-born, so are you; where did you get the idea, soldier, that I hate you?

Me duele que a veces tú
te olvides de quién soy yo;
caramba, si yo soy tú,
lo mismo que tú eres yo.

Pero no por eso yo
he de malquererte, tú;
si somos la misma cosa,
yo,
tú,
no sé por qué piensas tú,
soldado, que te odio yo.

Ya nos veremos yo y tú,
juntos en la misma calle,
hombro con hombro, tú y yo,
sin odios ni yo ni tú,
pero sabiendo tú y yo,
a dónde vamos yo y tú . . .
¡No sé por qué piensas tú,
soldado, que te odio yo!

It hurts me that you sometimes forget who I am; for God's sake, since I am you just as much as you are me.

But not because of that, will I bear you a grudge; since we are the same, you, I, I don't know why you think, soldier, that I hate you.

You and I will see ourselves together in the same street, shoulder to shoulder, you and I, without hatred, neither I nor you, but knowing, you and I, where we're going, I and you. . . . I don't know why you think, soldier, that I hate you!

EUGENIO FLORIT (b. 1903)

Estrofas a una estatua

MONUMENTO ceñido
de un tiempo tan lejano de tu muerte.
Así te estás inmóvil a la orilla
de este sol que se fuga en mariposas.

Tú, estatua blanca, rosa de alabastro,
naciste para estar pura en la tierra
con un dosel de ramas olorosas
y la pupila ciega bajo el cielo.

No has de sentir cómo la luz se muere
sino por el color que en ti resbala
y el frío que se prende a tus rodillas
húmedas del silencio de la tarde.

Cuando en piedra moría la sonrisa
quebró sus alas la dorada abeja
y en el espacio eterno lleva el alma
con recuerdo de mieles y de bocas.

Stanzas to a Statue

A MONUMENT girded by a time so distant from your death. Thus you stand motionless on the edge of this sun, which runs away in butterflies.

You, white statue, alabaster rose, were born to be pure on the earth, with a canopy of fragrant boughs, and a blind eye beneath the heavens.

You will not feel how the light dies, except for the colour which slips over you, and the cold which clings to your knees, damp with the silence of the afternoon.

When the smile died into stone, the gilded bee broke his wings, and took his soul into the eternal space, with memories of honeys and mouths.

Ya tu perfecta geometría sabe
que es vano el aire y tímido el rocío;
y cómo viene el mar sobre esa arena
con el eco de tantos caracoles.

Beso de estrella, luz para tu frente
desnuda de memorias y de lágrimas:
la firme superficie de alabastro
donde ya no se sueña.

Por la rama caída hasta tus hombros
bajó el canto de un pájaro a besarte.
Qué serena ilusión tienes, estatua,
de eternidad bajo la clara noche.

A la mariposa muerta

TU júbilo, en el vuelo;
tu inquietud, en el aire;
tu vida, al sol, al aire, al vuelo.

Qué pequeña tu muerte
bajo la luz de fuego vivo.

Already your perfect geometry knows that the air is empty and the dew timid; and how the sea comes over the sand, with the echo of so many shells.

Kiss of the star, light for your forehead, stripped of memories and tears; the firm surface of alabaster where there is no dreaming.

Along the fallen branch to your shoulders came down the song of a bird to kiss you. How serene, O statue, is your illusion of eternity beneath the clear night.

To the Dead Butterfly

YOUR jubilation, in flight; your restlessness, in the air; your life, in the sunshine, in the air, in flight.

How tiny your death, under the light of living fire. How serene

Qué serena la gracia de tus alas
ya para siempre abiertas en el libro.

Y en ti, tan suave, en tu morir callado,
en tu sueño sin sueños,
cuánta ilusión perdida al aire,
cuánto desesperado pensamiento.

the grace of your wings, now [pressed] open for ever in the book.

And in you, so gentle, in your silent death, in your dreamless dream, how many illusions lost in the air, how many despairing thoughts.

EMILIO BALLAGAS (1908–54)

Nocturno

¿Cómo te llamas, noche de esta noche?
Dime tu nombre. Déjame
tu santo y seña
para que yo te reconozca
siempre
a través de otras noches diferentes.

Tú me ofreces su frente en medialuna
(medialuna de carne),
sus labios (pulpa en sombra)
y su perfil al tacto . . .
(Mañana mi derecha
jugará a dibujar su contorno en el aire.)

¿Cómo te llamas, noche de esta noche?
Dime tu nombre, déjame
tu santo y seña
para que yo te reconozca
siempre
a través de otras noches diferentes.

Nocturne

What is your name, night of this night? Tell me your name. Give me your password, that I may always recognize you, through other different nights.

You offer me her brow, half-moon (half-moon of flesh), her lips (fruit in the shadows) and her profile to the touch. . . . (Tomorrow my right hand will play at drawing her shape in the air.)

What is your name, night of this night? Tell me your name, leave me your password, that I may always recognize you through

¡Y que pueda llamarte gozoso,
trémulo,
por tu nombre!

Poema impaciente

¿Y si llegaras tarde,
cuando mi boca tenga
sabor seco a cenizas,
a tierras amargas?

¿Y si llegaras cuando
la tierra removida y oscura (ciega, muerta)
llueva sobre mis ojos,
y desterrado de la luz del mundo
te busque en la luz mía,
en la luz interior que yo creyera
tener fluyendo en mí?
(Cuando tal vez descubra
que nunca tuve luz
y marche a tientas dentro de mí mismo,
como un ciego que tropieza a cada paso
con recuerdos que hieren como cardos.)

other different nights. And, that I, joyous, tremulous, may call you by your name!

Poem of Impatience

AND if you were to come late, when my mouth has the dry taste of ashes, or bitter earth?

And if you were to come when the dark ploughed earth (blind, dead) rains over my eyes, and, banished from the light of the world, I seek you in my light, in the interior light I believe is flowing in me? (When ,at such a time, I might discover that I never did have light, and go groping deeper into myself, like a blind man stumbling at every step, over memories which prick like thistles.)

¿Y si llegaras cuando ya el hastío
ata y venda las manos;
cuando no pueda abrir los brazos
y cerrarlos después como las valvas
de una concha amorosa que defiende
su misterio, su carne, su secreto;
cuando no pueda oír abrirse
la rosa de tu beso ni tocarla
(tacto mío marchito entre la tierra yerta)
ni sentir que me nace otro perfume
que le responda al tuyo,
ni enseñar a tus rosas
el color de mis rosas?
¿Y si llegaras tarde
y encontraras (tan sólo)
las cenizas heladas de la espera?

And if you were to come when tedium already binds and ties the hands; when the arms cannot be opened or closed afterwards like the shells of the amorous clam, which defends its mystery, its flesh, its secret; when I can no longer hear the rose of your kiss opening, no longer touch it (my withered touch in the stiff earth) nor feel that another perfume is born in me which responds to yours, nor show your roses the colour of my roses? And if you were to come late, and were to find (only) the frozen ashes of waiting?

JOSÉ LEZAMA LIMA (b. 1912)

Pez nocturno

LA oscura lucha con el pez concluye;
su boca finge de la noche orilla.
Las escamas enciende, sólo brilla
aquella plata que de pronto huye.

Hojosa plata la noche reconstruye
sus agallas, caverna de luz amarilla
en coágulos de fango se zambulle.
Frío el ojo del pez nos maravilla.

Un temblor y la mirada extiende
su podredumbre, lo que comprende
ligera aísla de lo que acapara.

Aquel fanal se pierde y se persigue.
La espuma de su sueño no consigue
reconstruir la línea que saltara.

Nocturnal Fish

THE dark fight with the fish concludes; its mouth imitates the edge of night. The scales shimmer, only that silver, that suddenly runs away, glitters.

Overlapping silver, the night reconstructs its gills, cavern of yellow light, it dives into clots of mud. Cold, the eye of the fish astounds us.

A tremor, and the glance extends its rottenness, and lightly insulates that which it comprises from that which it seizes.

That beacon-light is lost and persecuted. The froth of its dream cannot reconstruct the line it jumped over.

Llamado del deseoso

DESEOSO es aquel que huye de su madre,
Despedirse es cultivar un rocío para unirlo con la secularidad de la saliva.
La hondura del deseo no va por el secuestro del fruto.
Deseoso es dejar de ver a su madre.
Es la ausencia del sucedido de un día que se prolonga
y es a la noche que esa ausencia se va ahondando como un cuchillo.
En esa ausencia se abre una torre, en esa torre baila un fuego hueco.
Y así se ensancha y la ausencia de la madre es un mar en calma.
Pero el huidizo no ve el cuchillo que le pregunta,
es de la madre, de los postigos asegurados, de quien se huye.
Lo descendido en vieja sangre suena vacío.
La sangre es fría cuando desciende y cuando se esparce circulizada.
La madre es fría y está cumplida.
Si es por la muerte, su peso es doble y ya no nos suelta.

Cry of the Wishful Man

THE wishful man is he who runs away from his mother, to say goodbye is to cultivate a dew to unite it to the secularity of saliva. The depth of desire does not go after the sequestration of the fruit. To be wishful is to stop seeing one's mother. It is the absence of what happened on one prolonged day and it is at night that that absence deepens like a knife. In that absence a tower opens, in that tower dances a hollow fire. And thus it widens and the absence of a mother is like a calm sea. But the evasive man does not see the questioning knife, he belongs to the mother, to bolted shutters, to the person from whom he runs. That which has descended into old blood rings hollow. Blood is cold when, having circulated, it descends and spreads. The mother is cold and is fulfilled. If it is through death, its weight is double and does not let us go. It is not

No es por las puertas donde se asoma nuestro abandono.
Es por un claro donde la madre sigue marchando, pero
ya no nos sigue.
Es por un claro, allí se ciega y bien nos deja.
Ay del que no marcha esa marcha donde la madre ya no
le sigue, ay.
No es desconocerse, el conocerse sigue furioso como en
sus días,
pero el seguirlo sería quemarse dos en un árbol,
y ella apetece mirar el árbol como una piedra,
como una piedra con la inscripción de ancianos juegos.
Nuestro deseo no es alcanzar o incorporar un fruto ácido.
El deseoso es el huidizo
y de los cabezazos con nuestras madres cae el planeta
centro de mesa
y ¿dé dónde huimos, si no es de nuestras madres de
quien huimos
que nunca quieren recomenzar el mismo naipe, la misma
noche de igual ijada descomunal?

through the doors where our abandonment appears. It is through an opening where the mother continues her walk, but no longer follows us. It is through an opening and there she blinds herself and finally leaves us. Alas for the man who does not walk the walk where his mother no longer follows him, alas. It is not to be unacquainted with oneself, self-knowledge continues furiously like it did in her time, but to follow it would be burning both in one tree, and she seeks to look at the tree as if it were a stone, a stone bearing the inscription of old games. Our desire is not to reach or incorporate acid fruit. The wishful man is the evasive, and from banging our heads against our mothers' falls the planet, the table's centrepiece, and from whence do we run if not from our mothers from whom we run if we never seek to begin again the same game of cards, the same night, and its equal enormous haunches?

from *Primera glorieta de la amistad*

Para Fina García Marruz

SEÑORA piel . . . oleaje,
punto en boca del pez.
No el wagneriano crinaje,
si la hoja en su envés.

Luciérnaga del poro,
extensión con su pino
de Noel y el egipcio lino.
Se pliega, esfera de oro.

Incomprensiblemente se retrata
con una orquídea japonesa.
Su alianza es como la plata,

cuando en el examen reza.
Hable la fresa en su rocío
del baile de los elfos en el frío.

from *The First Bower of Friendship*

For Fina García Marruz

SEÑORA skin . . . the waves of the sea, a point in the mouth of a fish. Not the Wagnerian mane, if one side of the page is in the other.

The glow-worm of the pore, extension with its pine of Noel* and the Egyptian flax. It folds, a sphere of gold.

Incomprehensibly, she is painted with a Japanese orchid. Her composition is like silver.

Upon examination. Let the strawberry speak in its dew of the dance of the elves in the frost.

---

*Christmas tree.

Para Octavio Smith

ASPAS, bastos, flautines, ojos,
niebla, aliento, sombra, cerrojos.

Aproximación a las proclamas del estío,
cuando la madera chilla dentro del caserío.

La entonada raíz el agua mece
y el leñador pegando en la sombra acrece,

como dos vasos de agua removidos,
por barajas y linces estremecidos.

La niebla es el sombrero de una vida sumergida,
quitarse el sombrero es lo invisible que convida.

For Octavio Smith

WINDMILL-SAILS, clubs,* piccolos, eyes, fog, breath, shadow, bolts.

Approximation to the announcements of summer, when the timber creaks in the hamlet.

Water cradles the thrusting root, and the woodcutter, clattering in the shadows, makes it grow . . .†

Like two glasses of water stirred and frightened by packs of cards and lynxes.

Fog is the sombrero of a submerged life, to take off the sombrero is the invisible which invites.

---

*The suit in a pack of cards.

†The ambiguities of this stanza make it untranslatable. It could also be read 'The thrusting root cradles the water, and the woodcutter grows, clattering in the shadows.' A further difficulty is that *leñador* could be an abbreviation of *pájaro leñador*, or woodpecker.

from *Fragmentos*

Los murmullos tienen, plásticamente, una seda estrujada,
un gran pañuelo reducido por la mano, y después saltan.
La fluidez y contracciones, los graciosos dones líquidos,
desean un ceremonioso recogimiento, y después alegremente
vacilan ante su libertad. Murmullo que es esa vacilación
del candoroso repliegue entre dos lunas y la ancha boca
de ondas apoltronados y escote cuarentón.

Los murmullos agitan su nueva caldera de plata,
el príncipe y el condotieri sienten la ligereza
de la luna por las baldosas, cuando sorprenden el crecendo
que llega hasta el balcón, hostil plumón
en donde el sueño recibe el ancla del naufragio.
El pequeño oscuro tiene un oleaje contraído
y la perra cubriendo las baldosas ladra la fuga de un reflejo.

from *Fragments*

THE murmurs hold, in their plasticity, a crumpled silk, a large scarf squashed into the hand, and afterwards they leap out. Fluidity and contractions, the graceful liquid gifts, seek a ceremonious composure, and then joyfully hesitate before their liberty. Murmur which is that hesitation of the candid fold between two moons and the wide-open mouth of the indolent waves, and an ageing neckline.

Murmurs stir their new silver kettle, the prince and the Condottiere feel the swiftness of the moon through the tiles of the floor when they surprise the crescent moon, which reaches the balcony, the hostile eiderdown in which the dream receives the anchor of shipwreck. There is a choppy sea on the little black [horse] and the bitch covering the tiles on the floor barks at the fleeing reflection.

La seda nos toca con la cola de su ciego calamar.
La jactancia ilusoria de la seda vuelve a ser reconocida
por la caricia que se extiende llevando sueño
hasta sus términos; su jactancia se tolera lentamente
y con lentitud despiertan sus guardianes el contorno.
Tiende a caer la seda sobre la piel, navegamos entonces
sin tocar las entrañas del mar, la piel del monstruo nos
acoge.

Nerviosos animalejos de sumergidas cabezas,
mueven las piernas como lombrices avanzando por lo
húmedo,
caracteres de la lluvia a la salida del salón de otoño.
Alguien que espera que la verde mujer termine de dormir,
mientras las sonrientes paredes improvisan sus ventanas,
se abraza a la pierna reconociendo la esbeltez
de las antiguas humillaciones, desembarcando en una
ciudad quemada por los persas.

Silk touches us with the tentacle of its blind squid. The illusory boastfulness of the silk is again recognized by the caress which reaches out carrying dreams to their extremes; its boastfulness is slowly tolerated and with slowness its guardians awake the contour. Silk tends to fall on the skin, we sail then without putting in to the entrails of the sea, the monster's skin welcomes us.

Restless little animals, their heads submerged, move their legs like worms advancing through the humid earth, characters of the rain [advancing] to the way out of autumn's salon. Someone who waits for the green woman's sleep to end, while the smiling walls improvise their windows, embraces the leg perceiving the gracefulness of ancient humiliations, disembarking into a city the Persians burnt.

El cuerpo completo en su doctrina es que el que escoge,
se sumerge, cae o posesiona, como la tierra posee
el sentido curvo de su visión, los escalonados muros
derruídos por la espiral de la mirada, pues no es el espacio
sensibilizado sino la ocupación del temblor vaciado
por un golpe el que inaugura las bodas del conocimiento,
ya que el dolor del otro cuerpo es que comenzó por un
vaciado que recibe.

Reino de las imágenes por el artificio del inmóvil cono-
cido,
pues el cuerpo tiende a la otra extensión de su escultura
y a establecer en el sueño los juegos del rescate no pagado.
Si no llegasen los números del sueño retendríamos al
inmóvil desconocido,
lo que no se demuestra ni se puede dar por demostrado:
la gracia o aprovechamiento de las imágenes que des-
conocen las escalas de nuestro cuerpo.
Nuestro oleaje, al que desconocemos, es despreciado
como trampa.

The body, complete in its doctrine, is the chooser, who submerges, falls or possesses, as the earth possesses the curved sensation of its vision, the terraced walls knocked down by the spiral of seeing, for it is not the space sensitized, but the occupation of a tremor emptied by a blow which inaugurates the wedding of knowledge, because the pain of the other body is that it started as a receiving mould.

Kingdom of images through the artifices of the stationary known, because the body tends towards the other extension of its sculpture and to the establishment in dreams of games of ransoms unredeemed. If the numbers of the dream did not turn up, we would retain the stationary known, undemonstrated and undemonstrable: the grace or the use of the images which do not know the patterns of our body. The swell of our sea, unknown to us, is despised like a snare.

Las imágenes proclaman nuestro cuerpo,
caen en lo sucesivo o en la esfera, siempre en una voz
que le prestó el centro de su aliento.
Nuestro cuerpo llega a ser un obstáculo donde la ajenía
se revuelve. Ay, nuestro cuerpo a horcajadas en otras
imágenes,
que no eran para él, oscuro y musical impedimento
penetra en la desolación, el soplo que transfigura a la
hoja no es el que recibirá como terror.

Images proclaim our body, fall into the successive or the sphere, always in a voice borrowed from the centre of its inspiration. Our body becomes an obstacle where alien-ness revolves. Alas, our body straddles other images which were not for it, dark and musical impediment penetrating into the desolation, the inspiring breath which transfigures the leaf is not the same as will receive the terror.

ROBERTO FERNÁNDEZ RETAMAR (b. 1930)

El poema de hoy

EL poema de hoy, cuando ya el día
Quebró la frente oscura y dispersó
En múltiple caída las estrellas,
Y ocupó todo el mundo el sitio
Abandonado o desconocido;
El poema de hoy es el de siempre,
El de luego, el de entonces,
El solo poema que una mano
Traza sin cansarse y alegre
Sobre un papel que vuela vasto,
Y en donde pone cielos,
Astros, ígneas llamadas
Que a la tarde regresarán
A conversar con nosotros.

Patria

AHORA lo sé: no eres la noche: eres
Una severa y diurna certidumbre.

Today's Poem

TODAY'S poem, when day already struck the dark forehead, and dispersed the stars in a multiple fall, and the abandoned or unknown site occupied the whole world; today's poem is the poem of ever, of later on, of then, the sole poem which a hand draws without tiring, happily on a paper in vast flight, and where it places skies, stars, burning calls, which in the evening will return to talk to us.

Homeland

NOW I know it: you are not the night: you are a severe and diurnal

Eres la indignación, eres la cólera
Que nos levantan frente al enemigo.
Eres la lengua para comprendernos
Muchos hombres crecidos a tu luz.
Eres la tierra verdadera, el aire
Que siempre quiere el pecho respirar.
Eres la vida que ayer fue promesa
De los muertos hundidos en tu entraña.
Eres el sitio del amor profundo,
De la alegría y del coraje y de
La espera necesaria de la muerte.
Eres la forma de nuestra existencia,
Eres la piedra en que nos afirmamos,
Eres la hermosa, eres la inmensa caja
Donde irán a romperse nuestros huesos
Para que siga haciéndose tu rostro.

certitude. You are the indignation, you are the wrath which lifts us up before the enemy. You are the tongue with which we, the many grown in your light, understand each other. You are the true land, the air the breast always yearns to breathe. You are the life which yesterday was the promise of the dead sunk in your womb. You are the place of profound love, of happiness, and of courage, and of the necessary waiting for death. You are the form of our existence, you are the rock on which we stand firm, you are the beautiful, you are the immense coffin where our bones will go to be broken so that your countenance should continue in its making.

PABLO ARMANDO FERNÁNDEZ (b. 1930)

Trajano

CANTAR no es fácil, joven.
No es ceñir cada palabra al canto
y apretadas, echarlas a volar.
Muchas veces tropiezan, caen y ruedan.
Difícil es alzarlas una a una
sin resentir sus alas; animarlas
de un aliento distinto,
no siempre poderoso pero firme.
Y hacer que de ellas nazca la voz
que el canto exige.
Joven, cantar es doloroso.
No confíes al acento del canto
su belleza; piensa que la tiniebla
y el silencio fueron primero.
Piensa que de ese encuentro
nacieron la palabra y lo que alumbra.

Trajan

YOUNG man, it is not easy to sing. It is not to bind every word to the song, and, when they have been imprisoned, launch them into flight. Often they stumble, fall, and roll away. It is difficult to lift them up one by one without hurting their wings; to breathe a distinct character into them, not always powerful, but firm. And to make sure that from them is born the voice which the song demands. Young man, it is painful to sing. Do not trust the beauty of the song to its accent; think that darkness and silence were there first. Think that from that encounter were born both the word, and that which illuminates [engenders].

Los héroes

DESDE los sueños el polvoriento corazón
del monte ardía
y de nuevo comenzaba a vivir
para un suceso puro.
Cantos y toques en la casa vieja del mundo
y ellos nacidos la víspera del fin.
Viven hacia la eternidad los héroes.
Para sus ojos múltiples de asombro
guarda el monte la única flor
que el tiempo no elabora, que la muerte no toca.
Eran desde los sueños, iguales y distintos.

The Heroes

FROM the dreams, the dusty heart of the bush-land burned, and started to live anew, for a pure event. Songs and martial noises in the old house of the world, and they, born on the eve of the end. The heroes live on into eternity. For their many eyes of wonder the bush-land guards the only flower which time does not make, nor death touch. From the dreams, they were like others, and [yet] different.

ECUADOR

JOSÉ JOAQUÍN DE OLMEDO (1780–1847)

from *La victoria de Junín*

EL trueno horrendo que en fragor revienta
y sordo retumbando se dilata
por la inflamada esfera,
al Dios anuncia que en el cielo impera.

Y el rayo que en Junín rompe y ahuyenta
la hispana muchedumbre
que, más feroz que nunca, amenazaba,
a sangre y fuego, eterna servidumbre,

y el canto de victoria
que en ecos mil discurre, ensordeciendo
el hondo valle y enriscada cumbre,
proclaman a Bolívar en la tierra
árbitro de la paz y de la guerra.

Las soberbias pirámides que al cielo
el arte humano osado levantaba
para hablar a los siglos y naciones

from *The Victory at Junín*

THE terrible noise of thunder that explodes and spreads with a muffled boom around the burning globe proclaims the God that rules in heaven.

And the thunderbolt that breaks in Junín and puts to flight the Spanish rabble that, fiercer than ever, with blood and fire, threatened eternal slavery,

And the song of victory that spreads in a thousand echoes, deafening the deep valleys and the rocky crags, acclaim Bolívar the arbiter on earth of peace and war.

The lofty pyramids that presumptuous human art once built to speak to the centuries and to the nations – temples where en-

– templos do esclavas manos
deificaban en pompa a sus tiranos – ,
ludibrio son del tiempo, que con su ala
débil, las toca y las derriba al suelo,
después que en fácil juego el fugaz viento
borró sus mentirosas inscripciones;
y bajo los escombros, confundido
entre la sombra del eterno olvido
– ¡oh de ambición y de miseria ejemplo! –
el sacerdote yace, el dios y el templo.
Mas los sublimes montes, cuya frente
a la región etérea se levanta,
que ven las tempestades a su planta
brillar, rugir, romperse, disiparse,
los Andes, las enormes, estupendas
moles sentadas sobre bases de oro,
la tierra con su peso equilibrando,
jamás se moverán. Ellos, burlando
de ajena envidia y del protervo tiempo
la furia y el poder, serán eternos
de libertad y de victoria heraldos,
que con eco profundo,
a la postrema edad dirán del mundo:

slaved hands deified their tyrants in splendour – are the object of time's scorn; time, which, with its weak wing, touches them and brings them down in ruins, after the fleeting wind, with playful ease, has wiped out their equivocal inscriptions; and amid the debris lies the priest – exemplary victim of ambition and wretchedness! – the god and the temple, submerged in the shadows of eternal oblivion. The sublime mountains, however, their faces raised in the ethereal regions, watching the storms flare up, roar, shatter and vanish at their feet, the huge and marvellous blocks on foundations of gold that balance the earth with their weight, the Andes will never move. Scorning the fury and the strength of foreign envy and peevish time, they will be the eternal heralds of freedom and victory, saying with deep echoes to the world's last age:

«Nosotros vimos de Junín el campo,
vimos que al desplegarse
del Perú y de Colombia las banderas,
se turban las legiones altaneras,
huye el fiero español despavorido,
o pide paz rendido.
Venció Bolívar, el Perú fue libre,
y en triunfal pompa Libertad sagrada
en el templo del Sol fué colocada».

¿Quién me dará templar el voraz fuego
en que ardo todo yo? Trémula, incierta,
torpe la mano va sobre la lira
dando discorde son . . . ¿Quién me libera
del dios que me fatiga . . . ?

Siento unas veces la rebelde Musa,
cual bacante en furor, vagar incierta
por medio de las plazas bulliciosas,
o sola por las selvas silenciosas,
o las risueñas playas
que manso lame el caudaloso Guayas;
otras el vuelo arrebatada tiende

'We have seen the field of Junín, we have seen the haughty legions become alarmed before the unfurled flags of Peru and Colombia; we have seen the proud Spaniard flee in terror or, exhausted, sue for peace. Bolívar was victorious, Peru was free, and sacred Liberty was set in triumphal splendour in the temple of the Sun.'

Who will help me to assuage the voracious fire that consumes my whole being? Tremulous, uncertain and heavy, my hand runs over the lyre giving a discordant sound . . . . Who will free me from the God that exhausts me . . . ?

Sometimes I hear the rebellious Muse wandering uncertainly, like a bacchante in a frenzy, through the noisy squares, or alone through the silent forests or the charming shores lapped gently by the mighty Guayas; at other times, startled, she takes flight over

sobre los montes, y de allí desciende
al campo de Junín, y ardiendo en ira,
los numerosos escuadrones mira,
que el odiado pendón de España arbolan,
y en cristado morrión y peto armada,
cual amazona fiera,
se mezcla entre las filas la primera
de todos los guerreros,
y a combatir con ellos se adelanta,
triunfa con ellos y sus triunfos canta.

Tal en los siglos de virtud y gloria,
donde el guerrero sólo y el poeta
eran dignos de honor y de memoria,
la musa audaz de Píndaro divino,
cual intrépido atleta,
en inmortal porfía
al griego estadio concurrir solía;
y en estro hirviendo y en amor de fama
y del metro y del número impaciente,
pulsa su lira de oro sonorosa
y alto asiento concede entre los dioses
al que fuera en la lid más valeroso,

the mountains and from there descends on to the field of Junín; burning with rage, she watches the numerous squadrons that fly the hated Spanish flag, and armed in crested morion and breastplate, mingles with the ranks like a fierce Amazon, the first among the warriors; marching forward into battle with them, she is victorious with them and sings their triumphs.

Thus, in the centuries of virtue and glory, where only the warrior and the poet were worthy of honour and of memory, divine Pindar's daring muse, like an intrepid athlete, used to attend the immortal contest in the Greek stadium; burning with inspiration and the love of fame, and impatient with metre and with rhythm, she plucks her sonorous golden lyre and grants a high place among the gods to him who was most valiant in the fight, or to

o al más afortunado;
pero luego, envidiosa
de la inmortalidad que les ha dado,
ciega se lanza al circo polvoroso,
las alas rapídisimas agita
y al carro vencedor se precipita,
y desatando armónicos raudales
pide, disputa, gana,
o arrebata la palma a sus rivales.
¿Quién es aquél que el paso lento mueve
sobre el collado que a Junín domina?
¿que el campo desde allí mide, y el sitio
del combatir y del vencer desina?
¿que la hueste contraria observa, cuenta,
y en su mente la rompe y desordena,
y a los más bravos a morir condena,
cual águila caudal que se complace
del alto cielo en divisar la presa
que entre el rebaño mal segura pace?
¿Quién el que ya desciende
pronto y apercibido a la pelea?
Preñada en tempestades la rodea
nube tremenda; el brillo de su espada

the most fortunate; but then, jealous of the immortality she has given them, blindly throws herself into the dusty amphitheatre, flaps her wings very fast and rushes at the victor's carriage; and, unleashing torrents of harmony, she claims, disputes. wins or snatches away the palm from her rivals.

Who is the man moving with a slow step over the hill that dominates Junín? Who measures the field from that vantage point, and designates the site of the battle and the victory? Who watches the rival host, counts it, and breaks and routs it in his mind, condemning the bravest among them to death, like a red-tailed eagle who is pleased to pick out from high up in the sky, the prey that grazes unprotected amid the flock? Who is the man who now descends for battle, prompt and forearmed? He is enveloped in a huge cloud bulging with storms; the shining of his sword is

es el vivo reflejo de la gloria;
su voz un trueno, su mirada un rayo.
¿Quién aquél que al trabarse la batalla,
ufano como nuncio de victoria,
un corcel impetuoso fatigando,
discurre sin cesar por toda parte . . . ?
¿Quién sino el hijo de Colombia y Marte?

the living reflection of glory, his voice is a clap of thunder, his glance a thunderbolt. Who is that man, proud harbinger of victory, who, when the battle begins, covers the whole field, and exhausts an impetuous charger. . .? Who else but the son of Colombia and Mars?

JORGE CARRERA ANDRADE (b. 1903)

Vocación del espejo

CUANDO olvidan las cosas su forma y su color
y, acosados de noche, los muros se repliegan
y todo se arrodilla, o cede o se confunde,
sólo tú estás de pie, luminosa presencia.

Impones a las sombras tu clara voluntad.
En lo oscuro destella tu mineral silencio.
Como palomas súbitas
a las cosas envías tus mensajes secretos.

Cada silla se alarga en la noche y espera
un invitado irreal ante un plato de sombra,
y sólo tú, testigo transparente,
una lección de luz repites de memoria.

Vocation of the Mirror

WHEN things, assailed by night, forget their form and colour, and the walls fold up and everything falls to its knees or yields or becomes confused, only you, shining presence, are on your feet.

You impose your clear will on the shadows. In the darkness your mineral silence shimmers. Like sudden pigeons you send your secret messages to things.

Every chair lengthens in the night and awaits an imaginary guest before a plate of shadow, and only you, transparent witness, repeat by heart a lesson of light.

Defensa del domingo

ISLA de soledades y campanas,
los días nos arrojan hacia tu acantilado,
tu cima de reposo y de candor,
tu inmensidad que surcan las horas y los pájaros.

Tu masa de luz nueva surge en medio del tiempo
y tu oro semanal repartes gradualmente
animando jardines
y volviéndonos ricos de parcelas celestes.

Como a lecho o espuma ansiada tocan
nuestros cansados pies a tu último peldaño
o conmovida cúpula con pájaros de vino
que celebran la dulce vacación de las manos.

Náufragos semanales llegamos a tus costas
a saciarnos de luces
y a buscar la palmera del reposo
o el plano del tesoro escondido en las nubes.

Defence of Sunday

ISLAND of solitudes and bells, the days dash us against your cliffs, your peak of rest and candour, your immensity cut through by the hours and the birds.

Your mass of new light emerges out of time, and little by little you share out your weekly gold, reviving gardens and making us rich in celestial allotments.

Our tired feet touch your last step as if it were a bed, or coveted foam, or an agitated cupola where birds of wine celebrate the hands' sweet holiday.

We reach your coasts each week as shipwrecked men, to fill ourselves with lights and to seek out the palm tree of repose or the plans for the treasure hidden in the clouds.

El reloj

RELOJ:
picapedrero del tiempo.

Golpea en la muralla más dura de la noche,
pica tenaz, el péndulo.

La despierta vainilla
compone partituras de olor en los roperos.

Vigilando el trabajo del reloj
anda con sus pantuflas calladas el silencio.

Imagen entera

De pronto me vi
imagen entera,
con un gesto aprendido
a través de los años.
Yo era hombre de cristal
que reflejaba el mundo
sin nada retener.

The Clock

CLOCK: stone-cutter of time.

The pendulum, a tenacious hammer, chips at the hardest wall of the night.

The heliotrope, still awake, composes scores of smell in wardrobes.

Watching over the clock's work, in muted slippers, walks silence.

Complete Image

SUDDENLY I saw myself, a complete image, with an expression rehearsed over the years. I was a man of crystal who reflected the world, holding nothing back. I saw myself different from the other

Me vi distinto
a las otras imágenes
de mí mismo
vivas en el espejo:
más sombra en mi cabeza,
a mis pies más abismo,
en mi interior más selva,
inconciencia de planta
obediente a la brisa,
junco de soledad,
ya no pensante,
– ¡soledad terrenal,
única compañía! –
Me vi en fugaz reflejo,
mirando desde afuera
al ser que vive dentro,
recluso enmascarado
en su ambulante encierro.

images of me alive in the mirror: a [darker] shadow on my head, a [deeper] abyss at my feet, a [thicker] wood within me; the unconsciousness of a plant, obedient to the breeze, a reed of solitude, no longer thinking – earthly solitude, my only company! I saw myself in a fleeting reflection, looking from outside at the being who lives within, a masked recluse in his wandering seclusion.

GUATEMALA

LUIS CARDOZA Y ARAGÓN (b. 1904)

Canto a la soledad

SOLO de soledad y solitario y solo
como el loco en el centro de su locura,
yo digo lo que tú me has dicho
con la ahogada voz del mar
en mis oídos de ceniza que canta.

He escuchado tu paso eglógico y naval
de gacela y anémona, cayendo sobre el tiempo
de un sueño que tejen estatuas mutiladas;
la alondra que agoniza debajo de la nieve,
el musgo deletreando la vida sobre roca,
el trigo de la lluvia, el túnel ciego
que va de la simiente hasta la rosa,
hermosura del mundo, su más alto gemido.
Vencidamente sigo tu llama congelada,
tus desiertos espejos y tus lentos metales
que no se rendirán jamás a las campanas,
tu huella de reliquia incinerada.

Song to Solitude

SOLE of solitude and solitary and sole, like the madman in the centre of his madness, I say what you have said to me with the drowning voice of the sea in my ears, made of ashes which sing.

I have heard your step, pastoral and naval, of gazelle and anemone, falling across the time of a dream woven by mutilated statues; the lark dying under the snow, the moss spelling life on the rock, the harvest-fields of rain, the blind tunnel which leads from the seed to the rose, the beauty of the world, its greatest lamentation. Conquered, I follow your frozen flame, your deserted mirrors and your slow metals which will never submit to the bells, your footprint of burnt-out remains.

No sé si pulpa o hueso eres de fruto
de misterio y locura,
de orgullosa agonía anticipada,
o si estamos soñándonos los dos
en el huracán y en el suspiro,
en la breve inmensidad de un lunar,
en lo que yo he querido,
como agua y fuego en sangre,
como amores sin olvido.

Yo recuerdo tu descanso de lluvia
cayendo sobre el mar.
Tu afán de hiedra fiel
y niña amada nuevamente,
Yo recuerdo tus duelos pensativos,
tu gozo doloroso y tu arrobo yacente
en mi corazón y en los luceros.
Tu norma de nube, única y lenta,
sobre un cielo de llagas;
de llanto inútil sobre muerte pura
y mano desolada en la inmensidad
de un cuerpo que se entrega.
No estás, lo sé, fuera de mí, en el viento,

I do not know if you are the flesh or the bone of the fruit of mystery and madness, of the proud and awaited agony, or if we are both dreaming ourselves in the hurricane and in the sigh, in the brief immensity of a blemish, in that which I have wished for, like water and fire in the blood, like loves without forgetfulness.

I remember your repose of rain falling over the sea. Your anxiety of faithful ivy, and of a little girl loved again. I remember your pensive sorrows, your dolorous joy, and your recumbent ecstasy in my heart and in the morning stars. Your pattern of cloud, unique and slow, over a sky of sores; of useless weeping over pure death, and a desolate hand in the immensity of a body which yields itself. You are not, I know, outside me, in the wind, or in the fare-

ni en el adiós, la tumba o la derrota,
ni en la nieve que suele prolongar
la sombra del olvido y el eco de jamás.

Ni en la falta de amor,
que cuando más amor me ha consumido,
ella más era yo, su carne y sueño,
su ansia desvelada,
y hasta besable se tornaba entonces
su azul, insomne garra.
Y cuando de golpe todo es triste,
porque el amor llega completo,
triste como si hubieses muerto,
¡ah!, qué cerca de mí, remota,
sueño mío en la patria del sueño.

Ya sin sombra, con amor, y sin cuerpo,
en la clara materia del silencio
que todo lo besa hacia el enigma,
me recuerdo de mí después de muerto.

El espacio donde cato y sufro
es cascada de luto de piedra consolada
y una mancha de humedad sobre el muro.

well, the tomb or the defeat, or in the snow which sometimes prolongs the shadow of forgetfulness and the echo of nevermore.

Nor, when love was gone, when a greater love had consumed me, was she more part of me, her flesh and dream, and her waking anxiety, and her blue, sleepless grasp even became kissable. And when suddenly all is sad, because love comes complete, as sad as if you had died, ah! how close to me, [how] remote, my dream in the homeland of dreams.

Already shadowless, with love, and without body, in the clear fabric of silence, which everything kisses into an enigma, I remember myself after death.

The space where I taste and suffer is a cascade of mourning of consoled stone and a stain of damp on the wall. And already I do

Y ya no me concibo sino siendo la soledad misma
en el solo tiempo y ámbito hacia adentro.
Pétreo delirio de pasión votivo
donde el deseo existe, único y solo
y el amor es terrible y eterno y sin límites.

Eres el grito opaco y prolongado
de la piedra contra la viva sangre,
hiriendo su misterio de salud y amapola.
¡Oh poesía!, soledad y vida,
eterna Eva primera,
¿quién cercena las manos
de los pobres amantes?

Yo sé mi soledad agónica y hermana
de mirto seco y cúpulas dormidas.
Yo sé que naces como el fuego,
frotando dos misterios
mi sueño y mi esqueleto.

La sangre, tenazmente derramada,
escucha tu palabra antigua
buscando, soledad, tu rumbo.
Cuando muera, si alguna vez lo sé,

not conceive of myself without being solitude itself in the one time and place inside me. Stony votive delirium of passion where desire exists, unique and alone, and love is terrible and eternal, and boundless.

You are the dull prolonged shout of the stone against the living blood, hurting its mystery of health and poppies. Oh poesy! solitude and life, first and eternal Eve, who chops off the hands of poor lovers?

I know my agonizing solitude, sister of the dry myrtle and sleeping cupolas. I know you are born like fire, rubbing together two mysteries, my dream and my skeleton.

Blood, tenaciously shed, hears your ancient word, seeking, solitude, your way. When I die, if I ever know it, I will be more in

estaré más en ti, seré tu trigo,
tu pulso y tu verdad inconsolable.
¡Oh poesía!, soledad y muerte,
eterna Eva primera,
está llorando el mar.

La soledad no es estar a solas con la muerte
y en la vida por ella ser amado.
Es algo más triste, deslumbrante y alto;
estar a solas con la vida.

Muerto de sed en medio de los mares,
tus formas en mi voz y otras estrellas.
La soledad está en la esperanza,
en el triunfo, en la risa y en la danza.

you, I will be your wheat, your pulse and your inconsolable truth. Oh poesy! solitude and death, eternal and first Eve, the sea is crying.

Solitude is not being alone with death, and being loved by her in life. It is something sadder, dazzling and high: it is to be alone with life.

Dying of thirst amid the seas, your forms in my voice and other stars. Solitude is in hope, in triumph, in laughter and in the dance.

MEXICO

SALVADOR DÍAZ MIRÓN (1853–1928)

Cleopatra

La vi tendida de espaldas
entre púrpura revuelta . . .
Estaba toda desnuda
aspirando humo de esencias
en largo tubo escarchado
de diamantes y perlas.

Sobre la siniestra mano
apoyada la cabeza,
y cual el ojo de un tigre
un ópalo daba en ella
vislumbres de sangre y fuego
al oro de su ancha trenza.

Tenía un pie sobre el otro
y los dos como azucenas,
y cerca de los tobillos
argollas de finas piedras,
y en el vientre un denso triángulo
de rizada y rubia seda.

Cleopatra

I saw her stretched out on her back amid a purple swirl. . . . She lay in all her nakedness inhaling scented smoke from a long pipe encrusted with diamonds and pearls.

Her head rested on her left hand, where an opal, like the eye of a tiger, gave a glimmer of blood and fire to the gold of her thick tresses.

She had one foot over the other, both like white lilies, and, around her ankles, bangles of precious stones, and on her abdomen a thick triangle of curly blonde silk.

En un brazo se torcía
como cinta de centella
un áspid de filigrana
salpicado de turquesas,
con dos carbunclos por ojos
y un dardo de oro en la lengua.

Tibias estaban sus carnes,
y sus altos pechos eran
cual blanca leche vertida
dentro de dos copas griegas,
convertida en alabastro,
sólida ya pero aún trémula.

¡Ah! hubiera yo dado entonces
todos mis lauros de Atenas
por entrar en esa alcoba
coronado de violetas,
dejando con los eunucos
mis coturnos a la puerta.

Around one arm there twisted a ribbon of sparks, an asp in filigree studded with turquoises, with two garnets for eyes and a golden dart on its tongue.

Her flesh was cool and her erect breasts like white milk poured into two Greek goblets, transformed into alabaster, now firm yet still trembling.

Oh! at that moment I would have given all my Athenian laurels to enter that alcove decorated with violets, leaving my buskins with the eunuchs at the door.

El fantasma

BLANCAS y finas, y en el manto apenas
visibles, y con aire de azucenas
las manos, que no rompen mis cadenas.

Azules y con oro enarenados,
como las noches limpias de nublados,
los ojos, que contemplan mis pecados.

Como albo pecho de paloma el cuello;
y como crin de sol barba y cabello;
y como plata el pie descalzo y bello.

Dulce y triste la faz; la veste zarca . . .
Así, del mal sobre la inmensa charca,
Jesús vino a mi unción, como a la barca.

Y abrillantó a mi espíritu la cumbre,
con fugaz cuanto rica certidumbre
como con tintas de refleja lumbre.

The Apparition

HANDS that do not break my chains, as white and delicate as lilies and hardly visible beneath the cloak.

Eyes that contemplate my sins, blue and flecked with gold like cloudless nights.

His neck like the snowy breast of a dove; beard and hair like a mane of sunlight, and his perfect unshod foot like silver.

His face sweet and sad; his raiment light blue. . . . Thus Jesus came to my anointment across the immense sea of evil, as he came to the boat.

And the blessing made my spirit shine with a certainty as exquisite as it was fleeting, as if with tints of reflected light.

Y suele retornar; y me reintegra
la fe que salva y la ilusión que alegra;
y un relámpago enciende mi alma negra.

And he returns often, and restores to me the faith that saves and the vision that brings joy; and a flash of lightning fires my black soul.

MANUEL JOSÉ OTHÓN (1858–1906)

Una estepa del Nazas

NI un verdecido alcor, ni una pradera!
Tan sólo miro, de mi vista enfrente,
la llanura sin fin, seca y ardiente
donde jamás reinó la primavera.

Rueda el río monótono en la austera
cuenca, sin un cantil ni una rompiente
y, al raz del horizonte, el sol poniente,
cual la boca de un horno, reverbera.

Y en esta grama gris que no abrillanta
ningún color; aquí, do el aire azota
con ígneo soplo la reseca planta,

sólo, al romper su cárcel, la bellota
en el pajizo algodonal levanta
de su cándido airón la blanca nota.

*A Steppe on the Nazas**

NOT one green hill or prairie! Stretched out endlessly before my gaze, I can only look across the dry and burning plain, where spring has never reigned.

The river flows monotonously across the austere river basin, without a steep bank or a reef and, at the edge of the horizon, the dying sun reverberates like the mouth of a furnace.

And in this grey and lifeless grass that no colour brightens; here, where the wind whips the dry plants with burning breath,

Only the dandelion, breaking out of its prison in the straw-coloured cotton plant, raises the white flag from its white plumed rest.

---

*The River Nazas has its source in the state of Durango, flowing thence through Coahuila and into the Laguna de Mayran. It is 580 kilometres long.

Las brujas

– TODAS las noches me convierto en cabra
para servir a mi señor el chivo,
pues, vieja ya, del hombre no recibo
ni una muestra de amor, ni una palabra.

– Mientras mi esposo está labra que labra
el terrón, otras artes yo cultivo.
¿Ves? Traigo un niño ensangrentado y vivo
para la cena trágica y macabra.

– Sin ojos, pues así se ve en lo oscuro,
como ven los murciélagos, yo vuelo
hasta escalar del camposanto el muro.

– Trae un cadáver frío como el hielo.
Yo a los hombres daré del vino impuro
que arranca la esperanza y el consuelo.

The Witches

'EVERY night I turn myself into a she-goat in order to serve my master the goat, for, since I'm an old woman now, men give me neither a sign nor a word of love.'

'While my husband is working away at the clod, I cultivate other arts. Can you see? I am carrying a living child stained with blood for the tragic and macabre supper.'

'Eyeless – for that's the way to see in the dark like the bats – I fly until I am over the cemetery wall.'

'Bring me a corpse as cold as ice. I shall give men some of the impure wine that tears out all hope and consolation.'

MANUEL GUTIÉRREZ NÁJERA (1859–95)

Para entonces

QUIERO morir cuando decline el día,
en alta mar y con la cara al cielo;
donde parezca sueño la agonía
y el alma un ave que remonta el vuelo.

No escuchar en los últimos instantes,
ya con el cielo y con el mar a solas,
más voces ni plegarias sollozantes
que el majestuoso tumbo de las olas.

Morir cuando la luz triste retira
sus áureas redes de la onda verde,
y ser como ese sol que lento expira:
algo muy luminoso que se pierde.

Morir, y joven: antes que destruya
el tiempo aleve la gentil corona,
cuando la vida dice aún «soy tuya»,
aunque sepamos bien que nos traiciona.

When That Time Comes

I WANT to die when day is fading, on the high seas and with my face to the sky, where the agony may seem like a dream and the soul like a bird that soars in flight.

In the last moments, alone with the sky and the sea, hearing no voices or sobbing prayers other than the majestic crash of the waves.

To die when the light sadly withdraws its golden nets from the green waves, and to be like the sun that expires gently; something very luminous that is lost.

To die, and in youth; before treacherous time destroys the gracious crown, while life is still saying 'I'm yours', although we know well that she is betraying us.

To Be

¡INMENSO abismo es el dolor humano!
¿Quién vio jamás su tenebroso fondo?
Aplicad el oído a la abra oscura
de los pasados tiempos . . . Dentro cae
lágrima eterna. A las inermes bocas
que en otra edad movió la vida nuestra
acercaos curiosos . . . ¡Un gemido
sale temblando de los blancos huesos!

La vida es el dolor. Y es vida oscura
pero vida también la del sepulcro.
La materia disyecta se disuelve;
el espíritu eterno, la sustancia,
no cesa de sufrir. En vano fuera
esgrimir el acero del suicida.
El suicidio es inútil. ¡Cambia el modo,
el ser indestructible continúa!

En ti somos, Dolor, en ti vivimos!
La suprema ambición de cuanto existe
es perderse en la nada, aniquilarse,

To Be

HUMAN suffering is a great abyss! Who has ever seen into its dark, awesome depths? Put your ear to the threshold of times past. . . . Within falls an eternal tear. Come, you curious ones, come close to the defenceless mouths that our life made to move in another age. . . . A cry emerges trembling from the white bones!

Life is pain. Life in the tomb is dismal but it is still life. Discarded matter dissolves; the eternal spirit, the soul, does not cease to suffer. It would be futile to wield the suicide's sword. Suicide is useless. The manner changes; the indestructible spirit lives on!

We are in you, Suffering, we live in you! The highest ambition of everything that exists is to lose itself in nothingness, to anni-

dormir sin sueños . . . Y la vida sigue
tras las heladas lindes de la tumba.

¡No hay muerte! En vano la llamáis a voces,
almas sin esperanza. Proveedora
de seres que padezcan, la implacable
a otro mundo nos lleva. No hay descanso.
Queremos reposar un solo instante
y una voz en la sombra dice: ¡Anda!

Sí: la vida es mal. Pero la vida
no concluye jamás. El dios que crea
es un esclavo de otro dios terrible
que se llama el dolor. Y no se harta
el inmortal Saturno. Y el espacio,
el vivero de soles, lo infinito,
son la cárcel inmensa, sin salida,
de almas que sufren y morir no pueden.

¡Oh, Saturno inflexible, al fin acaba,
devora lo creado y rumia luego,
ya que inmortales somos, nuestras vidas!

hilate itself, to sleep without dreaming. . . . And life goes on beyond the frozen confines of the tomb.

There is no death! Souls without hope, you call aloud for it in vain. Implacable Death, the provider of suffering beings, takes us to another world. There is no repose. Should we want to rest for a single instant, a voice from the shadows says 'get moving!'.

Yes: life is evil. Yet life never ends. The god that creates is the slave of another terrible god whose name is Suffering. Immortal Saturn is never satisfied. And space, the breeding place of suns, the infinite, are the immense prison without exit for souls that suffer and cannot die.

Oh inflexible Saturn, stop it once and for all; devour all created things and, since we are immortal, ruminate later over our lives.

¡Somos tuyos, Dolor, tuyos por siempre!
Mas perdona a los seres que no existen
sino en tu mente que estimula el hambre . . .
¡Perdón, oh Dios, perdón para la nada!
Sáciate ya. Que la matriz eterna,
engendradora del linaje humano,
se torne estéril . . . que la vida pare . . .
¡Y ruede el mundo cual planeta muerto
por los mares sin olas del vacío!

We are yours, oh Suffering, yours forever! But pardon the beings who only exist in your mind which hunger stimulates. . . . Forgiveness, oh God, forgiveness for the Void! Be satisfied now. Let the eternal womb, begetter of the human line, become sterile . . . let life cease. . . . And let the world turn like a dead planet through the waveless seas of emptiness!

ENRIQUE GONZÁLEZ MARTÍNEZ
(1871–1952)

Un fantasma

El hombre que volvía de la muerte
se llegó a mí, y el alma quedó fría,
trémula y muda . . . De la misma suerte
estaba mudo el hombre que volvía
de la muerte . . .

Era sin voz, como la piedra . . . Pero
había en su mirar ensimismado
el solemne pavor del que ha mirado
un gran enigma, y torna mensajero
del mensaje que aguarda el orbe entero . . .
El hombre mudo se posó a mi lado.

Y su faz y mi faz quedaron juntas,
y me subió del corazón un loco
afán de interrogar . . . Mas, poco a poco,
se helaron en mi boca las preguntas . . .

A Spectre

The man who was returning from the dead approached me, and my heart stood cold, trembling and mute . . . . Neither did he speak, the man who came back from the dead . . .

He was as silent as stone. . . . Yet in his self-absorbed expression there was the solemn dread of one who has looked at a great enigma, and becomes the bearer of the message that the whole globe awaits. . . . The man who did not speak paused at my side.

And his face and mine came together, and there arose in my heart a violent desire to ask questions. . . . But, little by little, the questions froze on my lips . . .

Se estremeció la tarde con un fuerte
gemido de huracán . . . Y paso a paso
perdióse en la penumbra del ocaso
el hombre que volvía de la muerte . . .

Plus ultra

SILBÓ la flecha y se clavó en la entraña
escondida;
pero el ay fué más hondo que la herida.

El chorro de cristal tendió su claro
hilo de luz en la caverna oscura . . .
La voz de la canción era más pura.

En su sed infinita de horizontes
la vida se lanzó, de salto en salto,
cruzando abismos y salvando montes . . .
El ímpetu del sueño iba más alto.

The evening shook with a loud howl of a hurricane. . . . And step by step the man who came back from the dead disappeared into the half-light of the declining day . . .

Plus Ultra

THE arrow whistled and pierced the hidden recess of the heart; but the oh was deeper than the wound.

The crystal stream extended its clear thread of light into the dark cavern. . . . The tone of the song was purer.

In its infinite thirst for horizons life leaped forward, jump over jump, crossing chasms and vaulting mountains. . . . The impulse to dream went higher.

JOSÉ JUAN TABLADA (1871–1945)

El pavo real

Pavo real, largo fulgor,
por el gallinero demócrata
pasas como una procesión . . .

La tortuga

Aunque jamás se muda,
a tumbos, como carro de mudanzas,
va por la senda la tortuga.

Los sapos

Trozos de barro,
por la senda en penumbra
saltan los sapos.

Peacock *

PEACOCK, long brilliance, you pass through the democratic chicken-run like a procession . . .

Tortoise *

THOUGH he never moves house, in lurches, like a removal van, the tortoise goes along the path.

Toads *

BITS of mud, along the path in penumbra jump the toads.

---

* Translated by John Hill.

Peces voladores

Al golpe del oro solar
estalla en astillas el vidrio del mar.

Sandía

Del verano, roja y fría
carcajada,
rebanada
de sandía.

El insomnio

En su pizarra negra
suma cifras de fósforo.

Flying Fish *

AT the impact of solar gold the windowpane of the sea breaks into splinters.

Water-Melon *

RED, cold laughter of summer, a slice of water-melon.

Insomnia *

ON its black slate it collects ciphers of phosphorus.

* Translated by John Hill.

Nocturno alterno

Neoyorquina noche dorada
  Fríos muros de cal moruna
Rector's champaña fox-trot
  Casas mudas y fuertes rejas
Y volviendo la mirada
  Sobre las silenciosas tejas
El alma petrificada
  Los gatos blancos de la luna
Como la mujer de Loth

  Y sin embargo
    es una
      misma
        en New York
          y en Bogotá

            la Luna . . . !

*Alternate Nocturne**

GILDED New York night, *cold walls of Moorish limestone*, rector's champagne fox-trot, *dumb houses, strongly barred windows*, and glancing round *over the silent roofs*, the petrified soul, *the white cats of the moon*, like Lot's wife.

And yet, it's the same thing in New York and Bogotá,
The moon!

---

* Translated by John Hill.

RAMÓN LÓPEZ VELARDE (1888–1921)

La lágrima

ENCIMA
de la azucena esquinada
que orna la cadavérica almohada;
encima
del soltero dolor empedernido
de yacer como imberbe congregante
mientras los gatos erizan el ruido
y forjan una patria espeluznante;
encima
del apetito nunca satisfecho,
de la cal
que demacró las conciencias livianas,
y del desencanto profesional
con que saltan del lecho
las cortesanas;
encima
de la ingenuidad casamentera
y del descalabro que nada espera;
encima
de la huesa y del nido,
la lágrima salobre que he bebido.

The Tear

ABOVE the angular lily that adorns the cadaverous pillow; above the lonely and deep-seated pain of lying like an ingenuous congregant while the cats make the noise bristle and forge a hair-raising homeland; above the insatiable appetite of the lime that drained the colour from the lustful minds, and above the professional disenchantment with which the courtesan jumps out of bed; above the matchmaking ingenuity and the misfortune that waits for nothing; above the grave and the nest, the salty tear that I have drunk.

Lágrima de infinito
que eternizaste el amoroso rito;
lágrima en cuyos mares
goza mi áncora su náufrago baño
y esquilmo los vellones singulares
de un compungido rebaño;
lágrima en cuya gloria se refracta
el iris fiel de mi pasión exacta;
lágrima en que navegan sin pendones
los mástiles de las consternaciones;
lágrima con que quiso
mi gratitud salar el Paraíso;
lágrima mía, en ti me encerraría
debajo de un deleite sepulcral
como un vigía
en su salobre y mórbido fanal.

Hormigas

A LA cálida vida que trascurre canora
con garbo de mujer sin letras ni antifaces,

Tear of the infinite that immortalized the ritual of love; tear in whose seas my anchor enjoys its shipwrecked bathe and I rob a repentant flock of its extraordinary fleeces; tear in whose lustre is refracted the faithful rainbow of my precise passion; tear in which masts of distress sail without pennants; tear with which my gratitude tried to season Paradise; my tear, I would lock myself inside you beneath a sepulchral pleasure, like a watchman on his morbid and salty lighthouse.

Ants

IN the intoxication of the enchanted hour, a burning of ants in my voracious veins responds to the warm life that flows melodiously,

a la invicta belleza que salva y enamora,
responde, en la embriaguez de la encantada hora,
un encono de hormigas en mis venas voraces.

Fustigan el desmán del perenne hormigueo
el pozo del silencio y el enjambre del ruido,
la harina rebanada como doble trofeo
en los fértiles bustos, el Infierno en que creo,
el estertor final y el preludio del nido.

Mas luego mis hormigas me negarán su abrazo
y han de huir de mis pobres y trabajados dedos
cual se olvida en la arena un gélido bagazo;
y tu boca, que es cifra de eróticos denuedos,
tu boca, que es mi rúbrica, mi manjar y mi adorno,
tu boca, en que la lengua vibra asomada al mundo
como réproba llama saliéndose de un horno,
en una turbia fecha de cierzo gemebundo
en que ronde la luna porque robarte quiera
ha de oler a sudario y a hierba machacada,
a droga y a responso, a pabilo y a cera.

with the grace of a woman without learning or masks, the invincible beauty that saves and inspires love.

The well of silence and the swarm of noise, the dough cut like a double trophy on the fertile breasts, the hell in which I believe, the death rattle and the prelude to the nest, lash out at the wild and endless crawling of the ants.

But then my ants will deny me their embrace, and they will flee from my poor worn fingers just as one leaves a frozen bagasse on the sand; and your mouth that is an emblem of erotic adventures; your mouth that is my mark, my food, my adornment; your mouth, whose tongue darts out, peeping at the world like a reprobate flame coming out of a furnace; on a cold, turbulent day, when the north wind moans and the moon hovers because it wants to steal you, your mouth will smell like a shroud and like crushed grass, like a drug and a responsory for the dead, like a burnt wick and like wax.

Antes de que deserten mis hormigas, Amada,
déjalas caminar camino de tu boca
a que apuren los viáticos del sanguinario fruto
que desde sarracenos oasis me provoca.
Antes de que tus labios mueran, para mi luto,
dámelos en el crítico umbral del cementerio
como perfume y pan y tósigo y cauterio.

Before my ants desert me, my Love, let them travel along your mouth to consume the viaticum of bloody fruit that tempts me from Saracen oases. Before your lips die, and I should mourn their loss, give them to me on the critical threshold of the grave, as perfume and bread, as a poison and a cautery.

ALFONSO REYES (1889–1959)

Pesadilla

POR esas casas que visito en sueños,
confusas galerías y salones,
escalinatas donde vaga el miedo
y ruedan las tinieblas en temblores,

pálido el rostro, los amigos muertos
asoman en lo alto de las torres,
o vienen hasta mí con labios secos,
blandas manos de sombra y tristes flores.

Cunde la noche, la tiniebla absorbe
la diáfana verdad. No se conoce
si son fantasmas o si son recuerdos,

amenazas o solicitaciones . . .
Y es la manada de gigantes huecos
que en torno al pozo de la sangre corren.

Nightmare

IN those houses that I visit in dreams, blurred galleries and drawing-rooms, flights of steps where fear wanders and the mists swirl and tremble,

My dead friends, their faces pale, appear on top of the towers, or they come towards me with dry lips, soft hands of shadow and sad flowers.

The darkness spreads, the mist absorbs transparent truth. One does not know whether they are apparitions or memories,

Threats or supplications. . . . And it is the crowd of hollow giants who at night run carousing around the well of blood.

Virtud del recuerdo

CUANDO la soledad me da licencia,
repaso con la mente mi destino,
ansioso de buscar la consecuencia
en tan aventurado desatino.

Ni quiere ni resiste la conciencia
ceder al trance que jamás previno,
aunque se burlan de su resistencia
todos los sobresaltos del camino.

Me desesperan los torcidos trazos,
en la madeja del azar me pierdo
y pugno por soltarme de los lazos.

Pero renazco vencedor y cuerdo,
porque juntan y zurcen los retazos
los virtuosos hilos del recuerdo.

The Strength of Memory

WHEN solitude permits, I go over my destiny in my mind, eagerly in search of the consequences of such an uncertain and foolish act.

The mind neither desires nor resists surrender to the peril that it did not foresee, even though all the surprises along the way mock it for its resistance.

The tortuous lines drive me to despair, I lose myself in the tangled skeins of the unforeseen and struggle to free myself from the knots.

But I am born again triumphant and wise, for the fine strong threads of memory gather up the pieces and sew them together.

CARLOS PELLICER (b. 1899)

Soneto

MI voluntad de ser no tiene cielo;
sólo mira hacia abajo y sin mirada.
¿Luz de la tarde o de la madrugada?
Mi voluntad de ser no tiene cielo.

Ni la penumbra de un hermoso duelo
ennoblece mi carne afortunada.
Vida de estatua, muerte inhabitada
sin la jardinería de un anhelo.

Un dormir sin soñar calla y sombrea
el prodigioso imperio de mis ojos
reducido a los grises de una aldea.

Sin la ausencia presente de un pañuelo
se van los días en pobres manojos.
Mi voluntad de ser no tiene cielo.

Sonnet

THERE is no heaven above my will to live; it simply looks sightlessly downwards. Light of the evening or the dawn? There is no heaven above my will to be.

Not even the shadow of a noble grief dignifies my fortunate flesh. The life of a statue, a deserted death uncultivated by a strong desire.

Sleep without dreams silences and gives shade to the marvellous empire before my gaze, reduced to the grey colours of a village.

Without the present absence of a handkerchief the days pass in sad clusters. There is no heaven above my will to live.

Deseos

A Salvador Novo

TRÓPICO para qué me diste
las manos llenas de color.
Todo lo que yo toque
se llenará de sol.
En las tardes sutiles de otras tierras
pasaré con mis ruidos de vidrio tornasol.
Déjame un solo instante
dejar de ser grito y color.
Déjame un solo instante
cambiar de clima el corazón,
beber la penumbra de una cosa desierta,
inclinarme en silencio sobre un remoto balcón,
ahondarme en el manto de pliegues finos,
dispersarme en la orilla de una suave devoción,
acariciar dulcemente las cabelleras lacias
y escribir con un lápiz muy fino mi meditación.
¡Oh, dejar de ser un solo instante
el Ayudante de Campo del sol!
¡Trópico, para qué me diste
las manos llenas de color!

Wishes

TROPIC, what did you give me hands full of colour for. Everything that I touch will be filled with sun. On gentle evenings in other lands, I shall pass by with my sounds of iridescent glass. Let me for one moment cease to be a cry and a colour. Let me for a single instant change the climate in my heart, drink the half-light of a deserted thing, lean in silence over a remote balcony, bury myself in a cloak of delicate folds, scatter myself on the banks of a gentle devotion, gently stroke the straight hair and write down my meditations with a very fine pen. Oh, if I could stop for a moment being aide-de-camp to the sun! Tropic, why did you give me hands full of colour!

JOSÉ GOROSTIZA (b. 1901)

Presencia y fuga

I

EN el espacio insomne que separa
el fruto de la flor, el pensamiento
del acto que germina su aislamiento,
una muerte de agujas me acapara.

Febril, abeja de la carne, avara,
algo estrangula en mí a cada momento.
Usa mi voz, se nutre de mi aliento,
impone muecas turbias a mi cara.

¿Qué amor, no obstante, en su rigor acierta
a destruir este hálito enemigo
que a compás con mi pulso me desierta?

¡Templado hielo, sí, glacial abrigo!
¡Cuánto – para que dure en él – liberta
en mí, que ya no morirá conmigo!

Presence and Flight

IN the sleepless void dividing the fruit from the flower, the thought of the act that brings forth isolation, a death of needles totally controls me.

Febrile, miserly, a bee in my flesh, every moment something chokes in me. It uses my voice, feeds on my breath, imposes blurred grimaces on my face.

What love, however, is firm enough to succeed in destroying this hostile breath that makes me a desert in time with my pulse?

Hardened ice, yes, an icy shelter! How much does it liberate in me so that it should endure there, for it will not die with me!

II

Te contienes, oh Forma, en el suntuoso
muro que opones de encarnada espuma,
al oscuro apetito de la bruma
y al tacto que te erige luminoso.

Dueña así de un dinámico reposo,
marchas igual a tu perfecta suma
ay, como un sol, sin que el andar consuma
ni el eco mismo de tu pie moroso.

¡Isla del cielo, viva, en las mortales
congojas de tus bellos litorales!
Igual a ti, si fiel a tu diseño,

colmas el cauce de tu ausencia fría;
igual, si emanas de otra tú, la mía,
que nace a sus insomnios en mi sueño.

You contain yourself, oh Form, in the sumptuous wall of scarlet foam that you set against the hidden appetite of the mist and the shining touch that constructs you.

Thus, mistress of a dynamic repose, you progress towards your perfect quantity, oh, like a sun, and yet walking does not even extinguish the echo of your heavy tread.

An island in the sky, alive in the fatal anguish of your beautiful coasts! Consistent to yourself, if faithful to your design,

You fill to the brim the channel of your cold absence; consistent to yourself if you emerge from another you, mine, born of sleeplessness in my dream.

XAVIER VILLAURRUTIA (1903–50)

Muerte en el frío

Cuando he perdido toda fe en el milagro,
cuando ya la esperanza dejó caer la última nota
y resuena un silencio sin fin, cóncavo y duro;

cuando el cielo de invierno no es más que la ceniza
de algo que ardió hace muchos, muchos siglos;

Cuando me encuentro tan solo, tan solo,
que me busco en mi cuarto
como se busca, a veces, un objeto perdido,
una carta estrujada, en los rincones;

cuando cierro los ojos pensando inútilmente
que así estaré más lejos
de aquí, de mí, de todo
aquello que me acusa de no ser más que un muerto,

siento que estoy en el infierno frío,
en el invierno eterno

Death in the Cold

When I have lost all faith in miracles, when hope has shed its final note and an endless silence resounds, concave and hard;

When the winter sky is no more than the ashes of something that burned many, many ages ago;

When I feel so alone, so alone that I search for myself in my room as one sometimes looks in corners for a lost object, a crumpled letter;

When I close my eyes and think vainly that this way I shall be further away from here, from myself, from all those things that accuse me of being no better than a corpse,

I feel that I am in the cold hell, in the endless winter that freezes

que congela la sangre en las arterias,
que seca las palabras amarillas,
que paraliza el sueño,
que pone una mordaza de hielo a nuestra boca
y dibuja las cosas con una línea dura.

Siento que estoy viviendo aquí mi muerte,
mi sola muerte presente,
mi muerte que no puedo compartir ni llorar,
mi muerte de que no me consolaré jamás.

Y comprendo de una vez para nunca
el clima del silencio
donde se nutre y perfecciona la muerte.
Y también la eficacia del frío
que preserva y purifica sin consumir como el fuego.

Y en el silencio escucho dentro de mí el trabajo
de un minucioso ejército de obreros que golpean
con diminutos martillos mi linfa y mi carne estremecidas;
siento cómo se besan
y juntan para siempre sus orillas
las islas que flotaban en mi cuerpo;

the blood in one's arteries, that dries up the yellow words, that paralyses sleep, that puts a muzzle of ice over our mouth and draws everything with harsh lines.

I feel that now I am living out my death, my only death in the present, my death that I can neither share nor cry over, my death for which I shall find no consolation.

And I understand once and for ever the condition of the silence in which death is nourished and perfected. And also the efficacy of the cold that preserves and purifies yet does not consume like fire.

And in the silence I hear a minute army of workers toiling within me, striking with tiny hammers at my trembling lymph and flesh; I can feel how the islands that were floating in my body kiss and unite their banks for ever;

cómo el agua y la sangre
son otra vez la misma agua marina,
y cómo se hiela primero
y luego se vuelve cristal
y luego duro mármol,
hasta inmovilizarme en el tiempo más angustioso y lento,
con la vida secreta, muda e imperceptible
del mineral, del tronco, de la estatua.

How water and blood are again the same sea water, and how it first freezes and then becomes glass and later solid marble until, in the gentlest and most anguished time, I am immobilized together with the dumb and imperceptible secret life of minerals, of trunks of trees, of statues.

SALVADOR NOVO (b. 1904)

Elegía

Los que tenemos unas manos que no nos pertenecen,
grotescas para la caricia, inútiles para el taller o la azada,
largas y flácidas como una flor privada de simiente
o como un reptil que entrega su veneno
porque no tiene nada más que ofrecer.

Los que tenemos una mirada culpable y amarga
por donde mira la Muerte no lograda del mundo
y fulge una sonrisa que se congela frente a las estatuas
desnudas
porque no podrá nunca cerrarse sobre los anillos de oro
ni entregarse como una antorcha sobre los horizontes
del Tiempo
en una noche cuya aurora es solamente este mediodía
que nos flagela la carne por instantes arrancados a la
eternidad.

Los que hemos rodado por los siglos como una roca
desprendida del Génesis

Elegy

THOSE of us who have hands that do not belong to us, grotesque in the caress, useless for the workshop or the spade, long and flaccid like a flower robbed of seed, or like a reptile that gives up its poison because it has nothing else to offer.

We who have a bitter and guilty expression through which Death looks, the death the world has not attained, and a smile flashes, that freezes before the naked statues, because it will never close over the gold rings nor, one night when dawn is only this midday that whips our flesh in moments torn out of eternity, will it give itself up like a torch above the horizons of Time.

We who have wandered through the ages like a rock broken

sobre la hierba o entre la maleza en desenfrenada carrera
para no detenernos nunca ni volver a ser lo que fuimos
mientras los hombres van trabajosamente ascendiendo
y brotan otras manos de sus manos para torcer el rumbo
de los vientos o para tiernamente enlazarse.

Los que vestimos cuerpos como trajes envejecidos
a quienes basta el hurto o la limosna de una migaja que
es todo el pan y la única hostia
hemos llegado al litoral de los siglos que pesan sobre
nuestros corazones angustiados
y no veremos nunca con nuestros ojos limpios
otro día que este día en que toda la música del universo
se cifra en una voz que no escucha nadie entre las palabras
vacías
y en el sueño sin agua ni palabras en la lengua de la arcilla
y del humo.

loose from Genesis, over the grass and through the undergrowth in a wild, unbridled race, never to stop nor to be again what we were, while men go on laboriously climbing and other hands bloom from their hands to twist the direction of the winds or to twine tenderly around each other.

Those of us who wear bodies like worn clothes, who are satisfied with theft or the charity of a crumb that is all the bread and the only host; we have reached the bank of the centuries that weigh heavily on our anguished heart, and we shall never see with our clean eyes a day other than today, when all the music of the universe places its hopes on one voice that no one listens to amid the empty words, and on the dream without water or words on the tongue of the clay or the smoke.

OCTAVIO PAZ (b. 1914)

Temporal

EN la montaña negra
El torrente delira en voz alta
A esa misma hora
Tú avanzas entre precipicios
Por tu cuerpo dormido
El viento lucha a oscuras con tu sueño
Maraña verde y blanca
Encina niña encina milenaria
El viento te descuaja y te arrastra y te arrasa
Abre tu pensamiento y lo dispersa
Torbellino tus ojos
Torbellino tu ombligo
Torbellino y vacío
El viento te exprime como un racimo
Temporal en tu frente
Temporal en tu nuca y en tu vientre
Como una rama seca te avienta
El viento
A lomos del torrente de tu sueño
Manos verdes y pies negros
Por la garganta

Tempest

IN the dark mountain the torrent rants and raves aloud. At that same moment, you advance between precipices in your sleeping body. The wind fights with your dream in the dark; green and white jungle: child oak, millenarian oak. The wind uproots you and drags you down and destroys you. It opens your thoughts and scatters them, whirlwind your eyes, whirlwind your centre, whirlwind and void. The wind presses you like a cluster. Tempest on your forehead. Tempest on the nape of your neck and on your belly. Like a dry branch the wind winnows you. The wind astride the torrent in your dream. Green hands and black feet through the

De piedra de la noche
Anudada a tu cuerpo
De montaña dormida
El torrente delira
Entre tus muslos
Soliloquio de piedras y de agua
Por los acantilados
De tu frente
Pasas como un río de pájaros
El bosque dobla la cabeza
Como un toro herido
El bosque se arrodilla
Bajo el ala del viento
Cada vez más alto
El torrente delira
Cada vez más hondo
Por tu cuerpo dormido
Cada vez más noche

Complementarios

EN mi cuerpo tú buscas al monte,
A su sol enterrado en el bosque.
En tu cuerpo yo busco la barca
En mitad de la noche perdida.

stone throat of the night, tied to your body, that is a sleeping mountain. The torrent rants between your thighs. Soliloquy of stones and water. Through the escarpments of your brow you pass like a river of birds. The forest bows its head like a wounded bull. The forest bends the knee beneath the wing of the wind, higher and higher. The torrent rants deeper and deeper through your sleeping body, darker and darker.

Complementaries

IN my body you search for the hills, for its sun buried in the forest. In your body I seek the boat lost in the middle of the night.

Alba última

TENDIDA en los confines
Tus cabellos se pierden en el bosque,
Tus pies tocan los míos.
Dormida eres más grande que la noche
Pero tu sueño cabe en este cuarto.
¡Cuánto somos qué poco somos tánto!
Afuera pasa un taxi
Con su carga de espectros.
El río que se va
Siempre
Está de regreso.

¿Mañana será otro día?

Ustica

LOS sucesivos soles del verano,
La sucesión del sol y sus veranos,
Todos los soles,
El solo, el sol de soles,

Last Dawn

STRETCHED out at the confines, your hair is lost in the forest, your feet touch mine. Asleep, you are greater than the night, yet there is space for dream in this room. How much we are how little we are so much! Outside a taxi passes with its load of ghosts. The river that flows away – always – is on its way back.

Will tomorrow be another day?

*Ustica**

THE successive suns of summer, the succession of sun and its summers, all the suns, the single one, the sun of suns, now become

*Author's note: Ustica is a volcanic desert island in the Sicilian sea. It was a Saracen graveyard.

Hechos ya hueso terco y leonado,
Cerrazón de materia enfriada.

Puño de piedra,
Piña de lava,
Osario,
No tierra,
Isla tampoco,
Peña despeñada,
Duro durazno,
Gota de sol petrificada.

Por las noches se oye
El respirar de las cisternas,
El jadeo del agua dulce
Turbada por el mar.
La hora es alta y rayada de verde.
El cuerpo oscuro del vino
En las jarras dormido
Es un sol más negro y fresco.

Aquí la rosa de las profundidades
Es un candelabro de venas rosadas
Encendido en el fondo del mar.
En tierra, el sol lo apaga,

obstinate and tawny bone, the darkness before the storm of freezing matter.

Fist of stone, pine cone of lava, ossuary, not earth, nor island, a rock falling down a precipice, a hard peach, petrified drop of sun.

During the night you hear the breathing of the cisterns, the panting of fresh water disturbed by the sea. The hour is late and striped with green. The dark body of the wine asleep in the jars is a darker and cooler sun.

Here the rose of the depths is a candlestick of pink-coloured veins alight at the bottom of the sea. On land the sun puts it out, a

Pálido encaje calcáreo
Como el deseo labrado por la muerte.

Rocas color de azufre,
Altas piedras adustas.
Tú estás a mi costado.
Tus pensamientos son negros y dorados.
Si alargase la mano
Cortaría un racimo de verdades intactas.
Abajo, entre peñas centelleantes,
Va y viene el mar lleno de brazos.
Vértigos. La luz se precipita.
Yo te miré a la cara,
Yo me asomé al abismo:
Mortalidad es transparencia.

Osario, paraíso:
Nuestras raíces anudadas
En el sexo, en la boca deshecha
De la Madre enterrada.
Jardín de árboles incestuosos
Sobre la tierra de los muertos.

pale chalky lacework [of holes] like desire carved out by death.

Sulphur-coloured rocks, tall stern stones. You are at my side. Your thoughts are black and golden. If I stretched out my hand I could cut a cluster of untouched truths. Below, among sparkling rocks, the sea, full of arms, comes and goes. Vertigos. The light rushes forward. I looked into your face, I leaned out over the abyss: mortality is transparency.

Ossuary, paradise: our roots united in sex, in the broken mouth of the buried Mother. Garden of incestuous trees on the land of the dead.

Ida y vuelta

CENAGOSO noviembre:
Piedras manchadas, huesos renegridos,
Indecisos palacios.

Yo atravesé los arcos y los puentes
Yo estaba vivo, en busca de la vida.

En el salón lunar
Se desangra la luz. Los hombres-peces
Cambian fríos reflejos.

Yo estaba vivo y vi muchos fantasmas,
Todos de carne y hueso y todos ávidos.

Torre topacio y sangre,
Las trenzas negras y los pechos ámbar,
La dama subterránea.

Tigre, novilla, pulpo, yedra en llamas:
Quemó mis huesos y chupó mi sangre.

There and Back

MUDDY November: stained stones, black bones, blurred palaces.

I crossed the arches and the bridges, I was alive, in search of life.

In the lunar sitting-room, light loses blood. The fish-men exchange cold reflections.

I was alive and saw many ghosts, all of flesh and blood and all eager.

Topaz tower and blood, the tresses black and the breasts of amber, the subterranean lady.

Tiger, heifer, octopus, ivy in flames: burned my bones and sucked my blood.

Lecho, planeta extinto,
Trampa de espejos fueron noche y cuerpo,
Montón de sal, la dama.

Come mis restos, sol del altiplano:
Yo estaba vivo y fui a buscar la muerte.

Cuento de dos jardines

UNA casa, un jardín,
No son lugares:
Giran, van y vienen.
Sus apariciones
Abren en el espacio
Otro espacio,
Otro tiempo en el tiempo.
Sus eclipses
No son abdicaciones:
Nos quemaría
La vivacidad de uno de esos instantes
Si durase otro instante.
Estamos condenados

Bed, extinct planet, where night and the body were a trick of mirrors, heap of salt, the lady.

Eat my remains, sun of the plateau: I was alive and I went in search of death.

*Fable of Two Gardens**

A HOUSE, a garden, are not places. They spin, come and go. Their apparitions unfold in space other space, other time within time. Their eclipses are not abdications. We would be scorched by the vitality of one of those moments if it lived a moment longer.

*Translated by John Hill.

A matar al tiempo:
Así morimos,
Poco a poco.
Un jardín no es un lugar:
Por un sendero de arena rojiza
Entramos
En una gota de agua,
Bebemos en su centro
Verdes claridades,
Ascendemos
Por la espiral de las horas
Hasta
La punta del día,
Descendemos
Hasta
La consumación de su brasa.
Ríos en la noche: fluyen los jardines.

Aquél de Mixcoac era un cuerpo
Cubierto de heridas,
Una arquitectura
A punto de desplomarse.
Yo era niño
Y el jardín se parecía a mi abuelo.
Trepaba por sus rodillas vegetales

We are condemned to kill time: thus we die, bit by bit. A garden is not a place: by the footpath of russet sand we enter a drop of water, and drink at its centre green clarities, we ascend by the spiral of the hours up to the peak of day, we descend down to the consummation of its dying ember. Rivers in the night: the gardens flow away.

The garden of Mixcoac was a corpse covered with wounds, an architecture almost toppling over. I was a little boy and the garden looked like my grandfather. I climbed over the vegetal knees, not

Sin saber que eran los mástiles de un barco
Varado.
El jardín lo sabía:
Esperaba su destrucción como el sentenciado
El hacha.
La higuera era la Madre,
La Diosa:
Zumbar de insectos coléricos,
Los sordos tambores de la sangre,
El sol
Y su martillo,
El verde abrazo de innumerables brazos,
La incisión del tronco.
El mundo se entreabrió:
Yo creí que había visto a la muerte
Al ver
La otra cara del ser,
La vacía:
El fijo replandor sin atributos.

En la frente del Ajusco
se apiñan
Las confederaciones blancas
Hasta no ser
Sino una masa cárdena:
El galope negro del aguacero

knowing they were the timbers of a grounded ship. The garden knew it. It awaited its destruction as a man sentenced to death awaits the axe. The fig-tree was Mother and Goddess: the buzz of angered insects, the deaf drums of blood, the sun and its hammer, the green embrace of numberless arms, the incision of the trunk. The world stood half opened: I believed I had seen death when I saw the other face of being, the empty face: the permanent, featureless brilliance.

On the brow of the Ajusco, the white confederations are clustered together till nothing exists but a purple mass: the black gallop of

Cubre todo el llano.
México:
Sobre la piedra ensangrentada
Danza el agua.
Meses de espejos.
El hormiguero,
Sus ritos subterráneos:
Inmerso en la luz cruel
Expiaba mi cuerpo-hormiguero,
Espiaba
La febril construcción de mi ruina.
Elitros:
El afilado canto del insecto
Corta yerbas secas.
Luz, luz:
Substancia del tiempo y sus inventos.
Cactos minerales,
Lagartijas de azogue
En las bardas de adobe,
El pájaro
Que perfora el espacio,
Sed, tedio, telvaneras:
Impalpables epifanías del viento.
Los pinos me enseñaron a hablar solo.
En aquel jardín aprendí a despedirme.

the downpour covers all the plain. Mexico: over the bloodstained stone dances the water. Months of mirrors. The ant-hill, its subterranean rituals: immersed in the cruel light I purified my ant-hill-body, and I lurked in the febrile building of my ruin. Insect-wings: the sharp song of the insect cuts the dry grasses. Light, light: substance of time and its inventions. Mineral cacti, quicksilver lizards in the adobe shacks, the bird piercing the space, thirst, tedium, sandstorms: impalpable epiphanies of the wind. The pines taught me to talk to myself. In that garden I learned to say goodbye.

Después no hubo jardines.
Un día,
Como si regresara,
No a mi casa:
Al comienzo del Comienzo,
Llegué a una claridad,
Ancha,
Construída para los juegos pasionales
De la luz y el agua.
Dispersiones, alianzas:
Del gorjeo del verde Al azul más húmedo
Al gris entre brasas
Al más llagado rosa
Al oro desenterrado
Al verde verde.
Esa noche me enfrenté al *nim*.
Sobre sus hombros
El cielo con todas sus joyas bárbaras.
El calor
Era una mano inmensa que se cerraba.
Se oía
El jadeo de las raíces,
La dilatación del espacio,
El desmoronamiento del año.
Con una máscara de polvo,
Armado de silencio,

Afterwards there were no gardens. One day, as if I were returning, not to my house: to the beginning of the Beginning, I reached a wide clarity, built by the impassioned play of light and water. Dispersions, alliances: from the chirrup of green, to the damper blue, to the grey between the embers, to the more wounded rose, to the gold disinterred, to the green greenness. That night I confronted *nim*. On its shoulders, the sky with all its barbarous jewels. The heat was an immense fist, clenching. The panting of the roots was heard, the dilation of space, the slow mouldering of the year. With a mask of dust, armed with silence,

El árbol no cedía.
Era grande como el monumento de la paciencia.
Era justo como la balanza que pesa instantes y siglos.
Casa de las ardillas, mesón de los mirlos.
Cabían
En sus brazos muchas lunas.
La fuerza
Es fidelidad,
El poder es acatamiento:
Nadie acaba en si mismo:
Un todo cada uno
En otro todo,
En otro uno:
Constelaciones.
El enorme *nim* sabía su pequeñez.
A sus pies
Supe que estaba vivo,
Supe que morir es ensancharse,
Negarse es crecer.
Entre gula y soberbia,
Codicia de vida
O fascinación por la muerte,
La vía de en medio.
En la fraternidad de los árboles

the tree did not yield. Its greatness was like a monument of patience. Its justice like the balance weighing instants and centuries. House of squirrels, hostelry of blackbirds. Many moons were at home in its arms. Force is fidelity, power is acceptance; nobody ends in himself: each one a whole in another whole, in another one: constellations. The enormous *nim* knew its littleness. At its feet I learned I was alive, I learned that to die is to extend one's being, that self-denial is growth. Between gluttony and pride, lust for life or fascination with death, the middle way. In the brotherhood

Aprendí a reconciliarme,
                    No conmigo:
Con lo que me levanta y me sostiene y me deja caer.

Me crucé con una muchacha.
                    El pacto
Del sol del verano y el sol del otoño:
                    Sus ojos.
Partidaria de acróbatas, astrónomos, camelleros.
Yo de fareros, lógicos, sadhúes.
Nuestros cuerpos se hablaron, se juntaron y se fueron.
Nosotros nos fuímos con ellos.
                    Era el monzón.
Cielos de yerba machacada
                    Y el viento en armas
En todas las encrucijadas.
                    Por la niña del cuento,
Marinera de un estanque en borrasca,
                    La llamé Almendrita.
No un nombre:
                    Un velero intrépido.
Llovía,
          La tierra se vestía y así se desnudaba,
Las serpientes salían de sus hoyos,
                    La luna

of the trees I learned to reconcile myself, not with myself, but with that which lifts me up and holds me up and lets me fall.

I encountered a girl. The pact between the sun of summer and the sun of autumn: her eyes. A lover of acrobats, astronomers, camel-drivers. I of light-house keepers, logicians, and saddhus. Our bodies spoke, and joined, and left. We left with them. It was the monsoon. Skies of pounded grass and the wind in arms at all the crossroads. After the girl in the fable, the sailor-girl of a storm-tossed lake, I called her Almendrita. Not a name: but a fearless skiff. The rain fell, and the earth was clothed, and so stripped herself, the snakes slithered from their holes, the moon was made

Era de agua,
El cielo se destrenza,
Sus trenzas
Eran ríos desatados,
Los ríos tragaban pueblos,
Muerte y vida se confundían,
Amasijo de lodo y sol,
Estación de lujuria y pestilencia,
Estación del rayo
Sobre el árbol de sándalo,
Tronchados astros genitales
Pudriéndose
Resucitando
En tu vagina,
Madre India,
India niña,
Empapada de savia, semen, jugos venenosos.

A la casa le brotaron escamas.
Almendrita:
Llama intacta entre el culebreo y el ventarrón,
En la noche de hojas de banano
Ascua verde,
Hamadríada,
Yakshi:
Risas en el matorral,

of water, the heaven let down her hair, her tresses were unbound rivers, the rivers carried away villages, death and life mingled as one, the dough of mud and sunlight, season of luxury and pestilence, season of the sunbeam over the sandalwood tree, the torn genital stars rotting, refertilizing in your vagina, mother India, maiden India, soaked with sap and sperm, and venomous juices.

The house budded with scales. Almendrita: intact flame between the writhing and the whirlwind, the green ember in the night of banana-leaves, hamadryad, *Yakshi*: laughter in the thicket, a

Manojo de albores en la espesura,
Más música
Que cuerpo,
Más fuga de pájaro
Que música,
Más mujer que pájaro:
Sol tu vientre,
Sol en el agua,
Agua de sol en la jarra,
Grano de girasol que yo planté en mi pecho,
Ágata
Leonada,
Mazorca de llamas en el jardín de huesos.

Chuang Tseu le pidió al cielo sus luminarias,
Sus címbalos al viento,
Para sus funerales.
Nosotros le pedimos al *nim* que nos casara.
Un jardín no es un lugar:
Es un tránsito,
Una pasión:
No sabemos hacia donde vamos,
Transcurrir es suficiente,
Transcurrir es quedarse.
Una vertiginosa inmovilidad.
Estaciones

handful of whiteness in the dark glade, more music than body, more flight of birds than music, more woman than bird: the sun your womb, sun in the water, water of sun in the pitcher, a grain of sunflower-seed I planted in my breast, the agate, lion-yellow, a head of corn aflame in a garden of bone.

Chuang Tseu begged of the sky its luminous stars, begged of the wind its cymbals, for his exequies. We beg of the *nim* that he marry us. A garden is not a place, it is a transition, a passion: we know not where we go, to elapse is enough, to elapse is to remain. A giddying immobility. Seasons like the succession of

Como la sucesión de grandes reyes,
                                        Cada invierno
Alta terraza sobre el año tendido.
                                        Luz bien templada,
Resonancias, transparencias,
                                        Esculturas de aire
Disipadas apenas pronunciadas,
                                        ¡Sílabas,
Islas afortunadas!
                              Engastado en la yerba,
El gato Demóstenes
                              Es un carbón luminoso.
La gata Semíramis persigue quimeras,
                                        Acecha
Sombras, ecos, reflejos.
                              Arriba:
Sarcasmos de cuervos,
                              El urogallo y su hembra,
Taciturnos príncipes desterrados,
                                        La upupa:
Pico y penacho, un alfiler engalanado,
La verde artillería de los pericos fulgurantes,
La inmovilidad del milano
                              Negro
En el cielo sin escollos.
                              Ahora,

great kings, every winter a high terrace above the lengthening year. A well-tempered light. Resonances, transparencies, sculptures of air no sooner pronounced but gone, syllables, the fortunate isles. Encrusted in the grass Demosthenes the cat is a glowing coal. The she-cat Semiramis chases chimeras, lies in wait for shadows, echoes, reflections. Overhead: the sarcasms of crows, the guinea-cock and his hen, taciturn exiled princes, the hoopoe, beak and crest, a decorated brooch, the green artillery of glittering parrots, the stillness of the black kite, effortless in the unhindering sky. Now,

Quieto,
Sobre la arista de una ola,
Instantáneo peñasco de espuma que se dispersa:
Un albatros.
No estamos lejos de Durban
(Allí estudió Pessoa.)
Cruzamos un petrolero.
Iba a Mombasa,
Ese puerto con nombre de fruta
(En mi sangre otros nombres,
Asamblea de estelas:
Camoens, Vasco de Gama y los otros.)
El jardín se ha quedado atrás.
¿Atrás o adelante?
No hay más jardines que los que llevamos dentro.
¿Qué nos espera en la otra orilla?
Pasión es tránsito:
La otra orilla está aquí,
Luz en el aire sin orillas:
Prainaparamita,
Nuestra Señora de la Otra Orilla,
Tú misma,
La muchacha del cuento,
La alumna del jardín.
Olvidé a Nagarjuna y a Dharmakirti
En tus pechos,

still, over the crest of a wave a momentary vanishing boulder of spray: an albatross. We are not far from Durban (where Pessoa studied). We pass a tanker. It was heading for Mombasa, the port with a name of fruit. (In my blood other names, a gathering of the wakes of ships, Camões, Vasco de Gama, and the rest.) The garden has been left behind. Behind or ahead? There are no gardens save those we carry within us. What awaits us on the other shore? Passion is transit: the shore is here, light in the shoreless air: *Prainaparamita*, Our Lady of the Other Shore, thou thyself, the girl of the fable, pupil of the garden. I forgot Nagarjuna and Dharmakirti in your breasts, in your scream I met them: *Maithuna*,

En tu grito los encontré:
Maithuna,
Dos en uno,
Uno en todo,
Todo en nada,
¡*Sunyata*,
Plenitud vacía,
Vacuidad redonda como tu grupa!

Sombras girando
Sobre un charco de luz.
Mergos y ¿peces?
Hélice de diecisiete sílabas
Dibujada en el mar
No por Basho:
Por mis ojos, el sol y los pájaros,
Hoy,
A eso de las cuatro,
A la altura de Mauritania.
Una ola estalla:
Mariposas de sal:
Desvanecimientos.
Metamorfosis de lo idéntico.
A esta misma hora
Delhi y sus piedras rojas,
Su río oscuro,
Sus domos blancos,

two in one, one in all, all is nothing, *Sunyata*, vacant plenitude, round emptiness, like your haunches.

Shadows turning over a pool of light. Diver-birds and . . . fishes? Helix of seventeen syllables sketched in the sea, not for Basho; for my eyes, the sun and the birds, today, at about four, at the latitude of Mauritania. The splash of a wave: butterflies of salt: faintings. Metamorphosis of the identical. At the same hour Delhi and her red stones, her dark river, her white domes, her centuries

Sus siglos en añicos,
Se transfigura:
Arquitecturas sin peso,
Cristalizaciones
Casi mentales,
Altos vértigos sobre un espejo.
Espiral
De transparencias.
Se abisma
El jardín en una identidad
Sin nombre
Ni sustancia.
Los signos se borran: yo miro la claridad.

Altamar, a bordo del Victoria, entre Bombay y Las Palmas, del 20 al 28 de noviembre de 1968.

in fragments, is transfiguring herself: architecture without weight crystallizations almost mental, high vertigos above a looking-glass. Spiral of transparencies. The garden plunges into introspection, into an identity without name or substance. The signs are blotted out; I stare into the clarity.

(At sea on board the *Victoria*, between Bombay and Las Palmas, from 20–28 November 1968.)

JAIME SABINES (b. 1926)

Oigo palomas

OIGO palomas en el tejado del vecino.
Tú ves el sol.
El agua amanece,
y todo es raro como estas palabras.
¿Para qué te ha de entender nadie, Tarumba?,
¿para qué alumbrarte con lo que dices
como con una hoguera?
Quema tus huesos y caliéntate.
Ponte a secar, ahora, al sol y al viento.

Si alguien te dice que no es cierto

SI alguien te dice que no es cierto,
dile que venga,
que ponga sus manos sobre su estómago y jure,
que atestigüe la verdad de todo.
Que mire la luz en el petróleo de la calle,

I Hear Pigeons

I HEAR pigeons on my neighbour's roof. You see the sun. The water dawns, and everything is as strange as these words. Why should anyone understand you, Tarumba? Why should anyone throw light on you through what you say as if it were a bonfire? Burn your bones and warm yourself. Put yourself out to dry now in the sun and the wind.

If Anyone Should Tell You That It Isn't So

IF anyone should tell you that it isn't so, tell him to come, to put his hands on his stomach and swear, bearing witness to the truth of it all. Tell him to look at the light in the petrol in the street, at

los automóviles inmóviles,
las gentes pasando y pasando,
las cuatro puertas que dan al este,
las bicicletas sin nadie,
los ladrillos, la cal amorosa,
las estanterías a tu espalda cayéndose,
las canas en la cabeza de tu padre,
el hijo que no tiene tu mujer,
y el dinero que entra con la boca llena de mierda.
Dile que jure, en el nombre de Dios invicto
en el torneo de las democracias,
haber visto y oído.
Porque ha de oír también el crimen de los gatos
y un enorme reloj al que dan cuerda pegado a tu oreja.

the immobile cars, the people that go on passing by, the four gates that look to the east, the riderless bicycles, the bricks, the gentle lime, the bookshelves falling apart at your back, the white hairs on your father's head, the son your wife hasn't had and the money that goes into a mouth full of shit. Tell him to swear, in the name of God the invincible that he has seen and heard in the contest of the democracies. Because he shall also hear the crime of the cats and an enormous watch which they wind up while it is pressed to your ear.

MARCO ANTONIO MONTES DE OCA
(b. 1932)

Pequeña moral

CORAZÓN mío y de todos:
clava tu arpón en la pulpa desvalida,
estrangula el silencio con una cuerda de violín,
abofetea la inválida sonrisa del juguete
y derriba tu palacio de abejas ardientes
si lo amado hasta la muerte no se te concede.
Dí que las urnas son acuarios mutilados,
destapa tu caja de imágenes venenosas
si esta realidad, tan terriblemente amada,
tras el tibio monóculo de una lágrima
no se deja sorprender.
Entretanto, desafía a la enterradora que acumula torsos
de espejeante sudor en un túnel vacío,
haz que la buscadora de éxtasis no enloquezca en el pajar
  del universo;
ayuda en esta hora miserable
a que las cosas sean lo que puedan ser.
Ama las imprevistas ternuras,

A Little Set of Morals

MY heart, everyone's heart; if what you love until death is not given to you, stick your harpoon into the helpless flesh, strangle the silence with a violin string, aim blows at the toy's crippled smile and knock down your palace of burning bees. Say that the [glass] cases are maimed aquariums, take the lid off your box of venomous images if this reality, so terribly loved, will not allow itself to be taken unawares behind the warm monocle of a tear. Meanwhile, don't trust the woman who digs graves, who piles up torsos with glistening sweat, in an empty tunnel; make sure that the woman who searches for ecstasies doesn't go mad in the hayloft of the universe; at this wretched time, help things to be what they could be. Love the unexpected acts of tenderness, the

los recuerdos que se clavan en nosotros hasta la em-
puñadura de la luz,
las voces que descienden imperiosas
sin otro hilo conductor
que su esperanza de ser oídas.

memories that are driven into us up to the hilt of light, the voices that imperiously descend drawn by no other thread than by the hope of being heard.

JOSÉ EMILIO PACHECO (b. 1939)

Aceleración de la historia

ESCRIBO unas palabras
y al minuto
ya dicen otra cosa
significan
una intención distinta
son ya dóciles
al Carbono 14
Criptogramas
de un pueblo remotísimo
que busca
la escritura en tinieblas

The Acceleration of History

I WRITE down some words and a minute later they mean something different, they indicate a different intention; they are docile now to Carbon 14, the cryptograms of a very remote people that is searching in the dark for the written word.

Pompeya

Qui su l'arida schiena
Del formidabil monte
Sterminator Vesèvo . . .
–Giacomo Leopardi, *La ginestra*

LA TEMPESTAD de fuego nos sorprendió en el acto
de la copulación.
No fuimos muertos por el río de lava.
Nos ahogaron los gases; la ceniza
nos sirvió de sudario. Nuestros cuerpos
continuaron unidos en la roca:
petrificado espasmo interminable.

El espejo de los enigmas: los monos

The monkey is an organized sarcasm upon the human race.
–Henry Ward Beecher

CUANDO el mono te clava la mirada
estremece pensar
si no seremos
su espejito irrisorio
y sus bufones.

Pompeii

THE fire storm caught us in the act of copulation. We were not killed by the river of lava. We were suffocated by the gases; the ash was our shroud. Our bodies remained united in the rock; an endless petrified spasm.

The Mirror of the Enigmas: Monkeys

WHEN the monkey fixes his gaze on you, it's a shuddering thought that we might be his derisive little mirror and his fools.

Mosquitos

NACEN en los pantanos del insomnio.
Son negrura viscosa que aletea.
Vampiritos inermes,
sublibélulas,
caballitos de pica
del demonio.

Mosquitoes

THEY are born in the swamps of sleeplessness. They are viscous flapping blackness. Unarmed little vampires, inferior versions of the dragonfly, the devil's little picadors.

NICARAGUA

RUBÉN DARÍO (1867–1916)

A los poetas risueños

ANACREONTE, padre de la sana alegría;
Ovidio, sacerdote de la ciencia amorosa;
Quevedo, en cuyo cáliz licor jovial rebosa;
Banville, insigne orfeo de la sacra Harmonía;

y con vosotros, toda la grey hija del día,
a quien habla el amante corazón de la rosa,
abejas que fabrican sobre la humana prosa
en sus Himetos mágicos mieles de poesía:

prefiero vuestra risa sonora, vuestra musa
risueña, vuestros versos perfumados de vino,
a los versos de sombra y a la canción confusa

que opone el numen bárbaro al resplandor latino;
y ante la fiera máscara de la fatal Medusa,
medrosa huye mi alondra de canto cristalino.

To the Joyful Poets

ANACREON, father of healthy joy; Ovid, priest of the art of love; Quevedo, whose cup runs over with a sparkling liquor; Banville, renowned Orpheus of sacred Harmony;

And with you, all those born of the day, to whom the loving heart of the rose speaks, bees that in their magical mountains of Hymettus make honey of poetry on human prose:

I prefer your sonorous laughter, your charming muse, your wine-perfumed verse, to the gloomy verses and the confused song

That barbarian inspiration offers in contrast to Latin brilliance; and my lark, with its clear and crystalline song, flees timorously before the fierce mask of the fatal Medusa.

Yo persigo una forma

Yo persigo una forma que no encuentra mi estilo,
botón de pensamiento que busca ser la rosa;
se anuncia con un beso que en mis labios se posa
al abrazo imposible de la Venus de Milo.

Adornan verdes palmas el blanco peristilo;
los astros me han predicho la visión de la Diosa;
y en mi alma reposa la luz, como reposa
el ave de la luna sobre un lago tranquilo.

Y no hallo sino la palabra que huye,
la iniciación melódica que de la flauta fluye
y la barca del sueño que en el espacio boga;

y bajo la ventana de mi Bella-Durmiente,
el sollozo continuo del chorro de la fuente
y el cuello del gran cisne blanco que me interroga.

I Seek a Form

I SEEK a form my style cannot find, the bud of thought that would be a rose; it is proclaimed to the impossible embrace of the Venus de Milo with a kiss that is set upon my lips.

Green palms bedeck the white colonnade; the stars have foretold to me the vision of the Goddess; and the light settles in my soul as the bird of the moon settles on a placid lake.

And all that I can find is the word that escapes me, the melodic introduction that flows from the flute and the ship of dreams that sails through space;

And beneath the window of my Sleeping Beauty, the constant weeping of the water flowing from the fountain and the neck of the great white swan that questions me.

Filosofía

SALUDA al sol, araña, no seas rencorosa.
Dá tus gracias a Dios, oh sapo, pues que eres.
El peludo cangrejo tiene espinas de rosa
y los moluscos reminiscencias de mujeres.

Sabed ser lo que sois, enigmas, siendo formas;
dejad la responsabilidad de las Normas,
que a su vez la enviarán al Todopoderoso . . .
(Toca, grillo, a la luz de la luna, y dance el oso.)

Un soneto a Cervantes

A Ricardo Calvo

HORAS de pesadumbre y de tristeza
paso en mi soledad. Pero Cervantes
es buen amigo. Endulza mis instantes
ásperos, y reposa mi cabeza.

Philosophy

WELCOME the sun, spider, no need to be spiteful. Give your thanks to God, oh toad, since you do exist. The hairy crab displays rose-thorns and the molluscs something reminiscent of women.

Learn to be what you are, enigmas given form; give up the responsibility for Norms; in time it will be passed on to the Almighty. . . . (Cricket, play in the light of the moon, and let the bear dance.)

A Sonnet to Cervantes

I SPEND my hours of solitude troubled and sad. But Cervantes is a faithful friend. He sweetens my bitter moments and cradles my head.

Él es la vida y la naturaleza,
regala un yelmo de oros y diamantes
a mis sueños errantes.
Es para mí: suspira, ríe y reza.

Cristiano y amoroso y caballero
parla como un arroyo cristalino.
¡Así le admiro y quiero,

Viendo cómo el destino
hace que regocije al mundo entero
la tristeza inmortal de ser divino!

Allá lejos

BUEY que vi en mi niñez echando vaho un día
bajo el nicaragüense sol de encendidos oros,
en la hacienda fecunda plena de la armonía
del trópico; paloma de los bosques sonoros
del viento, de las hachas, de pájaros y toros
salvajes, yo os saludo, pues sois la vida mía.

He is life and nature; he presents my wandering dreams with a helmet of gold and diamonds. He suits me well; he sighs, laughs and prays.

A generous and loving Christian, he speaks like a clear, bright stream. Thus I admire and love him,

When I see how fate has planned it so that the whole world rejoices in the immortal sadness of being divine.

Far Away

BULLOCK that I saw in my childhood on the fertile farmstead full of the harmony of the tropics, sweating one day under the Nicaraguan sun of burning gold; dove of the woods that ring with the wind, the axes, wild birds and bulls; I salute you all, for you are my life.

Pesado buey, tú evocas la dulce madrugada
que llamaba a la ordeña de la vaca lechera,
cuando era mi existencia toda blanca y rosada;
y tú, paloma arrulladora, y montañera,
significas en mi primavera pasada
todo lo que hay en la divina Primavera.

En una primera página

CÁLAMO, deja aquí correr tu negra fuente.
Es el pórtico en donde la Idea alza la frente
luminosa y al templo de sus ritos penetra.
Cálamo, pon el símbolo divino de la letra
en gloria del vidente cuya alma está en su lira.
Bendición al que entiende, bendición al que admira.
De ensueño, plata o nieve, ésta es la blanca puerta.
Entrad los que pensáis o soñáis. Ya está abierta.

Ponderous bullock, you evoke the sweet dawn that called for the milking of the cow, when my life was still all pink and white; and you, dove who lulls, dove who climbs, you stand in the springs of my past for everything there is in the divine Spring.

On an Opening Page

CALAMUS, let your black spring flow here. It is the portico where the Idea raises its shining countenance to enter the temple of its rituals. Calamus, set down the divine symbol of the letter in honour of the seer whose soul is in his harp. A blessing on him that understands, a blessing on him that admires. This is the unmarked door to illusion, silver or snow. Come in those of you who think you dream. It is open now.

Vesperal

HA pasado la siesta
y la hora del Poniente se avecina,
y hay ya frescor en esta
costa, que el sol del Trópico calcina.
Hay un suave alentar de aura marina,
y el Occidente finge una floresta
que una llama de púrpura ilumina.
Sobre la arena dejan los cangrejos
la ilegible escritura de sus huellas.
Conchas color de rosa y de reflejos
áureos, caracolillos y fragmentos de estrellas
de mar, forman alfombra
sonante al paso, en la armoniosa orilla.
Y cuando Venus brilla,
dulce, imperial amor de la divina tarde,
creo que en la onda suena
o són de lira, o canto de sirena.
Y en mi alma otro lucero, como el de Venus, arde.

Vesperal

THE siesta has passed and the hour of sunset draws near, and already there is a coolness on this coast, scorched by the tropical sun. There is a soft breath of sea air, and the west feigns a forest illuminated by a purple flame. The tracks of crabs leave an illegible script on the sand. Pink shells, and shells the colour of golden reflections, little snails and fragments of starfish form a carpet noisy to the step, on the harmonious shore. And when Venus sparkles, sweet, imperial love of the divine evening, I believe that the sound of a lyre or the siren's song resounds amid the waves. And in my soul there burns another bright star, like Venus.

Raza

HISOPOS y espadas
han sido precisos,
unos regando el agua
y otros vertiendo el vino
de la sangre. Nutrieron
de tal modo a la raza los siglos.
Juntos alientan vástagos
de beatos e hijos
de encomenderos con
los que tienen el signo
de descender de esclavos africanos,
o de soberbios indios,
como el gran Nicarao, que un puente de canoas
brindó al cacique amigo
para pasar el lago
de Managua. Esto es épico y es lírico.

Race

ASPERGILLS and swords have been required, some to sprinkle [holy] water and others to spill the wine of blood. Thus did the centuries nourish the race. Together they inspire the descendants of the pious, and the sons of *encomenderos*,* and those that carry the mark of descent from African slaves, or from proud Indians, like the great Nicarao, who offered his friend the cacique a bridge of canoes to cross the lake of Managua. This is epic and this is lyrical.

**encomendero*: the name given to a Spanish colonist who had authority over an Indian territory, or *encomienda*.

El gallo

Un botonazo de luz,
luz amarilla, luz roja.
En la contienda, disparo
de plumas luminosas.
Energía engalanada
de la cresta a la cola
– ámbar, oro, terciopelo –
lujo que se deshoja
con heroico silencio
en la gallera estentórea.
Rueda de luz trazada
ante la clueca remolona,
la capa del ala abierta
y tendida en ronda . . .

Gallo, gallo del trópico.
Pico que destila auroras.
Relámpago congelado.
Paleta luminosa.
¡Ron de plumas que bebe
la Antilla brava y tórrida!

The Cock

A THRUST of light, yellow light, red light. In the contest, explosion of luminous plumes. Energy adorned from the crest to the tail – amber, gold, velvet – finery that is stripped away in heroic silence in the noisy cock-pit. A circle of light traced out before the indolent broody hen; the wing's cape open and spread out in the round . . .

Cock, cock of the tropics. Beak that makes dawns fall in drops. Frozen lightning. Palette of luminous colours. Rum of feathers that the wild and torrid Antilles drink.

ERNESTO CARDENAL (b. 1925)

Es la hora del Oficio Nocturno

Es la hora del Oficio Nocturno, y la iglesia
en penumbra parece que está llena de demonios.
Esta es la hora de las tinieblas y de las fiestas.
La hora de mis parrandas. Y regresa mi pasado.

«Y mi pecado está siempre delante de mí».

Y mientras recitamos los salmos, mis recuerdos
interfieren el rezo como radios y como roconolas.
Vuelven viejas escenas de cine, pesadillas, horas
solas en hoteles, bailes, viajes, besos, bares.
Y surgen rostros olvidados. Cosas siniestras.
Somoza asesinado sale de su mausoleo. (Con
Sehón, rey de los amorreos, y Og, rey de Basán).
Las luces del «Copacabana» rielando en el agua negra

It Is the Time for the Evening Service

It is the time for the evening service, and in the half-light the church seems full of demons. This is the time of darkness and feasts. The time for my revels. And my past returns.

'And my sin is always before me.'

And while we recite the psalms, my memories intrude into the prayer like radios and juke boxes. Old film scenes come back to me, nightmares, solitary hours in hotels, dances, journeys, kisses, bars. And forgotten faces appear. Sinister things. The assassinated Somoza* emerges from his mausoleum. (With Sihon, king of the Amorites and Og, king of Bashan.) The lights of the 'Copacabana' are gleaming under the jetty in the black water that flows from the

*The absolute tyranny of the Somoza family in Nicaragua has lasted since 1936. In 1956 Anastasio was assassinated, but the country continues to be run by his sons Luis and Anastasio.

del malecón, que mana de las cloacas de Managua.
Conversaciones absurdas de noches de borrachera
que se repiten y se repiten como un disco rayado.
Y los gritos de las ruletas, y las roconolas.

«Y mi pecado está siempre delante de mí».

Es la hora en que brillan las luces de los burdeles
y las cantinas. La casa de Caifás está llena de gente.
Las luces del palacio de Somoza están prendidas.
Es la hora en que se reúnen los Consejos de Guerra
y los técnicos en torturas bajan a las prisiones.
La hora de los policías secretos y de los espías,
cuando los ladrones y los adúlteros rondan las casas
y se ocultan los cadáveres. – Un cuerpo cae al agua.
Es la hora en que los moribundos entran en agonía.
La hora del sudor en el huerto, y de las tentaciones.
Afuera los primeros pájaros cantan tristes,
llamando al sol. Es la hora de las tinieblas.
Y la iglesia está helada, como llena de demonios,
mientras seguimos en la noche recitando los salmos.

sewers of Managua. Absurd conversations on drunken nights that repeat and repeat themselves like scratched records. And the shouts from the roulette wheels and the juke boxes.

'And my sin is always before me.'

It is the time when lights shine from brothels and bars. Caiaphas' house is full of people. The lights of the Somoza palace are switched on. It is the time when the Councils of War meet and experts on torture go down into the prisons. The time of secret police and spies, when thieves and adulterers hover around the houses and corpses are hidden. A body falls into the water. It is the time when the dying enter their final agony. The hour of sweat in the orchard and the time for temptations. The first birds sing sadly outside, calling out for the sun. It is the time of darkness. And the church is freezing, as if full of demons, while we go on reciting the psalms in the night.

PERU

MANUEL GONZÁLEZ PRADA (1848–1918)

Cosmopolitismo

¡CÓMO fatiga y cansa y me abruma
el suspirar mirando eternamente
los mismos campos y la misma gente,
los mismos cielos y la misma bruma!

Huir quisiera por la blanca espuma
y al sol lejano calentar mi frente.
¡Oh, si me diera el río su corriente!
¡Oh, si me diera el águila su pluma!

Yo no seré viajero arrepentido
que al arribar a playas extranjeras,
exhale de sus labios un gemido.

Donde me estrechen generosas manos,
donde me arrullen tibias primaveras,
ahí veré mi patria y mis hermanos.

Cosmopolitanism

HOW it wearies, tires, and crushes me to sigh, eternally watching the same fields and the same people, the same skies and the same fog!

I would like to escape through the white foam and warm my forehead at the distant sun. Oh, if only the river would give me its current, if only the eagle would give me its plumage!

I will not be a regretful traveller, who on arriving at foreign shores breathes out a lamentation from his lips.

Where gentle hands press me, where warm springs lull me, there I will see my country and my brothers.

Rondel

AVES de paso que en flotante hilera
recorren el azul del firmamento,
exhalan a los aires un lamento
y se disipan en veloz carrera,
son el amor, la dicha y el contento.

¿Qué son las mil y mil generaciones
que brillan y descienden al ocaso,
que nacen y sucumben a milliones?
Aves de paso.

Inútil es, ¡oh pechos infelices!,
al mundo encadenarse con raíces.
Impulsos misteriosos y pujantes
nos llevan entre sombras, al acaso,
que somos, ¡ay!, eternos caminantes.
Aves de paso.

Rondel

LOVE, happiness and content are birds of passage that travel the blue of the firmament in a floating line, breathe out a lament to the air, and disperse in swift flight.

What are the thousands upon thousands of generations that shine and sink at sunset, that are born and succumb in millions? Birds of passage.

Oh unhappy souls, it is useless to bind yourself to the world with roots. Powerful and mysterious impulses carry us among shadows, aimlessly; for we are, alas, but eternal wanderers. Birds of passage.

JOSÉ SANTOS CHOCANO (1875–1934)

El sueño del caimán

ENORME tronco que arrastró la ola,
yace el caimán varado en la ribera:
espinazo de abrupta cordillera,
fauces de abismo y formidable cola.

El sol lo envuelve en fúlgida aureola;
y parece lucir cota y cimera,
cual monstruo de metal que reverbera
y que al reverberar se tornasola.

Inmóvil como un ídolo sagrado,
ceñido en mallas de compacto acero,
está ante el agua extático y sombrío,

a manera de un príncipe encantado
que vive eternamente prisionero
en el palacio de cristal de un río.

The Dream of the Cayman

ENORMOUS trunk that the wave dragged along, the stranded cayman rests on the river bank; spine a steep mountain range, jaws of the abyss, formidable tail.

The sun wraps him in a resplendent halo; armour and crest appear to shine, like a metal monster that reverberates, and on reverberating changes colour.

Immobile as a sacred idol, corseted in a mesh of solid steel, he faces the water, ecstatic and sombre;

Like an enchanted prince eternally prisoner in the crystal palace of a river.

La visión del cóndor

UNA vez bajó el cóndor de su altura
a pugnar con el boa, que, hecho un lazo,
dormía astutamente en el regazo
compasivo de trágica espesura.

El cóndor picoteó la escama dura;
y la sierpe, al sentir el picotazo,
fingió en el césped el nervioso trazo
con que la tempestad firma en la anchura.

El cóndor cogió el boa; y en un vuelo
sacudiólo con ímpetu bravío,
y lo dejó caer desde su cielo.

Inclinó la mirada al bosque umbrío;
y pudo ver que, en el lejano suelo,
en vez del boa, serpenteaba un río . . .

The Vision of the Condor

ONCE upon a time the condor came down from his peak to fight the boa, who, coiled like a lariat, was sleeping cunningly in the compassionate lap of a tragic thicket.

The condor pecked at the hard scales and the serpent, on feeling the peck, feigned in the grass a jerky trail, like that with which the tempest marks the shore.

The condor caught up the boa, and in flight shook it with ferocious violence and let it fall from the sky.

He gazed down to the shady forest, and could see that, on the distant ground, in place of the boa, a river meandered.

JOSÉ MARÍA EGUREN (1882–1942)

La Tarda

DESPUNTA por la rambla amarillenta,
donde el puma se acobarda;
viene de lágrimas exenta
la Tarda.

Ella, del esqueleto madre,
el puente baja, inescuchada;
y antes que el rondín ladre
a la alborada,
lanza ronca carcajada.

Y con sus epitalamios rojos,
con sus vacíos ojos
y su extraña belleza
pasa sin ver, por la senda bravía,
sin ver que hoy me muero de tristeza
y de monotonía.

Va a la ciudad que duerme parda,
por la yerta avenida,
y sin ver el dolor distraída
la Tarda.

La Tarda

RISING from the yellow sandy gully, where the puma loses courage, La Tarda comes, without tears.

From the maternal skeleton she passes under the bridge, unheeded; and before the sentry's round barks at the dawn, she throws out a raucous guffaw.

And with her red nuptial songs, her empty eyes and her strange beauty, she passes without seeing along the untamed pathway – without seeing that today I am dying of sadness and monotony.

Distractedly she goes on to the grey, sleeping city, along the motionless avenue, without seeing the pain – La Tarda.

El caballo

VIENE por las calles,
a la luna parva,
un caballo muerto
en antigua batalla.

Sus cascos sombríos . . .
trepida, resbala;
de un hosco relincho,
con sus voces lejanas.

En la plúmbea esquina
de la barricada,
con ojos vacíos
y con horror, se para.

Más tarde se escuchan
sus lentas pisadas,
por vías desiertas,
y por ruinosas plazas.

The Horse

HE comes through the streets under the full moon, a horse killed in an ancient battle.

His dull hooves . . . he trembles, he slips . . . gives a gloomy neigh with his distant voice.

At the leaden corner of the barricade he stops with empty eyes and horror.

Later one can hear his slow tread, through deserted streets and through ruined squares.

CÉSAR VALLEJO (1892–1938)

Líneas

CADA cinta de fuego
que, en busca del Amor,
arrojo y vibra en rosas lamentables,
me da a luz el sepelio de una víspera.
Yo no sé si el redoble en que lo busco,
será jadear de roca,
o perenne nacer de corazón.

Hay tendida hacia el fondo de los seres,
un eje ultranervioso, honda plomada.
¡La hebra del destino!
Amor desviará tal ley de vida,
hacia la voz del Hombre;
y nos dará la libertad suprema
en transubstanciación azul, virtuosa,
contra lo ciego y lo fatal.

¡Que en cada cifra lata,
reclusa en albas frágiles,
el Jesús aún mejor de otra gran Yema!

Lines

EACH ribbon of fire that, in searching for love, darts and vibrates in lamentable roses, gives birth to the burial of a day before. I do not know if the drum-roll in which I seek it will be the gasping of a rock, or the perennial birth of the heart.

Extended towards the depth of beings is a hypersensitive axis, a deep plumb-line. The thread of destiny! Love will deflect such a law of life towards the voice of man, and will give us supreme liberty in blue transubstantiation, virtuous, against the blind and the fatal.

Let there palpitate, in every pure cipher, kept apart in fragile dawns, the better Jesus from another great Beginning!

Y después . . . La otra línea . . .
Un Bautista que aguaita, aguaita, aguaita . . .
Y, cabalgando en intangible curva,
un pie bañado en púrpura.

Amor prohibido

SUBES centellante de labios y ojeras!
Por tus venas subo, como un can herido
que busca el refugio de blandas aceras.

Amor, en el mundo tú eres un pecado!
Mi beso es la punta chispeante del cuerno
del diablo; mi beso que es credo sagrado!

Espíritu es el horópter que pasa
¡puro en su blasfemia!
¡el corazón que engendra al cerebro!
que pasa hacia el tuyo, por mi barro triste.
¡Platónico estambre
que existe en el cáliz donde tu alma existe!

And afterwards. . . . The other line. . . . A Baptist who watches, watches, watches. . . . And rides in an intangible curve, one foot bathed in purple.

Forbidden Love

YOU rise sparkling from lips and shadowed eyes! I rise through your veins like a wounded dog seeking the refuge of soft pavements.

Love, in the world you are a sin! My kiss is the sparkling point of the devil's horn; my kiss that is a sacred creed.

Spirit is the horopter that passes – pure in its blasphemy! The heart that breeds the brain! – yours through my sad clay. Platonic stamen that dwells in the calyx where your soul dwells!

¿Algún penitente silencio siniestro?
¡Tú acaso, lo escuchas? Inocente flor!
. . . Y saber que donde no hay un Padrenuestro,
el Amor es un Cristo pecador!

from *Trilce*

XIII

PIENSO en tu sexo.
Simplificado el corazón, pienso en tu sexo,
ante el hijar maduro del día.
Palpo el botón de dicha, está en sazón.
Y muere un sentimiento antiguo
degenerado en seso.

Pienso en tu sexo, surco más prolífico
y armonioso que el vientre de la Sombra,
aunque la Muerte concibe y pare
de Dios mismo.

Oh Conciencia,
pienso, sí, en el bruto libre
que goza donde quiere, donde puede.

Some sinister silent penitent? Do you, by chance, hear him? Innocent flower! . . . And to know that where there is no Paternoster, Love is a sinning Christ!

from *Trilce*

I THINK of your sex. The heart simplified, I think of your sex before the ripe matrix of the day. I touch the bud of happiness, it is in season. And an ancient sentiment dies, decayed in the brain.

I think of your sex, a furrow more prolific and harmonious than the womb of the Shadow, although Death conceives and gives birth from God himself.

Oh Conscience, I think, yes, of the free beast who rejoices where he wishes, wherever he can.

Oh, escándalo de miel de los crepúsculos.
Oh estruendo mudo.
¡Odumodneurtse!

XVIII

OH las cuatro paredes de la celda.
Ah las cuatro paredes albicantes
que sin remedio dan al mismo número.

Criadero de nervios, mala brecha,
por sus cuatro rincones cómo arranca
las diarias aherrojadas extremidades.

Amorosa llavera de innumerables llaves,
si estuvieras aquí, si vieras hasta
qué hora son cuatro estas paredes.
Contra ellas seríamos contigo, los dos,
más dos que nunca. Y ni lloraras,
di, libertadora!

Ah las paredes de la celda.
De ellas me duelen entretanto más

Oh, honeyed scandal of twilights. Oh mute clamour. Ruomalcetum!

OH the four walls of the cell. Ah the four whitening walls, without fail looking upon the same number.

Breeding-ground of nerves, wicked breach, how you wrench the daily chained extremities in your four corners.

Loving custodian with innumerable keys, if you were here, if you could but see up to what hour the walls are always four. We would be together against them, two, more two than ever. And you wouldn't cry, would you, my liberator?

Ah the walls of the cell. Meanwhile the two long ones hurt me

las dos largas que tienen esta noche
algo de madres que ya muertas
llevan por bromurados declives
a un niño de la mano cada una.

Y sólo yo me voy quedando,
con la diestra, que hace por ambas manos,
en alto, en busca de terciario brazo
que ha de pupilar, entre mi donde y mi cuando,
esta mayoría inválida de hombre.

Intensidad y altura

QUIERO escribir, pero me sale espuma,
quiero decir muchísimo y me atollo;
no hay cifra hablada que no sea suma,
no hay pirámide escrita, sin cogollo.

Quiero escribir, pero me siento puma;
quiero laurearme, pero me encebollo.
No hay voz hablada, que no llegue a bruma,
no hay dios ni hijo de dios, sin desarrollo.

most, having somehow the air of mothers who, already dead, convey through bromided declivities a child each by the hand.

And I remain here alone, with the right hand that has to do for both hands, on high, searching for the third arm, that between my where and my when will father this crippled coming of age of a man.

Intensity and Height

I WANT to write, but only foam comes out, I want to say such a lot and I get into difficulties; there is no spoken number that is not a sum, there is no written pyramid without a core.

I want to write, but I feel myself a puma; I want to crown myself with laurels, but they smell of onions. There is no spoken voice that does not reach into mist, there is neither god nor son of god, without progress.

Vámonos, pues, por eso, a comer yerba,
carne de llanto, fruta de gemido,
nuestra alma melancólica en conserva.

Vámonos! Vámonos! Estoy herido;
Vámonos a beber lo ya bebido,
vámonos, cuervo, a fecundar tu cuerva.

Sombrero, abrigo, guantes

ENFRENTE a la Comedia Francesa, está el Café
de la Regencia; en él hay una pieza
recóndita, con una butaca y una mesa.
Cuando entro, el polvo inmóvil se ha puesto ya de pie.

Entre mis labios hechos de jebe, la pavesa
de una cigarillo humea, y en el humo se ve
dos humos intensivos, el tórax del Café,
y en el tórax, un óxido profundo de tristeza.

So, because of this, let us go therefore; to eat grass, the flesh of weeping, the fruit of lamentation, our pickled melancholy soul.

Let us go! Let us go! I am wounded! Let us go to drink the already drunk; let us go, crow, to impregnate your mate.

*Hat, Coat, Gloves**

OPPOSITE the Comédie Française stands the Regency Café; in it there is a hidden room, with an easy chair and a table. When I go in, the still dust has already stood up.

Between my rubber lips the stub of a cigarette smoulders, and in the smoke are seen two intensive smokes, the thorax of the cafe, and in the thorax, a profound oxide of sadness.

---

*Translated by John Hill.

Importa que el otoño se injerte en los otoños,
importa que el otoño se integre de retoños,
la nube, de semestres; de pómulos, la arruga.

Importa oler a loco postulando
¡qué cálida es la nieve, qué fugaz la tortuga,
el cómo qué sencillo, qué fulminante el cuándo!

A lo mejor, soy otro

A LO mejor, soy otro: andando, al alba, otro que marcha
en torno a un disco largo, a un disco elástico:
mortal, figurativo, audaz diafragma.
A lo mejor, recuerdo al esperar, anoto mármoles
donde índice escarlata, y donde catre de bronce,
un zorro ausente, espúreo, enojadísimo.
A lo mejor, hombre al fin,
las espaldas ungidas de añil misericordia,
a lo mejor, me digo, más allá no hay nada.

It matters that the autumn be grafted into the autumns, it matters that the autumn be integrated into young shoots, the cloud into half-years; the wrinkle into the cheekbones.

It matters to smell like a madman postulating how hot is the snow, how fleeting the tortoise, how simple the how, how deadly the when!

*As Like as Not I Am Another**

AS like as not I am another; going, in the dawn, another man who walks round a long disc, an elastic disc; mortal, figurative, audacious diaphragm. As like as not I remember as I wait, I annotate marbles, where there's a scarlet index and a hammock of bronze, an absent, spurious, extremely angry fox. As like as not, a man in the end, his shoulders anointed with indigo mercy, as like as not, I say to myself, there is nothing after you are dead.

---

*Translated by John Hill.

Me da la mar el disco, refiriéndolo,
con cierto margen seco, a mi garganta;
¡nada, en verdad, más ácido, más dulce, más kanteano!

Pero sudor ajeno, pero suero
o tempestad de mansedumbre,
decayendo o subiendo, ¡eso, jamás!

Echado, fino, exhúmome,
tumefacta la mezcla en que entro a golpes,
sin piernas, sin adulto barro, ni armas,
una aguja prendida en el gran átomo . . .
¡No! ¡Nunca! ¡Nunca ayer! ¡Nunca después!

Y de ahí este tubérculo satánico,
esta muela moral de plesiosaurio
y estas sospechas póstumas,
este índice, esta cama, estos boletos.

The sea gives me the disc, referring it, with a certain dry margin, to my throat; nothing, in truth, more acid, more sweet, more Kantian!

But alien sweat, but serum or tempest of mildness, decaying or climbing, that, never!

Thrown, fine, I exhume myself, tumescent the mixture into which I hammer my way, legless, without adult clay, or arms, a needle caught in the great atom. . . . No! Never! Never yesterday! Never afterwards!

And from that, this satanic tubercle, this moral plesiosaurian molar, and these posthumous suspicions, this index, this bed, these tickets.

España, aparta de mí este cáliz

NIÑOS del mundo
si cae España – digo, es un decir –
si cae
del cielo abajo su antebrazo que asen,
en cabestro, dos láminas terrestres;
niños, ¡qué edad la de las sienes cóncavas!
¡qué temprano en el sol lo que os decía!
¡qué pronto en vuestro pecho el ruido anciano!
¡qué viejo vuestro 2 en el cuaderno!

¡Niños del mundo, está
la madre España con su vientre a cuestas;
está nuestra maestra con sus férulas,
está madre y maestra,
cruz y madera, porque os dió la altura,
vértigo y división y suma, niños;
está con ella, padres procesales!

Si cae – digo, es un decir – si cae
España, de la tierra para abajo,
niños, ¡cómo vais a cesar de crecer!

Spain, Take This Chalice from Me

CHILDREN of the world, if Spain falls – I say it for the sake of argument – if she falls from the sky let her forearm be seized in a sling by two terrestrial sheets; children, what an age, that of the concave temples! How early in the sun, that which I told you! How soon the old noise in your chest! How old your figure 2 in the notebook!

Children of the world, mother Spain is burdened by her womb; she is our mistress who canes, is mother and mistress, cross and wood, because she gave you height, vertigo, division and addition, children; it rests with her, processal parents!

If she falls – I say it for the sake of argument – if Spain falls downwards from the earth, children, how you are going to stop

¡cómo va a castigar el año al mes!
¡cómo van a quedarse en diez los dientes,
en palote el diptongo, la medalla en llanto!
¡Cómo va el corderillo a continuar
atado por la pata al gran tintero!
¡Cómo vais a bajar las gradas del alfabeto
hasta la letra en que nació la pena!

Niños,
hijos de los guerreros, entretanto
bajad la voz, que España está ahora mismo repartiendo
la energía entre el reino animal,
las florecillas, los cometas, y los hombres.
¡Bajad la voz, que está
con su rigor, que es grande, sin saber
qué hacer, y está en su mano
la calavera hablando y habla y habla,
la calavera, aquélla de la trenza,
la calavera, aquélla de la vida!

Bajad la voz, os digo;
bajad la voz, el canto de las sílabas, el llanto
de la materia y el rumor menor de las pirámides, y aun

growing! How the year will punish the month! How your teeth will remain in tens, the diphthong in a pen stroke, the medal in tears! How the little lamb will go on tied by the leg to the great inkwell! How you will descend the steps of the alphabet to the letter where grief was born!

Children, sons of warriors, meanwhile lower your voice, for Spain is at this moment distributing energy among the animal kingdom, the small flowers, the comets and the men. Lower your voice, for she remains with her rigour, which is great, not knowing what to do; and in her hand the skull is speaking, and it speaks and speaks; the skull with its plaits, the skull of life!

Lower your voice, I tell you: lower your voice, the song of the syllables, the weeping of matter, and the lessened rumour of the

el de las sienes que andan con dos piedras!
¡Bajad el aliento, y si
el antebrazo baja,
si las férulas suenan, si es la noche,
si el cielo cabe en dos limbos terrestres,
si hay ruido en el sonido de las puertas,
si tardo,
si no veis a nadie, si os asustan
los lápices sin punta, si la madre
España cae – digo, es un decir –
salid, niños del mundo; id a buscarla! . . .

Himno a los voluntarios de la República

VOLUNTARIO de España, miliciano
de huesos fidedignos, cuando marcha a morir tu corazón,
cuando marcha a matar con su agonía
mundial, no sé verdaderamente
qué hacer, dónde ponerme; corro, escribo, aplaudo,
lloro, atisbo, destrozo, apagan, digo
a mi pecho que acabe, al bien, que venga,

pyramids; and even that of the temples of the head between two stones! Lower your breath, and if the forearm comes down, and the canes sound, if it is night, if there is room for the sky in two terrestrial limbos, if there is noise in the sound of the doors, if I am late, if you don't see anyone, if the blunted pencils scare you, if mother Spain falls – I say it for the sake of argument – go out, children of the world: go and search for her! . . .

*Hymn to the Volunteers of the Republic**

VOLUNTEER of Spain, militiaman, your bones worthy of faith, when your heart marches to die, when it marches to kill with its world-wide agony, I truly do not know what to do, where to stand; I rush about, I write, I applaud, I cry, I peep, I destroy, they extinguish things, I say to my heart that it's over, to the good that

*Translated by John Hill.

y quiero desgraciarme;
descúbrome la frente impersonal hasta tocar
el vaso de la sangre, me detengo,
detienen mi tamaño esas famosas caídas de arquitecto
con las que se honra el animal que me honra;
refluyen mis instintos a sus sogas,
humea ante mi tumba la alegría
y, otra vez, sin saber qué hacer, sin nada, déjame,
desde mi piedra en blanco, déjame,
solo,
cuadrumano, más acá, mucho más lejos,
al no caber entre mis manos tu largo rato extático,
quiebro contra tu rapidez de doble filo
mi pequeñez en traje de grandeza!

Un día diurno, claro, atento, fértil
¡oh bienio, el de los lóbregos semestres suplicantes,
por el que iba la pólvora mordiéndose los codos!
¡oh dura pena y más duros pedernales!
¡oh frenos los tascados por el pueblo!
Un día prendió el pueblo su fósforo cautivo, oró de
cólera

it comes, and I try to disgrace myself; I uncover my impersonal forehead till I touch the blood-vessel, I restrain myself, my size is obstructed by those famous falls of the architect, along with those which the animal who honours me honours; my instincts swirl back to their ropes, joy smokes before my tomb, and, another time, not knowing what to do, without anything, leave me, from my stone in its whiteness, leave me, alone, a quadruped human, closer, much further off, unable to hold in my hands your long ecstatic time, I break my grandeur-clad pettiness against your double-edged speed.

One diurnal, clear, intent, fertile day, Oh biennale, you of the lugubrious and supplicant half-years, through which went gun-powder biting its elbows! Oh bitter pain, and flints more bitter still! Oh bits clenched in the people's teeth! One day the people struck their captive match, prayed in anger and, in supremacy, full,

y soberanamente pleno, circular,
cerró su natalicio con manos electivas;
arrastraban candado ya los déspotas
y en el candado, sus bacterias muertas . . .
¿Batallas? ¡No! ¡Pasiones! Y pasiones precedidas
de dolores con rejas de esperanzas,
de dolores de pueblo con esperanzas de hombres!
¡Muerte y pasión de paz, las populares!
¡Muerte y pasión guerreras entre olivos, entendámosnos!
Tal en tu aliento cambian de agujas atmosféricas los
vientos
y de llave las tumbas en tu pecho,
tu frontal elevándose a primera potencia de martirio.

El mundo exclama: «¡Cosas de españoles!» Y es verdad.
Consideremos,
durante una balanza, a quema ropa,
a Calderón, dormido sobre la cola de un anfibio muerto
o a Cervantes, diciendo: «Mi reino es de este mundo, pero
también del otro»: ¡punta y filo en dos papeles!
Contemplemos a Goya, de hinojos y rezando ante un
espejo,
a Coll, el paladín en cuyo asalto cartesiano

circular, shut their nativities with the hands of choice; then the despots dragged their padlock, and in the padlock, their dead bacteria. Battles? No! Passions! And passions preceded by griefs with bars of hopes, the people's griefs with the hopes of men! Death and passion of peace, the people! Death and passion at war amidst olives, let us understand each other! Thus in your breath the winds change their atmospheric needles, and in your breast tombs change key, the bone of your brow raising itself to the first power of martyrdom.

The world exclaims: 'These are Spanish things.' And it is true. Let us consider, during a [point of] balance, point-blank, Calderón, asleep on the tail of a dead amphibian, or Cervantes, saying: 'My kingdom is of this world, but also of the next': the sword's point and edge on two bits of paper! Let us contemplate Goya, kneeling in prayer before a mirror, Coll, the paladin in whose Cartesian

tuvo un sudor de nube el paso llano
o a Quevedo, ese abuelo instantáneo de los dinamiteros
o a Cajal, devorado por su pequeño infinito, o todavía
a Teresa, mujer, que muere porque no muere
o a Lina Odena, en pugna en más de un punto con
    Teresa . . .
(Todo acto a voz genial viene del pueblo
y va hacia él, de frente o transmitidos
por incesantes briznas, por el humo rosado
de amargas contraseñas sin fortuna.)
Así tu criatura, miliciano, así tu exangüe criatura,
agitada por una piedra inmóvil,
se sacrifica, apártase,
decae para arriba y por su llama incombustible sube,
sube hasta los débiles,
distribuyendo españas a los toros,
toros a las palomas . . .

Proletario que mueres de universo, ¡en qué frenética
    armonía
acabará tu grandeza, tu miseria, tu vorágine impelente,
tu violencia metódica, tu caos teórico y práctico, tu gana

attack the straight step had a sweat of clouds, or Quevedo, that instantaneous grandfather of the dynamiters, or Cajal, devoured by his small infinity, or still Teresa, woman, who dies because she does not die, or Lina Odena, battling on more than one issue against Teresa. . . . (Every decently-voiced action comes from, and goes back towards, the people, directly or transmitted by incessant fragments, by the pink smoke of bitter, luckless passwords.) So your child, militiaman, your bloodless child, stirred by a motionless stone, sacrifices itself, vanishes, falls away upwards and rises up through its incombustible flame, climbs to the weak, giving Spains to bulls, bulls to doves.

Proletarian dying of the universe, in what frenetic harmony will be ended your greatness, your misery, your outward-spinning vortex, your methodical violence, your practical and theoretical

dantesca, españolísima, de amar, aunque sea a traición, a
tu enemigo!
¡Liberador ceñido de grilletes,
sin cuyo esfuerzo hasta hoy continuaría sin asas la
extensión,
vagarían acéfalos los clavos,
antiguo, lento, colorado, el día,
nuestros amados cascos, insepultos!
¡Campesino caído con tu verde follaje por el hombre,
con la inflexión social de tu meñique,
con tu buey que se queda, con tu física,
también con tu palabra atada a un palo
y tu cielo arrendado
y con la arcilla inserta en tu cansancio
y la que estaba en tu uña, caminando!
¡Constructores
agrícolas, civiles y guerreros,
de la activa, hormigueante eternidad: estaba escrito
que vosotros haríais la luz, entornando
con la muerte vuestros ojos;
que, a la caída cruel de vuestras bocas,
vendrá en siete bandejas la abundancia, todo
en el mundo será de oro súbito

chaos, your Dantesque and extremely Spanish desire to betray your enemy with love! Liberator in handcuffs, without whose effort unholdable expansion would continue today, nails would wander headless, the day ancient, slow, reddened, our beloved helmets unburied! Peasant, fallen along with your green foliage for man, with the social inflection of your little finger, with your ox standing with his heels dug in, with your physics, and also with your word lashed to a pole, and your rented sky and with clay driven into your weariness and sticking under your nail, marching! Builders, labourers, civilians and soldiers of active teeming eternity: it was written that you would make light, shielding your eyes with death; so that, in the cruel fall of your mouths, abundance would come on seven platters, everything in the world would

y el oro,
fabulosos mendigos de vuestra propia secreción de sangre,
y el oro mismo será entonces de oro!

¡Se amarán todos los hombres
y comerán tomados de las puntas de vuestros pañuelos
  tristes
y beberán en nombre
de vuestras gargantas infaustas!
Descansarán andando al pie de esta carrera,
sollozarán pensando en vuestras órbitas, venturosos
serán y al son
de vuestro atroz retorno, florecido, innato,
ajustarán mañana sus quehaceres, sus figuras soñadas y
  cantadas!
¡Unos mismos zapatos irán bien al que asciende
sin vías a su cuerpo
y al que baja hasta la forma de su alma!
¡Entrelazándose hablarán los mudos, los tullidos andarán!
¡Verán, ya de regreso, los ciegos
y palpitando escucharán los sordos!
¡Sabrán los ignorantes, ignorarán los sabios!
¡Serán dados los besos que no pudisteis dar!

suddenly turn to gold, and the gold, legendary beggars of your own secretion of blood, and the gold would then itself be golden!

All men will love each other and eat together from the corners of your sad handkerchiefs and will drink together in the name of your accursed throats! They will rest going to the foot of this race, they will weep thinking of your orbits, they will be fortunate, and to the sound of your terrifying return, in flower, innate, they will settle up their daily affairs, their dreamed and sung figures! The same shoes will fit the man who ascends without roads to his body, and the man who climbs down to the form of his soul! Embracing, the dumb will speak, the lame will go! Returning, the blind will see, and quivering, the deaf will hear! The fools shall be wise and the wise shall be as fools! The kisses that could not be given will

¡Sólo la muerte morirá! ¡La hormiga
traerá pedacitos de pan al elefante encadenado
a su brutal delicadeza; volverán
los niños abortados a nacer perfectos, espaciales
y trabajarán todos los hombres,
engendrarán todos los hombres,
comprenderán todos los hombres!

¡Obrero, salvador, redentor nuestro,
perdónanos, hermano, nuestras deudas!
Como dice un tambor al redoblar, en sus adagios:
¡qué jamás tan efímero, tu espalda!
¡qué siempre tan cambiante, tu perfil!

¡Voluntario italiano, entre cuyos animales de batalla
un león abisinio va cojeando!
¡Voluntario soviético, marchando a la cabeza de tu pecho
universal!
¡Voluntarios del sur, del norte, del oriente
y tú, el occidental, cerrando el canto fúnebre del alba!
¡Soldado conocido, cuyo nombre
desfila en el sonido de un abrazo!

be given! Only death will die! The ant will carry crumbs of bread to the elephant chained in his brutal delicacy; aborted children will be reborn perfect, spatial, and all men will work, all men will beget children, all men will understand!

Workman, saviour, our redeemer, brother, forgive us our trespasses! Thus speaks the rolling of the drum in its adagios: 'That never so ephemeral your back! That ever so changing, your profile.'

Italian volunteer, amongst whose animals of battle limps the Abyssinian lion! Soviet volunteer, marching at the head of your universal heart! Volunteers of the north, of the south, of the east, and you, western man, closing the funereal canto of the dawn! Known soldier, whose name marches in the sound of an embrace!

Combatiente que la tierra criará, armándote
de polvo,
calzándote de imanes positivos,
vigentes tus creencias personales,
distinto de carácter, íntima tu férula,
el cutis inmediato,
andándote tu idioma por los hombros
y el alma coronada de guijarros!
¡Voluntario fajado de tu zona fría,
templada o tórrida,
héroes a la redonda,
víctima en columna de vencedores:
en España, en Madrid, están llamando
a matar, voluntarios de la vida!

¡Porque en España matan, otros matan
al niño, a su juguete que se para,
a la madre Rosenda esplendorosa,
al viejo Adán que hablaba en alta voz con su caballo
y al perro que dormía en la escalera.
Matan al libro, tiran a sus verbos auxiliares,
a su indefensa página primera!
Matan el caso exacto de la estatua,
al sabio, a su bastón, a su colega,

Warrior whom the earth will create, arming yourself with dust, shod with positive magnets, your personal beliefs at work, your character clear-cut, your intimate walking-stick, immediate skin, your speech going on your shoulders, and your soul crowned with pebbles! Volunteer swathed in your cold, temperate, or torrid zone, heroes all around, victim in a column of conquerors: in Spain, in Madrid, you are called to kill, volunteers of life!

For they kill in Spain, others kill the boy, and his toy which comes to a stop, replendent mother Rosenda, old Adam who used to talk aloud to his horse, the dog that used to sleep on the stairs. They kill the book, fire on its auxiliary verbs, on its defenceless first page. They kill the exact declension of the statue, the wise man, his stick, his colleague, the barber next door – all right he might

al barbero de al lado – me cortó posiblemente,
pero buen hombre y, luego, infortunado;
al mendigo que ayer cantaba enfrente,
a la enfermera que hoy pasó llorando,
al sacerdote a cuestas con la altura tenaz de sus rodillas . . .

Voluntarios,
por la vida, por los buenos, matad
a la muerte, matad a los malos!
¡Hacedlo por la libertad de todos,
del explotado y del explotador,
por la paz indolora – la sospecho
cuando duermo al pie de mi frente
y más cuando circulo dando voces –
y hacedlo, voy diciendo,
por el analfabeto a quien escribo,
por el genio descalzo a su cordero,
por los camaradas caídos,
sus cenizas abrazadas al cadáver de un camino!
Para que vosotros,
voluntarios de España y del mundo, viniérais,
soñé que era yo bueno, y era para ver
vuestra sangre, voluntarios . . .
De esto hace mucho pecho, muchas ansias,

have cut me, but he was a good man, and, soon, an unlucky one, the beggar who yesterday was singing opposite, the nurse who today passed by in tears, the priest staggering under the stubborn height of his knees . . .

Volunteers, for life, for good men, kill death, kill the evil ones! Do it for the freedom of all, of the exploited and the exploiter, for painless peace – I sense it when I sleep at the foot of my forehead and more when I go round giving voice – and do it, I say to you, for the illiterate to whom I write, for the barefoot genius with his flocks, for the fallen comrades, their ashes embracing the corpse of a road. That you, volunteers of Spain and the world, should come, I dreamed that I was good, and that was that I should see your blood, volunteers. It's a long heart's time ago,

muchos camellos en edad de orar.
Marcha hoy de vuestra parte el bien ardiendo,
os siguen con cariño los reptiles de pestaña inmanente
y, a dos pasos, a uno,
la dirección del agua que corre a ver su límite antes que
arda.

ago many griefs and camels of an age to pray. Today burning good marches on your side, and the reptiles of immanent eyelids follow you with love and two steps behind, one step away, the direction of water rushing to see its limits before it burns.

MARTÍN ADÁN (b. 1908)

Stentato in ischerzo

No llamo desque nací,
vida mía,
sino a ti. – Encina

Mourir ainsi, mon corps, mourir serait le rêve. – Verhaeren

– ¡DAME mi eternidad, tú que la tienes,
Ánima y mano mía enajenada,
Alud de aserto, carne arrebatada,
Nombre ninguno, hueso que mantienes! . . .

– ¡Eterno, mío, yo, raptos, rehenes . . .
El amor que me tengo y se traslada! . . .
¡Cabezal parca parca inerme, y cabezada,
Para aurora del halo de las sienes! . . .

– ¡Ay, hado y nada soy . . . sino de ardores . . . !
¡El sueño, efímero! . . . ¡algún alma mía! . . .
¡Eros, divo, entre túes y grosores! . . .

*Stentato in ischerzo**

Since I was born
I only call you.
So to die, my body, would be a dream

GIVE me my eternity, you who have it, soul and my enraptured hand, avalanche of assertion, the frenzied flesh, no name, bone which supports! . . .

Eternal, mine, I, raptures, hostages. . . . The love I have for myself, and transports itself. . . . Chariot-head fury fury disarmed and charioted, for the aurora of the halo of the brows! . . .

Ay! I am destiny and nothing . . . fate of ardours . . . ! The dream, ephemeral! . . . sometime my soul! . . . Eros, god, between yours and thicknesses! . . .

*Translated by John Hill.

– ¡Más quiero eternidad, sea así poca,
Que es eterna, y consciente a oído y boca
Perder y perseguir de mi elegía!

Senza tempo. Afrettando ad libitum

Quo non adveniam? – Juvenal
Cette morte apparent, en qui revient-la vie,
Frèmit, riuvre les veux, m'illumine et me morde.
– Valéry

– ¡Mi estupor! . . . ¡quédateme . . . quedo . . . cada
Instante! . . . ¡mi agnición . . . porque me pasmo! . . .
¡Mi epifanía! . . . cegóme orgasmo! . . .
¡Vaciedad de mi pecho desbordada! . . .

– ¡Básteme infinidad de mi emanada . . .
Catástasis allende el metaplasmo! . . .
¡Que no conciba . . . yo el que me despasmo . ..
Entelequia . . . testigo de mi nada! . . .

– ¡Mi éxtasis . . . estáteme! . . . ¡inste ostento
Que no instó en este instante! . . . ¡tú consistas
En mí, o seas dios que se me añade! . . .

But I desire eternity, be it ever so small, which is eternal, and conscious to ear and mouth to lose and chase my elegy.

*Senza tempo. Afrettando ad libitum**

My awe! . . . stay with me . . . slowly . . . every instant! . . . my agnition! . . . because I'm overwhelmed! . . . My epiphany! . . . Orgasm blinded me! . . . The emptiness of my breast overflowed!

Let it suffice, the infinity emanated from me. . . . Catastasis beyond metaplasm! . . . Let me not conceive . . . I, the one who strips my wonder from myself. . . . Entelechy . . . witness of my nothingness! . . .

My ecstasy . . . stay with me! . . . urge I display which did not urge in this instant! may you consist in me, or may you be god who adds up in me! . . .

*Translated by John Hill.

– ¡Divina vanidad . . . donde me ausento
De aquel que en vano estoy . . . donde me distas,
Yo Alguno! . . . ¡dúrame, Mi Eternidad!

Divine vanity . . . where I absent myself from that which I am in vain . . . whence you distance me, I Someone! . . . Last out for me, My Eternity!

CARLOS GERMÁN BELLI (b. 1927)

En vez de humanos dulces

EN vez de humanos dulces,
por qué mis mayores no existieron
cual piedra, cual olmo, cual ciervo,
que aparentemente no disciernen
y jamás a uno dicen:
«no dejes este soto,
en donde ya conoces
de dó viene el cierzo, adó va el noto.»

Poema

FRUNCE el feto su frente
y sus cejas enarca cuando pasa
del luminoso vientre
al albergue terreno,
do se truecan sin tasa
la luz en niebla, la cisterna en cieno;
y abandonar le duele al fin el claustro,
en que no rugen ni cierzo ni austro,
y verse aun despeñado

Instead of Sweet Humans

INSTEAD of sweet humans, why did my ancestors not exist as stone, as elm, as deer, who apparently do not discriminate and never tell one: 'Don't leave this thicket, in which you already know from where the north wind comes, to where the south wind goes.'

Poem

THE foetus puckers its forehead and arches its eyebrows when it passes from luminous womb into its earthly lodging, where, without measure, light changes to mist, the cistern to slime. And at last it pains it to abandon the cloister in which neither north nor south wind howls; and it sees itself further precipitated from the

desde el más alto risco,
cual un feto no amado,
por tartamudo o cojo o manco o bizco.

¡Oh Hada Cibernética! . . .

¡OH Hada Cibernética!, ya líbranos
con tu eléctrico seso y casto antídoto,
de los oficios hórridos humanos,
que son como tizones infernales
encendidos de tiempo inmemorial
por el crudo secuaz de las hogueras;
amortigua, ¡oh señora!, la presteza
con que el cierzo sañudo y tan frío
bate las nuevas aras, en el humo enhiestas,
de nuestro cuerpo ayer, cenizas hoy,
que ni siquiera pizca gozó alguna,
de los amos ni ingas privativo
el ocio del amor y la sapiencia.

highest crag, as a foetus unloved, as a stutterer, a cripple, maimed, or cross-eyed.

Oh Cybernetic Fairy! . . .

OH cybernetic fairy, with your electric brain and chaste antidote, free us from the hideous human functions that are like infernal cinders kindled from time immemorial by the cruel servant of the bonfires: cushion, oh lady, the haste with which the north wind, furious and so cold, flails the new altars, erect in the smoke of our yesterday's body, ashes today which not a single crumb of the idleness of love and wisdom ever enjoyed, the exclusive right of neither masters nor Incas.

PUERTO RICO

LUIS LLORÉNS TORRES (1878–1944)

Bolívar

POLÍTICO, militar, héroe, orador y poeta.
Y en todo, grande. Como las tierras libertadas por él.
Por él, que no nació hijo de patria alguna,
sino que muchas patrias nacieron hijas de él.

Tenía la valentía del que lleva una espada,
tenía la cortesía del que lleva una flor.
Y, entrando en los salones, arrojaba la espada.
Y, entrando en los combates, arrojaba la flor.

Los picos del Ande no eran más a sus ojos
que signos admirativos de sus arrojos.
Fue un soldado poeta. Un poeta soldado.

Y cada pueblo libertado
era una hazaña del poeta y era un poema de soldado.
¡Y fue crucificado! . . .

Bolívar

POLITICIAN, soldier, hero, orator and poet. And great in all these things. Like the lands he liberated, he who was not born the son of any land, though many nations were born of him.

He had the courage of the man who wears a sword, he had the courtesy of the man who wears a flower. And when he entered the salons, he threw away the sword. And when he entered into battle he threw away the flower.

The peaks of the Andes were to his eyes no more than signs of admiration for his fearlessness. He was a soldier poet. A poet soldier.

And every liberated people was the poet's feat of arms and the soldier's poem. And he was crucified . . . !

Maceo

MÚSCULO que despierta de una raza dormida . . .
Sonoro escape de una fuerza comprimida . . .
Nos anuncia con el verbo de su vida
las epopeyas futuras de una legión no conocida.

Del Africa, que en el Globo pinta un gran corazón,
él se trajo el aguerrido corazón de león,
que el pecho le golpeaba bajo el negro vellón,
y era en cada honda palpitación,

la campana cubana de la revolución.
– Con los ojos sobre el pañuelo de esta elegía,
recordad, cubanos, recordad que un día,

mientras en las ciudades la molicie dormía,
una luz de la selva venía,
¡y el golpe de un hacha en la noche se oía! . . .

Maceo

THE awakening energy of a sleeping race. . . . Repressed strength bursting out with a loud thunder. . . . With the words of his life he points to the future epics of an unknown legion.

From Africa, that paints a great heart on the Globe, he brought his battle-scarred lion's heart with him, beating against his chest under the black fleece, and in every deep palpitation,

Was the Cuban revolutionary bell. 'With your eyes on the kerchief of this elegy, remember, Cubans, remember that one day,

While the soft ones slept in the city, a light was seen coming from the forest, and the sound of an axe-blow was heard in the night . . . !'

LUIS PALÉS MATOS (1898–1959)

Mulata-antilla

En ti ahora, mulata,
me acojo al tibio mar de las Antillas.
Agua sensual y lenta de melaza,
puerto de azúcar, cálida bahía,
con la luz en reposo
dorando la onda limpia,
y el soñoliento zumbo de colmena
que cuajan los trajines de la orilla.

En ti ahora, mulata,
cruzo el mar de las islas.
Eléctricos mininos de ciclones
en tus curvas se alargan y se ovillan,
mientras sobre mi barca va cayendo
la noche de tus ojos, pensativa.

En ti ahora, mulata . . .
¡oh despertar glorioso en las Antillas!
bravo color que el do de pecho alcanza,
música al rojo vivo de alegría,

Mulatta-Antilla

In you now, mulatta, I take shelter in the warm seas of the Antilles. Sensual and languorous molasses water, sugar port, warm bay, with the light at rest gilding the clean waves, and the dreamy buzzing of a beehive distilled from the coming and going on the shore.

In you now, mulatta, I cross the sea of the islands. Like cats, electrical cyclones stretch and curl in your curves, while the thoughtful night of your eyes is falling over my boat.

In you now, mulatta . . . oh glorious awakening of the Antilles! a noble colour the deep note attains, with the bright red music of

y calientes cantáridas de aroma
– limón, tabaco, piña –
zumbando a los sentidos
sus embriagadas voces de delicia.

Eres ahora, mulata,
todo el mar y la tierra de mis islas.
Sinfonía frutal cuyas escalas
rompen furiosamente en tu catinga.
He aquí en su verde traje la guanábana
con sus finas y blandas pantaletas
de muselina; he aquí el caimito
con su leche infantil; he aquí la piña
con su corona de soprano . . . Todos
los frutos ¡oh mulata! tú me brindas,
en la clara bahía de tu cuerpo
por los soles del trópico bruñida.

Imperio tuyo, el plátano y el coco,
que apuntan su dorada artillería
al barco transeúnte que nos deja
su rubio contrabando de turistas.
En potro de huracán pasas cantando

joy, and warm scented Spanish-flies, – scent of lemon, tobacco, pineapple – their intoxicated voices of delight ringing in the ears.

Now, mulatta, you are all the sea and the land of my islands. Fruit-bearing symphony whose scales break with fury into your Negro smell. Here the custard-apple in its green suit, with its fine soft muslin breeches; here the star-apple with its infant's milk; here the pineapple with its soprano's crown . . . oh mulatta, you cheerfully offer me all the fruits, in the clear bay of your body burnished by tropical suns.

Your empire, the plantain-tree and the cocoa-palm, aiming their golden artillery at the passing boat that leaves behind its blonde tourist contraband. You ride past on a colt of the storm, singing

tu criolla canción, prieta walkiria,
con centelleante espuela de relámpagos
rumbo al verde Walhalla de las islas.

Eres inmensidad libre y sin límites,
eres amor sin trabas y sin prisas;
en tu vientre conjugan mis dos razas
sus vitales potencias expansivas.
Amor, tórrido amor de la mulata,
gallo de rin, azúcar derretida,
tabonuco que el tuétano te abrasa
con aromas de sándalo y de mirra.
Con voces del Cantar de los Cantares,
eres morena porque el sol te mira.
Debajo de tu lengua hay miel y leche
y unguento derramado en tus pupilas.
Como la torre de David, tu cuello,
y tus pechos gemelas cervatillas.
Flor de Sarón y lirio de los valles,
yegua de Faraón, ¡oh Sulamita!

your creole song, dusky valkyrie, with a sparkling spur of lightning, making for the green Valhalla of the islands.

You are a vast and limitless freedom, you are love without shackles or haste; in your womb my two races conjugate their vital generative power. Love, torrid love of the mulatta, rooster of rum, melted sugar, *tabonuco** that burns your marrow with aromas of sandalwood and myrrh. With words from the Song of Songs, you are brown because the sun watches over you. Beneath your tongue are honey and milk, and balsam poured over your pupils. Your neck like the tower of David, and your breasts twin musk-deer. Flower of Sharon and lily of the valley, Pharaoh's mare, oh Sulamite!

**tabonuco*: a Puerto Rican tree from whose trunk flows a resin with a smell like camphor that is used as incense in churches.

Cuba, Santo Domingo, Puerto Rico,
fogosas y sensuales tierras mías.
¡Oh los rones calientes de Jamaica!
¡Oh fiero calalú de Martinica!
¡Oh noche fermentada de tambores
del Haití impenetrable y voduista!
Dominica, Tortola, Guadalupe,
¡Antillas, mis Antillas!
Sobre el mar de Colón, aupadas todas,
sobre el Caribe mar, todas unidas,
soñando y padeciendo y forcejeando
contra pestes, ciclones y codicias,
y muriéndose un poco por la noche,
y otra vez a la aurora, redivivas,
porque eres tú, mulata de los trópicos,
la libertad cantando en mis Antillas.

El dolor desconocido

HOY me he dado a pensar en el dolor lejano
que sentirá mi carne, allá en sus aposentos
y arrabales remotos que se quedan a oscuras

Cuba, Santo Domingo, Puerto Rico, impetuous and sensual lands of mine. Oh the warm rums of Jamaica! Oh proud *calalú** of Martinique! Oh night fermented with drums in impenetrable voodooist Haiti! Dominica, Tortola, Guadalupe; Antilles, my Antilles! On Columbus's sea, still erect, on the Caribbean sea, all united; dreaming and suffering and struggling against fever, cyclone and greed, and dying a little at night, and restored again at dawn, because you, mulatta of the tropics, are liberty singing in my Antilles.

The Unknown Pain

TODAY I began to think about the distant pain that my flesh will feel, there in the rooms and suburbs hidden in their world of shadow

**calalú*: vegetable broth.

en su mundo de sombras y de instintos espesos.
A veces, de sus roncos altamares ocultos,
de esas inexploradas distancias, vienen ecos
tan vagos, que se pierden como ondas desmayadas
sobre una playa inmóvil de bruma y de silencio.
Son mensajes que llegan desesperadamente
del ignorado fondo de estos dramas secretos:
gritos de auxilio, voces de socorro, gemidos,
cual de un navío enorme que naufraga a lo lejos.

¡Oh esos limbos hundidos en tinieblas cerradas;
esos desconocidos horizontes internos
que subterráneamente se alargan en nosotros
distantes de las zonas de luz del pensamiento!

Quizás las más profundas tragedias interiores,
los más graves sucesos,
pasan en estos mudos arrabales de sombra
sin que llegue a nosotros el más vago lamento,
y tal vez, cuando estamos riendo a carcajadas,
somos el tenebroso escenario grotesco
de ese horrible dolor que no tiene respuesta
y cuya voz inútil se pierde sobre el viento.

and impenetrable instinct. Sometimes, from its hidden hoarse-voiced high sea, from those unexplored distances, come echoes so vague that they lose themselves like swooning waves on an immobile coast of mists and silence. They are messages that reach us in desperation from the unknown depths of these secret dramas; cries for help, voices, moans like those from a huge ship that is being wrecked in the distance.

Oh those limbos buried in thick mists; those unknown inner horizons that extend subterraneously within us far from those areas that are alight with thought!

Perhaps the most profound internal tragedies, the gravest events happen in those silent outskirts of shadow; not the slightest lament reaches us, and perhaps, when we are laughing raucously, we are the gloomy and grotesque backcloth for that awful pain that has no answer, and whose useless voice is lost upon the wind.

URUGUAY

JULIO HERRERA Y REISSIG (1875–1910)

La velada

LA cena ha terminado: legumbres, pan moreno
Y uvas aún lujosas de virginal rocío . . .
Rezaron ya. La luna nieva un candor sereno
y el lago se recoge con lácteo escalofrío.

El anciano ha concluído un episodio ameno
y el grupo desnúdase con un placer cabrío . . .
Entretanto, allá fuera, en un silencio bueno,
los campos demacrados encanecen de frío.

Lux canta. Lidé corre. Palemón anda en zancos.
Todos ríen . . . La abuela demándales sosiego.
Anfión el perro, inclina, junto al anciano ciego,

ojos de lazarillo, familiares y francos . . .
Y al són de las castañas que saltan en el fuego
palpitan al unísono sus corazones blancos.

The Soirée

DINNER is over: vegetables, brown bread and grapes still resplendent with virgin dew. . . . The prayers have been said. The moon casts a serene snowy light and the lake draws back with a milky shiver.

The old man has finished a pleasant anecdote and the group undresses with goatish pleasure. . . . Meanwhile, out there, in a generous silence, the emaciated fields turn white with the cold.

Lux sings. Lidé runs. Palaemon walks on stilts. Everyone is laughing. . . . The grandmother calls for quiet. Near the blind old man, Anfion the dog lowers

His guide's eyes, intimate and frank. . . . And at the sound of chestnuts jumping in the fire their pure hearts beat in unison.

La cena

EN repique de lata la merienda circula . . .
Aploma el artesano su crasura y secuestra
media mesa en canónicas dignidades de bula,
comiendo con la zurda, por aliviar la diestra . . .

Mientras la grey famélica los manjares adula,
en sabroso anticipo, sus colmillos adiestra;
y por merecimiento, casi más que por gula,
duplica su pitanza de col y de menestra . . .

Luego que ante el rescoldo sus digestiones hipa,
sumido en la enrulada neblina de su pipa,
arrullan, golosinas domésticas de invierno:

la Hormiga y Blanca Nieves, Caperuza y el Lobo . . .
Y la prole apollada, bajo el manto materno,
choca de escalofríos, en un éxtasis bobo.

The Evening Meal

THE food goes round the table in a clamour of tin plates . . . . The artisan draws his fat body erect, and takes over half the table with grave canonical pronouncements like papal bulls, eating with his left hand, to relieve his right . . .

While the ravenous flock gloats in savoury anticipation on the morsels from the table, they grind their teeth; and more for merit than for gluttony, he doubles their ration of cabbage and broth . . .

After he has belched out what he has digested before the hot embers, enveloped in the swirling smoke from his pipe, domestic winter delicacies lull them:

The Travelling Ant and Snow White, Red Riding Hood and the Wolf. . . . And the coddled offspring, beneath the maternal cloak, jostle shivering in a foolish ecstasy.

Decoración heráldica

Señora de mis pobres homenajes.
Débote siempre amar aunque me ultrajes.
– Góngora

SOÑÉ que te encontrabas junto al muro
glacial donde termina la existencia,
paseando tu magnífica opulencia
de doloroso terciopelo oscuro.

Tu pie, decoro del marfil más puro,
hería, con satánica inclemencia,
las pobres almas, llenas de paciencia,
que aún se brindaban a tu amor perjuro.

Mi dulce amor que sigue sin sosiego,
igual que un triste corderito ciego,
la huella perfumada de tu sombra,

buscó el suplicio de tu regio yugo,
y bajo el raso de tu pie verdugo
puse mi esclavo corazón de alfombra.

Heraldic Declaration

Oh lady, who art the object of my attentions.
I shall always love you though you rebuff me.

I DREAMED that you were next to the icy wall where existence ends, displaying as you walked your opulent magnificence of pained dark velvet.

Your foot, an honour in purest ivory, with satanic pitilessness wounded the poor patient souls who still offered themselves up to your perjured love.

My gentle love, which like a sad little blind lamb, tirelessly follows the mark of your shadow's perfumed step,

Sought the torment of your regal yoke, and I placed my enslaved heart as a carpet beneath your satin executioner's foot.

EMILIO FRUGONI (1880–1969)

El círculo

TODOS nos vamos; pero queda todo.
No retornamos más a nuestro puerto.
Se fueron para siempre los que han muerto.
La flor que cae se descompone en lodo.

En ese lodo, al fin, bajo otro modo,
halla la esencia de la flor su huerto.
Por el aire, al morir, con rumbo incierto
iremos en los brazos del gran Todo.

Retornaremos, pero sin nosotros.
La sustancia inmortal cambia de forma
y unos se van para que vengan otros.

Es circular la cósmica avenida,
pero sin apartarse de su norma
nuestras vidas se funden en la Vida.

The Circle

WE all leave; but everything remains. We do not return again to our port. Those who have died have gone for ever. The flower that falls decomposes into mud.

Eventually, in another form, the essence of the flower finds its garden in that mud. When we die, we shall go through the air, with uncertain course, in the arms of the great Everything.

We shall return, but without ourselves. The immortal substance changes form and some go so that others may come.

The cosmic avenue is circular, yet without moving outside its pattern our lives fuse with Life.

Aventura

SOBRE la loma, envuelto en la mañana
– océano de luz que el campo inunda –
quiebro con mis rodillas la coyunda
de toda obligación civil y urbana.

Vuela en mi corazón una campana
y el alma entera se me va errabunda
huyendo de la cárcel ciudadana.

Aquí otra vida empieza.
No hay ayer ni mañana. Sólo siento
que el viento a una aventura me convida.
Y sin volver siquiera la cabeza
me alejo, arrebatado por el viento,
de la ciudad en el confín perdida,
donde quedan velando en mi aposento
todas las amarguras de mi vida.

Que encontraré cuando retorne el viento.

Adventure

ON the hillock, wrapped in the morning – an ocean of light that floods the countryside – I break with my knees the ties of all civil and urban duties.

A bell floats in my heart and my whole spirit leaves me, wandering, fleeing from the prison of the city.

Here another life begins. There is neither yesterday nor tomorrow. I only feel that the wind is inviting me to take part in an adventure. And without even turning my head I walk away, carried off by the wind, away from the city lost on the horizon, where all my life's bitter moments are waiting in my room.

And I shall find them when the wind turns back.

DELMIRA AGUSTINI (1886–1914)

Otra estirpe

Eros, yo quiero guiarte, Padre ciego . . .
pido a tus manos todopoderosas
¡su cuerpo excelso derramado en fuego
sobre mi cuerpo desmayado en rosas!

La eléctrica corola que hoy despliego
brinda el nectario de un jardín de Esposas;
para sus buitres en mi carne entrego
todo un enjambre de palomas rosas.

Da a las dos sierpes de su abrazo, crueles,
mi gran tallo febril . . . Absintio, mieles,
viérteme de sus venas, de su boca . . .

¡Así tendida, soy un surco ardiente
donde puede nutrirse la simiente
de otra Estirpe sublimemente loca!

Another Race

Eros, blind Father, let me guide you. . . . I ask your all-powerful hands for his sublime body, poured burning over my body swooning amid roses!

The electric corolla that I unfold today yields the nectar of a garden of Wives; in my flesh I deliver up to his vultures a whole swarm of pink doves.

Give my long febrile stem to the two cruel serpents of his embrace. . . . Absinthe, honeys, pour me from his veins, from his mouth . . .

Lying here in this way, I am an ardent furrow where the seed of another sublimely mad race can be nourished!

CARLOS SABAT ERCASTY (b. 1887)

from *Los adioses*

Interludios al modo antiguo

LVI

FECUNDO en mí las excesivas ilusiones,
y este soñar las cosas y verlas trasmutadas
por mi luz, y el correr y volar, las aladas
quimeras de hombre que se suben de mis prisiones.

Es como un juego, a veces, creer en las visiones
fantásticas, y levantar los sueños y las encantadas
formas de un pensamiento vivaz en superadas
ansias, y hacer el niño de repetidos dones.

¿Por qué no, si esas cosas al final caen solas,
si por adentro mueve la sombra enormes olas
que las más altas dichas pesadamente envuelven?

Ya ni siquiera el llanto tiene razón. Es tan sencillo
todo lo que nos pasa. Las ilusiones vuelven,
se van . . . Yo no las creo, pero me maravillo.

from *The Farewells*

Interludes in the Old Style

I FERTILIZE within me the immoderate illusions, and this dreaming of things, and seeing them transmuted by my light, and running and flying, the winged chimeras of men that rise out of my prisons.

Sometimes it is like a game to believe in fantastic visions, and build dreams and the enchanted forms of a lively thought within anxieties that are overcome, behaving like a child with many gifts.

Why not, if in the end these things fall by themselves; if within, the shadow moves enormous waves that the noblest fortunes heavily envelop?

Now not even tears are right. Everything that happens to us is so simple. The illusions turn and go away. . . . I do not believe in them, but I am struck with wonder.

from *Las sombras diáfanas*

LXXXVII

LOS astros son cabezas del Uno innumerable,
las ideas del Ser en el Ser sumergidas,
esferas del amor incendiadas de vidas,
escalas del deseo germinal e insondable.

Con el oído cósmico en la Tierra mudable
escucho el crecimiento, las formas ya nacidas,
las que aún van abriéndose, las que serán surgidas,
las que ni se soñaron en el Alma inmutable.

Nunca otra sinfonía, nunca otro arrobamiento! . . .
Oigo el fondo del fondo, que ya no es pensamiento,
lo que no tiene imagen y traspasa la esencia,

y a la vez que me embriagan las reales creaciones,
percibo, en el delirio de las revelaciones,
el nacimiento eterno de la inmortal potencia.

from *The Diaphanous Shadows*

THE stars are heads of the numberless One, ideas of Being submerged in Being, spheres of love alight with lives, steps of life-giving and fathomless desire.

I listen with my cosmic ear to growth on the changing Earth, the forms already born, those still emerging, those that shall have been born, those not even dreamed of in the unchanging Soul.

Never another symphony, never another rapture! . . . I hear the depths of the depths, that now is not thought, that has no image and transcends the essence,

And at the same time as the royal creations intoxicate me, I see, amid the delirium of revelations, the eternal birth of immortal potency.

LXXXVIII

Cuando, a veces, oprimo con mis nervios calientes,
mi propia vida cósmica, mi cuerpo y mi deseo,
como si descendiese donde ya no me veo,
en el Ser me perciben mis descensos videntes.

Atravieso los ciclos, los espacios ardientes,
y estoy, y en mis esencias me confirmo y me creo,
y en océanos diáfanos mi propio amor sondeo,
y aún más allá del caos me alcanzo, inmensamente.

Voy detrás de las órbitas, debajo de los mundos,
en planos del abismo cada vez más profundos,
en no pulsados tiempos, preuniversal, divino,

tras el velo insondable, tras la intención creadora,
tras el primer incendio de la primera aurora,
hasta el punto absoluto que subió mi destino.

When, from time to time, I subdue my own cosmic life, my body and my desire with my own burning nerves, my visionary descents see me in the Being, as if I were going where I can no longer see myself.

I cross the cycles, the burning spaces, and I exist; and in my essence I confirm and believe in myself, and in diaphanous oceans I explore my own love, and reach myself even further beyond chaos.

I go beyond the orbits, below worlds, on ever deeper levels of the abyss, in times without a pulse, pre-universal, divine,

Beyond the impenetrable veil, beyond the intention to create, beyond the first fire of the first dawn, until I reach the point in the absolute that my destiny ascended.

EMILIO ORIBE (b. 1893)

Las dos vertientes del tiempo

LOS cabellos de esa montaña
resplandecen de siglos
congelados.
Para este lado de ella,
y el otro,
es lo mismo; dos vertientes
de espejos verdes.
No me doy prisa,
Amo, desde un vértice temporal,
contemplar en mí dos vertientes de espejos.
Cuando quiero, digo:
uno es mi cuerpo;
el otro es mi pensamiento.

Y se me ocurre pensar:
uno es la cadena del hábito,
la sombra del ayer.
Otro es la libertad!

Allá voy!
Mi alma irá antes que los astros,

The Two Slopes of Time

THE hair of that mountain glistens with centuries, frozen.

On this side of it, and on the other, it is the same; two slopes of green mirrors.

I do not hurry; I love to contemplate further from a peak of time two slopes of mirrors. When I want to, I say;

One is my body; the other is my thought.

And it occurs to me to think: one is the chain of habit, the shadow of yesterday. The other is freedom!

There I go! My soul will go before the stars that it has vaguely

que ha entrevisto,
pues no lleva cadenas como ellos.
Y la eternidad me ha de ser futura
y nada más,
pues así lo cree el pensamiento,
en la infancia,
y éste es el único tiempo
en que somos profetas verdaderos.

Mas los cabellos del tiempo
resplandecen de siglos
congelados.

El poder de las cosas

CADA cosa
es un fragmento de tiempo
petrificado.

Para poseerla,
vano es proceder como la abeja
y en celdas ocultas
guardarla, junto a la miel de las categorías
o el concepto.

seen, for it does not wear chains like them. And eternity must lie in the future for me and that is all, because that is what thought believes, in infancy, and infancy is the only time when we are truly prophets.

But the hair of time glistens with centuries, frozen.

The Power of Things

EACH thing is a fragment of time, petrified.

In order to possess it, it is futile to imitate the bees and guard it in hidden cells, together with the honey of categories or concepts.

Las cosas se rebelarán
siempre
contra sus dueños.

Por eso en el umbral del mundo
se rebeló el ángel de las tinieblas,
arrastrando a los seres del paraíso;
porque los tres
                eran cuerpos;
                                es decir, cosas.
Los demás eran ángeles o ideas
y fueron fieles
                        puros,
                                    bienaventurados!

Things will always rebel against their masters.

That is why the angel of darkness rebelled at the threshold of the world, dragging the beings from paradise; for the three were bodies; things, that is. The rest were angels or ideas and were faithful, pure, blessed!

IDEA VILARIÑO (b. 1920)

Qué fue la vida

Qué fue la vida
qué
qué podrida manzana
qué sobra
qué deshecho.

Si era una rosa
si era
una nube dorada
y debió florecer
liviana
por el aire.

Si era una rosa si era
una llama feliz
si era cualquier cosa
que no pese
no duela
que se complazca en ser
cualquier cosa
cualquiera
que sea fácil
fácil.

What Was Life

What was life, what, what rotten apple, what leftover, what waste.

If it was a rose, if it was a golden cloud, and should have flowered, light, in the air.

If it was a rose, if it was a gay flame, if it was anything, weightless, that causes no pain, that is content to be, any thing, anything, that is easy, easy.

No pudo consistir en corredores
en madrugadas sórdidas
en asco
en tareas sin luz
en rutinas en plazos
no pudo ser
no pudo.

No eso
lo que fue
lo que es
el aire sucio
de la calle
el invierno
las faltas varias las
miserias
el cansancio

en un mundo desierto.

It could not have been made up of corridors, of sordid dawns, of revulsion, of unlit tasks, of routines, of credits, it could not have been, it could not.

Not that, what it was, what it is, the dirty air, of the street, the winter, the many errors, the miseries, exhaustion

In a deserted world.

VENEZUELA

ANDRÉS BELLO (1781–1865)

from *La agricultura de la zona tórrida*

¡SALVE, fecunda zona,
que al sol enamorado circunscribes
el vago curso, y cuanto ser se anima
en cada vario clima,
acariciada de su luz, concibes!
Tú tejes al verano su guirnalda
de granadas espigas; tú la uva
das a la hirviente cuba;
no de purpúrea fruta, o roja, o gualda,
a tus florestas bellas
falta matiz alguno; y bebe en ellas
aromas mil el viento;
y greyes van sin cuento
paciendo tu verdura, desde el llano
que tiene por lindero el horizonte,
hasta el erguido monte,
de inaccesible nieve siempre cano.

Tú das la caña hermosa,
de do la miel se acendra,
por quien desdeña el mundo los panales;

from *The Agriculture of the Torrid Zone*

HAIL, fertile region, who confine the wandering course of the lovesick sun, and give birth to all the beings that come to life in each of the varied climes caressed by its light! You weave for the summer her garland of ripe ears of corn; you give the grape to the boiling vat; not a single shade of purple, red or reseda fruit is absent from your beautiful forests, where the wind imbibes a thousand aromas, and countless flocks graze on your pastures, from the plain whose boundary is the horizon, to the noble inaccessible mountain always white-headed with snow.

You provide the fine cane from which is refined the molasses that makes the world discard the honeycomb; in coral jars you

tú, en urnas de coral, cuajas la almendra
que en la espumante jícara rebosa;
bulle carmín viviente en tus nopales,
que afrenta fuera al múrice de Tiro;
y de tu añil la tinta generosa
émula es de la lumbre del zafiro.
El vino es tuyo, que la herida agave
para los hijos vierte
del Anahuac feliz; y la hoja es tuya,
que, cuando de suave
humo en espiras vagarosas huya,
solazará el fastidio al ocio inerte.
Tu vistes de jazmines
el arbusto sabeo,
y el perfume le das, que, en los festines,
la fiebre insana templará a Lieo.
Para tus hijos la prócera palma
su vario feudo cría,
y el ananás sazona su ambrosía;
su blanco pan la yuca,
sus rubias pomas la patata educa;
y el algodón despliega al aura leve
las rosas de oro y el vellón de nieve.
Tendida para ti la fresca parcha

ripen the almond that overflows the foaming jar; in your cochineal trees bubbles a living carmine that would affront even the murex of Tyre, and the rich tint of your indigo emulates the splendour of the sapphire. Yours is the wine that the wounded agave spills for the children of fortunate Anahuac, and yours is the leaf that will relieve the boredom of sluggish leisure times as it disappears in drifting whorls of delicate smoke. You deck the Sabaean bush with jasmine and provide it with a scent that will soothe Lieo's insane passion at the feast. For your sons the noble palm brings forth its varied fee and the pineapple-tree ripens its ambrosia, the yucca-tree grows its white bread and the potato plant its golden fruit, and the cotton plant unfolds for gentle dawn the golden roses and the snowy fleece. The fresh passion-flowers are arranged for you in

en enramadas de verdor lozano,
cuelga de sus sarmientos trepadores
nectáreos globos y franjadas flores;
y para ti el maíz, jefe altanero
de la espigada tribu, hincha su grano;
y para ti el banano
desmaya al peso de su dulce carga:
el banano, primero
de cuantos concedió bellos presentes
Providencia a las gentes
del ecuador feliz con mano larga.
No ya de humanas artes obligado
el premio rinde opimo:
no es a la podadera, no al arado
deudor de su racimo:
escasa industria bástale, cual puede
hurtar a sus fatigas mano esclava:
crece veloz, y cuando exhausto acaba,
adulta prole en torno le sucede.

Mas ¡oh! ¡si cual no cede
el tuyo, fértil zona, a suelo alguno,
y como de natura esmero ha sido,
de tu indolente habitador la fuera!

lush green arbours, suspending from their climbing runners nectareal globes and fringed blooms; and for you the maize, arrogant chief of the eared tribe, swells its cob; and for you the banana palm faints beneath its sweet burden: the banana tree, first of many fine ones generously granted by Providence to the people of this happy equatorial region. Since it is not bound to human skills, it yields a rich prize; it is indebted for its bunches of fruit neither to the hook nor to the plough; it needs little cultivation, no more than the hand of a slave can steal from its labours; it grows quickly, and when it dies, exhausted, a fully grown progeny succeeds it in its turn.

But oh! if only your soil, fertile zone, which is bettered by none, were as industriously cared for by your indolent inhabitants as it

¡Oh! ¡si al falaz ruido
la dicha al fin supiese verdadera
anteponer, que del umbral le llama
del labrador sencillo,
lejos del necio y vano
fasto, el mentido brillo,
el ocio pestilente ciudadano!
¿Por qué ilusión funesta
aquellos que fortuna hizo señores
de tan dichosa tierra y pingüe y varia,
al cuidado abandonan
y a la fe mercenaria
las patrias heredades,
y en el ciego tumulto se aprisionan
de míseras ciudades,
de la ambición proterva
sopla la llama de civiles bandos,
o al patriotismo la desidia enerva;
de el lujo las costumbres atosiga,
y combaten los vicios
la incauta edad en poderosa liga?
No allí con varoniles ejercicios
se endurece el mancebo a la fatiga;

has been cared for by Nature! Oh! if only he could put true happiness before the false clamour, the false splendour, the rotten distractions of the city, that call him from the simple peasant home, far from the foolish and vain pomp! What pernicious illusion makes those whom Fortune made masters of such a fortunate, fertile and varied soil abandon the inherited lands at home to the care of others, to the mercenary faith, and imprison themselves within the blind tumult of wretched cities, where perverse ambition fans the flame of civilian factions and negligence enervates patriotism, where luxury poisons tradition and vices in powerful alliance challenge the years of innocence? It is not there that the young man hardens himself to toil through manful effort; instead he

mas la salud estraga en el abrazo
de pérfida hermosura,
que pone en almoneda los favores;
mas pasatiempo estima
prender aleve en casto seno el fuego
de ilícitos amores;
o embebecido le hallará la aurora
en mesa infame de ruinoso juego.
En tanto a la lisonja seductora
del asiduo amador fácil oído
de la consorte: crece
en la materna escuela
de la disipación y el galanteo
la tierna virgen, y al delito espuela
es antes el ejemplo que el deseo.
¿Y será que se formen de ese modo
los ánimos heróicos denodados
que fundan y sustentan los estados?
¿De la algazara del festín beodo,
o de los coros de liviana danza,
la dura juventud saldrá, modesta,
orgullo de la patria, y esperanza?

destroys his health in the embrace of a treacherous beauty, who sells her beauty to the highest bidder, but deems it amusing to light the perfidious flame of illicit love in a chaste breast; or dawn will find him drunk at a ruinous gaming table of ill fame. Meanwhile the seductive flattery of the assiduous lover is submissively heard by the consort: the tender virgin grows up in the maternal school of dissipation and flattery, and example rather than desire is the spur to sin. And can it be that the heroic spirits that establish and sustain nations should be thus formed? Will the strong, modest youth, pride and hope of the fatherland, emerge from the noise and laughter of the drunken feast and choruses of lascivious dances?

¿Sabrá con firme pulso
de la severa ley regir el freno;
brillar en torno aceros homicidas
en la dudosa lid verá sereno;
o animoso hará frente al genio altivo
del engreído mando en la tribuna,
aquel que ya en la cuna
durmió al arrullo del cantar lascivo,
que riza el pelo, y se unge, y se atavía
con femenil esmero,
y en indolente ociosidad el día,
o en criminal lujuria pasa entero?
No así trató la triunfadora Roma
las artes de la paz y de la guerra;
antes fió las riendas del estado
a la mano robusta
que tostó el sol y encalleció el arado;
y bajo el techo humoso campesino
los hijos educó, que el conjurado
mundo allanaron al valor latino.

Will the man who, when still in the cradle, slept through the murmur of bawdy songs, who curls his hair and perfumes himself and decks himself out with feminine care, and spends the whole day in idle distraction or in criminal lust, will he be able to hold the reins of a rigorous law with a strong hand? Will he remain calm when, in dubious battle, he sees murderous blades shining around him; or will he face up with courage to the haughty rage of those in power, grown conceited on the rostrum? Triumphant Rome did not treat the arts of peace and war in this way; rather did she entrust the reins of state to the robust hand burned by the sun and calloused by the plough, and educate under the smoking peasant roof the children that subdued the conspiring world to Latin valour.

El vino y el amor

– HIJO alado
de Dione,
no me riñas,
no te enojes,
si te digo
que los goces
no me tientan
de esos pobres
que mantienes
en prisiones.

Hechiceros,
¿quién lo niega?
son los ojos
de Filena;
pero mira
cómo el néctar
delicioso
de Madera
en la copa
centellea.

Tú prometes
bienandanza;
mas, ¿lo cumples?

Wine and Love

'WINGED son of Dione, don't rebuke me, don't be angry if I tell you that I am not tempted by the pleasures of those you hold imprisoned.

'Who will deny that Philena's eyes are bewitching? But look how Madeira's wine sparkles in the glass.

'You promise happiness, but do you keep your promise? A sly

¡Buena alhaja!
De los necios
que sonsacas,
unos llevan
calabazas;
otros viven
de esperanzas;
cuál se queja
de inconstancia;
cuál en celos
¡ay! se abrasa.
Baco alegre,
tú no engañas.

Hace el vino
maravillas;
esperanzas
vivifica;
da al cobarde
valentía;
a los rudos,
¡cómo inspira!
Aunque gruña
la avaricia,
tú le rompes
la alcancía.
Y otra cosa,
que a tu lima

one you are! Some of the fools that you entice are spurned, others live in hope; this one complains of inconstancy, that one, oh! is consumed with jealousy. You deceive no one, joyful Bacchus.

'Wine does wonderful things; it revives hope, gives courage to the coward; how it inspires the uncultured man! You break Greed's money box even though he grumbles. And what is more, nothing

no hay secretos
que resistan . . .

Los amantes
infelices
por las selvas
y jardines
andan siempre
de escondite;
cabizbajos
lloran, gimen;
mas, ¡cuán otro
quien te sirve!
dios amable
de las vides.
Compañeros
apercibe
que en su gozo
participen.
Canta, beben,
bullen, ríen. –

– Mas, Filena,
¿no tu mueve? –
– Niño alado,
vete, vete. –

remains hidden under your file . . .

'The unhappy lovers wander through woods and gardens, always hiding; downcast, they tremble and cry; but how different is he that serves you, gentle god of the vines. He summons companions to participate in his enjoyment. They sing, they drink, they bustle, they laugh.'

'But doesn't Philena excite you?' 'Go away, winged boy, go

– Sus miradas
inocentes,
sus amables
esquiveces . . . –
– ¿No te marchas,
alcahuete? . . . –
– Sus mejillas,
que parecen
frescas rosas
entre nieves . . . –
– Cupidillo,
no me tientes. –

– Sola ahora
por la calle
se pasea
de los sauces,
y las sombras
de la tarde
van cundiendo
por el valle.
Y la sigue
cierto amante
que maquina
desbancarte.

away.' 'Her shy glances, her gentle disdain . . . ' 'Aren't you leaving, you procurer?' 'Her cheeks that are like fresh roses amid snow.' 'Don't tempt me, little Cupid.'

'Alone now, she walks along the willow path, and evening's shadows spread through the valley. And a certain lover is following her and planning to supplant you.'

– ¿Tirsi acaso? –
– Tú los has dicho. –
– Oye, aguarda,
ya te sigo.
Compañeros,
me retiro.
Vuelo a verte,
dueño mío.

'Tirsi perhaps?' 'You have it.' 'Stop, wait, I understand you now. Friends, I am leaving. I fly to your side, my master.'

ANDRÉS ELOY BLANCO (1897–1955)

Buena como el pan

BUENA como el pan
y te lo dijeron
como si fueran a comerte,
como si tendieran la mesa del gesto
para almorzar con tu bondad.

Entonces me oliste
a desayuno de amor;
entonces tus manos
se desmigajaron
sobre la leche de tu cuerpo
y tu cuerpo
se tostó de piedad caliente
y tu corazón
se blanqueó para hacerse corazón de mi pan.

Y ése fue el octavo Sacramento
de tu blancura en mi Verbo
de tu bondad en mi Éxtasis,
de tu inminente traslación a mi sangre.

As Good as Bread

As good as bread, and they said it to you as if they were about to eat you, as if they were spreading the table of gestures to break their fast on your goodness.

I thought you smelled then like a breakfast of love; your hands crumbled at that time over the milk of your body and your body became brown with warm pity and your heart whitened, to become the heart of my bread.

And that was the Eighth Sacrament of your whiteness in my Word, of your goodness in my Ecstasy, of your imminent trans-

Y te apuraron mis poros
con un millón de hambres y un millón de sedes.

Ahora
sudé todos los odios y el alma no me pesa
más de lo que pesara tu pan entre mis manos
– Buena como el pan – y ahora
te tomo con el hambre de un niño sin pecado.

Coloquio bajo el ciprés

Y AHORA, en el crespúsculo, es la hora
de mirarnos las caras
con poco hablar y con decirlo todo,
seis ojos y tres ánimas,
la confluencia de todo en el silencio,
mi ser que se convoca, como el agua en el agua,
en un solo mirar mi turno entero,
mi vida entre mis tardes y tus albas,
porque es bueno pensar que cualquier día,
quizá muy pronto, sea para el ciprés mi alma

ference into my blood. And my pores consumed you with a million hungers and a million thirsts.

Now I have sweated out my hates and my soul weighs no more than would your bread in my hands – girl as good as bread – and now I take you with the hunger of a child without sin.

Conversation under the Cypress Tree

AND now, in the twilight, it is time to look into one another's face, talking little and saying everything, six eyes and three souls, everything gathered in the silence, my being, that, like water in the sea, takes into itself in a single glance the whole course of my life, between my evenings and your dawns; for it is good to think that any day, perhaps very soon, my soul will belong to the cypress

y en una tarde de las tardes mías
o en un amanecer de tus mañanas,
te apartes una gota de otra gota
para que entre en tus ojos mi última mirada.
Por eso, en este ocaso, ya es la hora
de entregarte mi lámpara,
ya nos llegó el momento
de que tu mano encienda la luz que se me apaga.
Mi luz, mi pobre luz a ti confío,
farol en tu pasillo, veladora en tu cama;
no digas que es linterna para encontrar a un Hombre
sino luz de sereno que ayude a los que pasan.
En las noches sin luna, cuélgala en el camino,
en las de tempestad ponla en la playa,
has de mi luz un hecho que ilumine tu mano
y de tu mano un hecho de tierra iluminada.

Y así como te doy el cuido de mi luz
y así como te pido cultivarla,
como te doy mi luz, te doy mi sombra,
sólo para tu amor y tu esperanza;
también la sombra puede cultivarse

and that in one of my evenings or in the dawn of one of your mornings, you might draw apart the drops so that my last look may penetrate your eyes. That is why, at this moment of decline, it is time to give my lamp into your care, for the moment has come for us when your hand must light the flame that is going out in me. I entrust my light to you, my poor light, a lantern along your corridor, a nightlight by your bed; don't say that it is a light to find a Man with, but that it is a night-watchman's light helping the passer-by. On moonless nights hang it by the road, on stormy nights put it on the beach; make out of my light something that will light your hand, and of your hand a piece of lighted ground.

And just as I give my light into your care and ask you to tend it, just as I give you my light I give you my shadow for your love and your hope only; shadows can also be cultivated if they

si se le da la vecindad del alma;
como se siembra un árbol en la tierra
puede sembrarse un sueño en la almohada.
Si hasta mi misma luz llega a faltarte,
mi sombra estará siempre detrás de tus pisadas.

Más que mi luz, tuya
mi sombra acostada,
no hay quien te la quite,
sombra no se apaga,
tuya para siempre;
hijo de mi alma,
la sombra es lo único
que no arrastra el agua.

are given a place near the heart; a dream can be sown in a pillow, just as a tree can be planted in the earth. Even if you should lose my light itself, my shadow will always be behind your footsteps.

More than my light, my sleeping shadow is yours, no one can take it away from you, the shadow that does not go out, it is yours for ever; child of my soul, the shadow is the only thing that water does not wash away.

RAFAEL CADENAS (b. 1930)

Derrota

YO que no he tenido nunca un oficio
que ante todo competidor me he sentido débil
que perdí los mejores títulos para la vida
que apenas llego a un sitio y ya quiero irme (creyendo que
mudarme es una solución)
que he sido negado anticipadamente y ayudado de manera
humillante y escarnecido por los más aptos

que me arrimo a las paredes para no caer del todo
que soy objeto de risa para mí mismo
que creí que mi padre era eterno
que he sido humillado por profesores de literatura
que un día pregunté en qué podía ayudar y la respuesta
fue una risotada
que no podré nunca formar un hogar, ni ser brillante, ni
triunfar en la vida
que he sido abandonado por muchas personas porque
casi no hablo
que tengo vergüenza por actos que no he cometido

Defeat

I WHO never had a trade, who have felt weak in the face of all competition, who lost the best claims to life, who scarcely arrive at a place before I want to leave (in the belief that moving on is a solution), who have been prematurely disowned and helped in a humiliating way and ridiculed by abler people,

I who cling to walls so that I do not fall completely, who am an object of laughter for myself, who believed that my father was eternal, who have been humiliated by teachers of literature, who was answered with a guffaw when once I asked how I could help, I who shall never build a home, nor sparkle, nor be a winner in life, who have been abandoned by many people because I hardly ever speak, who feel shame for acts I have not committed, who have

que poco me ha faltado para echar a correr por la calle
que he perdido un centro que nunca tuve
que me he vuelto el hazmerreír de mucha gente por vivir
en el limbo
que no encontraré nunca quien me soporte

que fui preterido en aras de personas más miserables que
yo
que seguiré todo le vida así y que el año entrante seré
muchas veces más burlado en mi ridícula ambición
que estoy cansado de recibir consejos de otros más
aletargados
que yo («Usted es muy quedado, avíspese, despierte»)
que nunca podré viajar a la India
que he recibido favores sin dar nada en cambio
que ando por la ciudad de un lado a otro como una pluma
que me dejo llevar por los otros

que no tengo personalidad ni quiero tenerla
que todo el día tapo mi rebelión
que no me he ido a las guerrillas

been close to starting to run down the street, who have lost a centre I never had, who have become the general laughing-stock because I live in limbo, who shall find no one to put up with me,

I who was ignored so that attention should be paid to those more abject than myself, who shall carry on my whole life like this and who next year will be mocked many more times for my ridiculous ambitions, who am tired of taking advice from others more lethargic than myself ('you're half asleep, get moving, wake up'), who shall never be able to travel to India, who have accepted favours and given nothing in return, who wander from one side of the city to the other like a feather and let myself be carried along by the others,

I who have no personality nor want one, who stifle my rebelliousness all day long, who have not joined the guerrillas, who have

que no he hecho nada por mi pueblo
que no soy de las FALN y me desespero por todas estas
cosas y por otras cuya enumeración sería interminable
que no puedo salir de mi prisión
que he sido dado de baja en todas partes por inútil
que en realidad no he podido casarme ni ir a París ni
tener un día sereno
que me niego a reconocer los hechos
que siempre babeo sobre mi historia

que soy imbécil y más que imbécil de nacimiento
que perdí el hilo del discurso que se ejecutaba en mí y no
he podido encontrarlo
que no lloro cuando siento deseos de hacerlo
que llego tarde a todo

que he sido arruinado por tantas marchas y contramarchas
que ansío la inmovilidad perfecta y la prisa impecable
que no soy lo que soy ni lo que no soy

done nothing for my people, who do not belong to the FALN* and who despair over all these things and others that would make an endless list, who cannot get out of my prison, who have been turned down everywhere because I am of no use, who, to tell the truth, have not been able to get married nor go to Paris nor spend a peaceful day, who refuse to recognize facts, who always dribble over my story,

Who since birth have been an imbecile and an imbecile twice over, who lost the thread of the speech that was being delivered within me and have not found it, I who do not cry when I want to cry, who am late for everything,

Who have been ruined by so many advances and retreats, who yearn for perfect immobility and impeccable promptness, who am neither what I am nor what I am not, who in spite of everything

---

*FALN: Fuerzas Armadas de Liberación Nacional – Armed Forces of National Liberation, military arm of the National Liberation Front of Venezuela.

que a pesar de todo tengo un orgullo satánico aunque a
ciertas horas haya sido humilde hasta igualarme a las
piedras
que he vivido quince años en el mismo círculo
que me creí predestinado para algo fuera de lo común y
nada he logrado
que nunca usaré corbata
que no encuentro mi cuerpo

que he percibido por relámpagos mi falsedad y no he
podido derribarme, barrer todo y crear de mi indolencia, mi flotación, mi extravío una frescura nueva, y
obstinadamente me suicido al alcance de la mano
me levantaré del suelo más ridículo todavía para seguir
burlándome de los otros y de mí hasta el día del juicio
final

have a satanic pride even though at certain moments my humility has made me feel no taller than the stones, who have lived for fifteen years within the same circle, I who believed myself predestined for something unusual and have achieved nothing, who shall never wear a tie, who cannot find my body.

Who have seen my duplicity in lightning flashes and have not been able to throw myself to the ground, to sweep everything away and to create a new freshness out of my indolence, my drifting, my eccentricity, and obstinately [continue] to commit suicide with whatever my hand touches. I shall get up from the ground more ridiculous than ever and go on mocking myself and others until the day of the last judgement.

APPENDIX: AN EXPLANATORY GUIDE TO MOVEMENTS IN LATIN-AMERICAN POETRY

E. Caracciolo-Trejo

THE PRECURSORS (1800–1830)

By the beginning of the nineteenth century most Latin-American countries were fighting for political independence from Spain after three centuries of colonial rule. The struggle for independence was accompanied by a strong desire for intellectual emancipation. Many patriotic songs and poems were written, exalting the courage, determination and abnegation of the freedom fighters. These were very much conditioned by a colonial education, based on classical studies, and the poets inevitably took as their models Ovid, Pindar, Virgil and Horace.

Andrés Bello, José Joaquín de Olmedo and José María Heredia belonged to a generation of poets who, aware of the revolution of ideas which had swept Europe during the eighteenth century, sought to create a new poetry which would be representative of Latin-American dreams and aspirations as well as of new aesthetic values. They believed that Latin Americans, with their different experience of the world, should differ in their poetry from Europeans, and that the subject matter of Latin-American poetry should be found in the new lands, and not in the books of the old masters which, although wise and perfect, were alien and remote.

The Venezuelan poet Andrés Bello proposed, in his 'Allocution to Poetry' (1823) a return to the 'world of Columbus'. In *Silvas americanas* (1823), Bello described the majestic scenery of the new continent and the activities of man in the new surroundings; his poetry, combining lofty verse with a great profusion of realistic detail, demonstrates his struggle to free himself from a long and deeply-rooted colonial cultural tradition.

José Joaquín de Olmedo of Ecuador, who had translated Pope, was a man totally committed to the fight for political independence. He found inspiration in the heroic actions of the patriots who fought against Spain during the campaigns for independence, and wrote his ode, *La victoria de Junín: Canto a Bolívar* (1825) as a tribute to the men who defeated the Spaniards at the battle of Junín (1824), a victory which put an end to Spanish rule in South America. Olmedo's patriotism is expressed in images of great splendour.

These poets of the early nineteenth century proclaimed their desire to assert a new concept of nationhood through their poetry, yet they still seemed to belong to the old world. Today their poetry reads as eloquent rhetoric, imposing enough, but lacking immediacy and spontaneous emotion. Critics have called this poetry 'Latin-American neo-classicism', but this is more a nickname than a valid literary classification.

Bello and Olmedo did not make any innovations in the actual structure of Latin-American poetry, but they opened up a whole new field of subject matter and this is where their merit lies.

ROMANTICISM (1830–80)

Bello and Olmedo had expanded the vision of poetry, but not poetic style: Bello wrote in traditional Spanish verse and Olmedo had found his model in the classics. The next generation of Latin-American poets looked for new poetic forms capable of expressing their new experience of the world. The Argentine writer Esteban Echeverría spent four years in France (1826–30) and became enthusiastic about European romanticism, which he saw as a liberation from stilted poetic forms and themes and a reassertion of the poet's individuality. In Latin America, romanticism took the form of an exaltation of the poet's feelings and an exploration of the relationship between poet and landscape – landscape conceived now as a comprehensive sensuous experience and not as something to be merely described. In 1837 Echeverría wrote a long poem, *La cautiva*, which tells a story set in the pampas. In the prologue to his volume *Rimas* (1837), in which *La cautiva* was first published, Echeverría explained his intentions:

El principal designio del autor de *La cautiva* ha sido pintar algunos rasgos de la fisonomía poética del Desierto; y para no reducir la obra a una mera descripción, ha colocado en las vastas soledades de la Pampa dos seres ideales, o dos almas unidas por el doble vínculo del amor y el infortunio.

The principal design of the author of *The Captive* has been to depict the poetical physiognomy of the Desert, and in order not to reduce the piece to a mere description, the poet has set in the vast solitudes of the Pampas two ideal beings, or two souls united by the double bond of love and misfortune.

The feeling of liberation from the past and from all tradition was accompanied by a reaction against Spain. Echeverría wrote:

Estas y otras composiciones del mismo género en este libro *Los consuelos* (1834) insertas las escribía preoccupado aún del estilo y formas usadas por los poetas españoles, cuyas liras rara vez han cantado la libertad. Si, recobrando mi patria su esplendor, me cupiese la dicha de celebrar otra vez sus glorias, seguiría distinto rumbo; pues sólo por no trillados senderos se descubren mundos desconocidos.

These and other compositions of the same genre included in this book *The Consolations* (1834) I wrote while still preoccupied with the style and forms used by Spanish poets whose lyres have rarely sung of liberty. If my fatherland regained its splendour and I were to have the happiness of celebrating its glories once again, I would follow a different path; because it is only along untrodden ways that unknown worlds can be discovered.

In discarding the past, Latin-American romantics had to rely on inspiration, but still produced poetry which was realistic in that it dealt with their own immediate environment: the Colombian Gregorio Gutiérrez González wrote *Memoria sobre el cultivo del maíz en Antioquía* (1868), a poeticized description of the cultivation of maize in a region of Colombia; and the

Brazilian Gonçalves Dias wrote in a subjective way of his native land, seeing nature as a part of his whole emotional being, and by doing so he brought himself closer to the themes and motifs which are central to the so-called 'Indianist' literature in Brazil.

The poetry of the Latin-American romantics is one of quest – both personal and collective – and from this quest grew an awareness of the social role of the poet. The Latin-American romantics were inspired by a deep love for their native land, which at times took on an almost political character. To us now, however, this attitude may often seem declamatory, hollow, and cliché-ridden.

An interesting development at this time was *gauchesco* poetry. The *gauchos* were white or half-caste inhabitants of the Pampas, famed for their wisdom and experiences. The gauchesco poets were not gauchos themselves, but city men, who used the gaucho language, writing in the metre of the Spanish romance, octosyllabic verse. Among these poets were Bartolomé Hidalgo, Hilario Ascasubi, and Estanislão del Campo. Two writers who transformed the genre, to some extent idealizing the gaucho, were Antonio Lussich and José Hernández. Gauchesco poetry, like the old romances, is narrative and dramatic rather than lyrical; the gaucho as a social entity was a rebel, and gauchesco poets were also rebelling against the tradition of 'preciousness' in literature. The finest example of gauchesco poetry is Hernández's *Martín Fierro* (1872 and 1879).

MODERNISMO (1880–1918)

The passion that characterized many poems of the romantic period was to turn eventually into empty rhetoric. The Cuban national hero José Martí was the first to react against this decayed form of romanticism and to turn to more controlled emotion. In 1882 he published *Ismaelillo*, which marked the beginning of a new development in Spanish-American poetry. This new development, which spread throughout Spanish-speaking America, is known as 'Modernismo', and can be divided into two periods. The first period lasted from 1882 to 1896, and its most important poets are the Cubans Martí and Julián del Casal, the Mexican Manuel Gutiérrez Nájera, the Colombian José Asunción Silva, and the Nicaraguan Rubén Darío. All died before 1896, except Darío, who formed an inspiring link with the second period, which began in 1896 and lasted until the First World War. Among the poets of this second phase of Modernismo are the Argentine Leopoldo Lugones, the Peruvian José Santos Chocano, the Colombian Guillermo Valencia, and the Mexicans Enrique González Martínez and Amado Nervo. The first man to divide Spanish-American Modernismo into two distinct periods in this way was the Dominican Pedro Henríquez Ureña (1884–1946), one of the most distinguished critics of Latin-American literature. (Brazil's literary tradition differs from that of the rest of Spanish America, largely because of its different language, Portuguese. By the time Modernismo appeared in Spanish America, Brazil had already begun an independent process of literary evolution. What is known as Brazilian Modernismo appeared much later, in 1922, and has different sources and characteristics. It will be discussed on p. 404).

Modernismo was a tendency that manifested itself in literature in all its forms, and in the visual arts. Its followers were called *modernistas*. Díez Canedo wrote: 'Modernismo is more than a school; it is a whole epoch and its influence goes beyond the literary field and exerts itself on all aspects of life.' It is not easy to define Modernismo, but certain features common to most of the *modernista* poets can be traced. In literature as a whole, two factors were important: reaction against Spain, and the influence of French literature. Latin-American poets, seeking to escape from the frustration and boredom of provincial literary life, found inexhaustible sources of inspiration, first in the Parnassians and later in the '*décadent*' and the Symbolists. They also looked further back in time, to French neo-classicism. An interest in the exotic developed: Chinese and Japanese 'objets d'art' acquired a particular fascination for *modernista* poets and this was reflected in their poetry. To these general trends were added more specific ones: poets sought new poetic forms, richer images, more variable rhythms, and new patterns of rhyming. A vitality resulted which was completely new in Latin-American writing.

Although the *modernista* contribution was an entirely aesthetic one, it helped to give Spanish-American countries more confidence in their creative abilities: this, the first literary movement to embrace the whole continent, had long-lasting effects on the cultural life of each country. Latin-American poets sought for aesthetic ideals in other cultures, and thus came closer to Europe instead of looking for sources in indigenous cultures or accommodating themselves to the smug fin-de-siècle positivism shared by so many Latin-American political leaders. Modernismo even influenced Spanish poetry in Europe. Although inevitably so large a movement produced a lot of indifferent, and today outdated, material, *modernista* poets at their best created both a body of poetry of lasting value and a new awareness of uniquely Latin-American creative possibilities. The influence has remained great: present-day writers – for example, Borges, Cortázar, Lezama Lima, and Paz – owe much to the *modernista* attitude.

If the first period of Modernismo arose partly out of a reaction against Spain, the second was to some extent based on new values: some poets began to feel obligations to their ancestral homeland, and a desire to reconsider the relationship between Latin America and Spain, particularly after the defeat of Spain in the Spanish-American War of 1898, a defeat which aroused new sympathies in those who saw that war as a confrontation between the Latin world and the Anglo-Saxon imperialism of the north. In 1896, Rubén Darío, the link between the two periods of Modernismo, published *Prosas profanas*, perhaps the best example of the poetry of the first period; in 1905 there appeared his *Cantos de vida y esperanza*, best illustrating the second. In *Prosas profanas* Darío considered politics as something completely alien to poetry, but he included in *Cantos de vida y espearanza* such poems as 'Salutación del optimista' (Salutation to the Optimist – a celebration of Hispanic origins) and 'A Roosevelt' (To Roosevelt):

> Eres los Estados Unidos,
> eres el futuro invasor
> de la América ingenua que tiene sangre indígena,
> que aún reza a Jesucristo y aún habla en español.
>
> You are the United States,
> You are the future invader
> of the innocent America of native blood
> that still prays to Jesus and still speaks Spanish.

'MUNDONOVISMO'

During the second phase of Modernismo, a new style of writing appeared. This is known as 'Mundonovismo' (from *mundo nuevo*: new world) – although the writers never actually gave themselves this name. It was marked by a decisive return to exclusively Latin-American themes. From the cosmopolitanism of Modernismo came a transition to the nationalism of 'Mundonovismo', the formal elements of the first being perfectly incorporated in the second: *Alma América* (1906), by the Peruvian José Santos Chocano, clearly illustrates this transition.

'SENCILLISMO'

In 1915, Baldomero Fernández Moreno published *Las iniciales del misal*, and in 1916, *Intermedio provinciano*; both books showed a reaction against the growing over-ornamentation by then prevalent in Modernismo. Like 'Mundonovismo', 'Sencillismo' – as this style came to be known (from *sencillo*: simple, direct) – was not a movement as such but more a coincidence of styles among separate writers working at the same time. 'Sencillismo' showed a return to the immediacy and simplicity that José Martí had advocated at the dawn of Modernismo.

Instead of the side themes of nationalism, subject matter became simpler: the contemplation of a spring day, or of a suburban street corner in Buenos Aires.

CREACIONISMO

The aftermath of the First World War brought new waves of immigrants to some areas of Latin America in the 1920s and life began to change, particularly in the cities, as, from a basically rural economy, Latin America began to evolve towards industrialization. By 1919 Modernismo had little left to offer poets. The Chilean Vicente Huidobro had lived in France for some time and had written a considerable amount in French, and was experimenting with new forms of expression. In 1917 Huidobro joined the group of writers and poets who, led by Guillaume Apollinaire and Pierre Reverdy, edited *Nord Sud*. It is interesting that Huidobro's *Horizon carré* (written in French) and Apollinaire's *Caligrammes* both appeared in 1918. In *Horizon carré*, Huidobro, a close friend of the Cubist painters Juan Gris and Fernand Léger, showed his interest in the ideas of Cubism. During this time of quest and change, Huidobro conceived the aesthetic ideas which are the basis of Creacionismo, the movement which he founded. In Huidobro's aesthetic order, the poet, as creator, reigned supreme.

ULTRAÍSMO

In 1919 the Argentine Jorge Luis Borges (who had been educated in Switzerland) went to Spain. There he met groups of Spanish experimental writers who were in touch with other European avant-garde movements. When he returned to Argentina he helped to found Ultraísmo. The *ultraísta* movement was made up of Spanish and Argentine poets interested in developing Spanish as a language for the new poetry. They advocated 'the greatest independence' for the metaphor, and in this way Latin-American poetry came closer to the Surrealist principles.

Prisma, revista mural was a magazine which was stuck on walls in order to 'bring poetry into the streets of Buenos Aires'. In 1922 it contained the following proclamation:

Hemos sintetizado la poesía en su elemento primordial: la metáfora, a la que concedemos una máxima independencia, más allá de los jueguitos de aquellos que comparan entre sí cosas de formas semejantes, equiparando con un circo a la luna. Cada verso de nuestros poemas posee su vida individual y representa una visión inédita. El Ultraísmo propende así a la formación de una mitología emocional y variable.

We have synthesized poetry into its primordial element: the metaphor, to which we grant the greatest independence, beyond the little games of those who compare things like each other *to* each other, equating a circus with the moon. Each line of our poems has its individual life and represents an original vision. Ultraísmo thus propounds the formation of an emotional, changeable, varied mythology.

A good example of *ultraísta* poetry is Oliverio Girondo's *Veinte poemas para ser leídos en el tranvía*, published in 1922. In the same year Girondo wrote:

Lo cotidiano, sin embargo, ¿no es una manifestación admirable y modesta de lo absurdo? Y cortar las amarras lógicas, ¿no implica la única y verdadera posibilidad?

The day-to-day, however, is it not an admirable and modest manifestation of the absurd? And cutting off the logical anchors, does it not imply the only true possibility?

Ultraísmo was only known as such in the Argentine and in Spain. José Juan Tablada, the Mexican poet who in 1919 published *Un día . . .*, a book in an *ultraísta* vein, and the Colombian León de Greiff, never became involved with the groups of Buenos Aires and Madrid, but can be grouped with the *ultraísta* poets because of their free use of the metaphor.

'POESÍA NEGRA'

Large Negro communities had developed in Latin America, especially in Brazil and the Caribbean area, and in the 1920s, Afro-American poetry began to be written: in most cases, however, this poetry was written by white men who were fascinated by the vitality and beauty of the Negro race. The way in which the Negroes used the Spanish and Portuguese languages, their special pronunciation which had become a part of life in some regions of Latin America but had never before been used as the language of poetry, appealed to some poets – for example, Luis Palés Matos in Puerto Rico, Nicolás Guillén and Emilio Ballagas in Cuba, Jorge de Lima in Brazil.

Afro-American poetry brought new and exciting rhythms into the Spanish and Portuguese languages. It was also the poetry of social protest, as, for example, *West Indies Ltd*, by Nicolás Guillén, published in 1934.

BRAZILIAN MODERNISMO

In 1922, the Semana de Arte Moderna was held in São Paulo, Brazil. This consisted not only of exhibitions of painting and sculpture but also of music, poetry readings, lectures and discussions. Among the many writers and artists taking part were Manuel Bandeira, Ronald de Carvalho, Mário de Andrade, Emiliano de Cavalcânti, Vicente do Rego Monteiro, and Heitor Vila-Lôbos. A militant group of young intellectuals fought to introduce new aesthetic principles which they hoped would lead to the abolition of the rhetoric and formalism they felt prevailed at the time; this group started the movement now known as Brazilian Modernismo.

In spirit, Brazilian Modernismo is comparable to Spanish-American Ultraísmo: *modernista* writers found the traditional genres too formal and suffocating, and sought to liberate themselves from these. They brought into their poetry rhythms not only imposed by formal requirements but arising also from their creative mood. New areas of experience were brought into poetry – humour, for instance – and *modernista* poets show a fine sense of irony and a feeling for paradox reminiscent of Apollinaire.

Between 1924 and 1930 Brazilian Modernismo was at its peak. In 1930 were published *Libertinagem* by Manuel Bandeira, *Remate de Males* by Mário de Andrade, *Alguma poesia* by Carlos Drummond de Andrade, and *Poèmas* by Murilo Mendes – collections of poetry written during these years. As a movement, Modernismo in Brazil continued until the 1940s, when a reaction, particularly in the work of the 'generation of 45' (geracão de 45) began to be felt. The most important poet of this post-*modernista* tendency is João Cabral de Melo Neto.

*

The poets who have appeared in Latin America since the 1920s are many and varied; they cannot be organized into any clear picture of schools or movements. The poetic image gained a great deal of freedom from movements such as Creacionismo and Ultraísmo, and further freedom from the advent of Surrealism. Surrealism, though, as it manifests itself in Latin America, is a creative attitude rather than a movement and so although it is possible to find a prevailing Surrealist tendency in the poetry of Latin America today, this is inevitable and the result of factors unconnected with literary movements within Latin America itself.

Certainly Surrealism has played its part in the careers of the great present-day poets of Latin America – the Peruvian César Vallejo, the Chilean Pablo Neruda, and the Mexican Octavio Paz. But each has evolved his own language of poetry and by doing so widened creative horizons for generations to come. The following notes on these three poets, in addition to the biographical information given in the contents list, may provide some further critical reference.

César Vallejo's first book, *Los heraldos negros*, appeared in

1918, and in 1922 he published *Trilce*, perhaps the most sustained attempt to carry the Spanish language to new frontiers of communication. But his originality was not recognized until after his death. In 1923 Vallejo went to Paris. He visited the Soviet Union several times, but never returned to Peru. He died in Paris in 1938.

In the 1920s, as has been briefly outlined above, many poetic trends coexisted and developed: it was a period of great creative vitality. Vallejo's poetry cannot be associated with any movement. When he arrived in Paris he was not impressed by the declamatory tone of the 'new poets'. He wrote:

Poesía 'nueva' ha dado en llamarse a los versos cuyo léxico está formado de las palabras 'cinema, motor, caballos de fuerza, avión, radio, jazz-band, telegrafía sin hilos', y, en general, de todas las voces de las ciencias e industrias contemporáneas, no importa que el léxico corresponda o no a una sensibilidad auténticamente nueva. Lo importante son las palabras. Pero no hay que olvidarse que esto no es poesía nueva, ni antigua, ni nada. Los materiales artísticos que ofrece la vida moderna, han de ser asimilados por el espíritu y convertidos en sensibilidad. El telégrafo sin hilos, por ejemplo, está destinado, más que a hacernos decir 'telégrafo sin hilos' a despertar nuevos temples nerviosos, profundas perspicacias sentimentales, ampliando videncias y comprensiones y densificando el amor: la inquietud entonces crece y se exaspera, el soplo de la vida se aviva. Esta es la cultura verdadera que da el progreso; éste su único sentido estético.

'New poetry' has come to be the term applied to those poems whose vocabulary is formed of the words 'cinema, motor, horsepower, aeroplane, radio, jazz-band, radio-telegraphy', and, in general, of all the terms of contemporary science and industry, no matter whether the vocabulary relates or not to an authentically new sensibility. The important thing is the words. But one must not forget that this is neither new poetry nor old, nor anything else. The materials offered by modern life have to be assimilated by the spirit and converted into a new sensibility. Radio-telegraphy, for example, is destined, rather than to make us say 'radio-telegraphy', to awaken in us new nervous dispositions, a deeper sentimental astuteness, widening our imaginative vision and comprehension and making more substantial our sense of love: our critical faculty then increases and becomes more acute and the breath of life becomes more lively. That is the real culture that progress gives; that is its only aesthetic sense.

Vallejo created a poetic image that can go beyond mere literary association – and this is why his poetry is sometimes obscure. His last book, *Poemas humanos*, was published posthumously in 1939 and written at a time when Vallejo realized that the cause of the Spanish Republic was doomed. In *Poemas humanos*, Vallejo's religious feeling, which had been so evident in his first book, fused with his belief in a juster world under Communism.

In 1924 Pablo Neruda published his *20 poemas de amor y una canción desesperada*, a book which was to become famous all over Latin America. Early in his career, as Neruda has himself recognized in *El hondero entusiasta* (1933), he was much influenced by the Uruguayan poet Carlos Sabat Ercasty, but it is clear that he already possessed the basic elements of his very personal language – a language which reached maturity in 1933 with his *Residencia en la tierra*. It is in *Residencia en la tierra* that a new technique is evident: a looser poetic structure through which reality is presented as a succession of apparently unconnected dreamlike visions held together by a common emotional core. This book and the later *Tercera residencia* (1947), a collection of poetry written between 1935 and 1945, show Neruda's Surrealist tendencies. But in *Tercera residencia* we also find the themes which are central to *Canto general* (1950) – 'España en el corazón', for example, records Neruda's experiences in the Spanish Civil War. In 1939 he wrote:

> El mundo ha cambiado y mi poesía ha cambiado. Una gota de sangre caída en estas líneas quedará viviendo sobre ellas, indeleble como el amor.

> The world has changed and my poetry has changed. A drop of blood fallen on these lines will live on, indelible like love.

Canto general includes 'Alturas de Macchu Picchu', one of Neruda's most important poems. In the books which followed *Canto general*, several styles evolved: these books include *Odas elementales* (1954), *Estravagario* (1958), *Cantos ceremoniales* (1961), *Plenos poderes* (1962), and *Memorial de la Isla Negra* (1964).

Octavio Paz's first book, *Luna silvestre*, was published in 1933, when he was twenty. His work as poet and critic has many phases. He has lived through a particularly rich period in Mexican art and letters, coming of age as a poet at a time when well-known older poets were in their prime: Xavier Villaurrutia, Carlos Pellicer, José Gorostiza. Paz's poetry shows a search for an integrated life, a life where the seemingly eternal dichotomies that affect Western man will disappear and a new, at present unattainable, harmony may be found. He sees the fragmentation of human life as the expression of Western intellectual history, and as leading only to frustration and despair:

Desde Parménides nuestro mundo ha sido el de la distinción neta y tajante entre lo que es y lo que no es. El ser no es no-ser. Este primer desarraigo – porque fue un arrancar al ser del caos primordial – constituye el fundamento de nuestro pensar.

Since Parmenides our world has been one of clear-cut distinctions between what *is* and what *is not*. Being is not not-being. This early uprooting – because indeed it was an uprooting of the being from its primordial chaos – constitutes one of the basic principles of our way of thinking.

Hence Paz's interest in Oriental philosophy. In search of his own essence, blurred and distorted rather than revealed by history, he comes to the poem:

Damos vueltas y vueltas en el vientre animal, en el vientre mineral, en el vientre temporal. Encontrar la salida: el poema.

We turn and turn in our animal womb, in our mineral womb and in the womb of time, looking for the way out: the poem.

Paz is alert and sensitive to his time; his latest books – *Viento entero* (1965), *Blanco* (1966), *Topoemas* (1968) – show his creative vitality: *Blanco* can be described as a study in poetical space, 'that which makes writing and reading possible, that where all writing and reading ends', not unlike Mallarmé's exercises: *Topoemas* are imaginative rediscoveries of the 'calligramme' as a poetic instrument. Paz's experience of the East is documented in his recent collection, *Ladera este* (1969), which consists of poems written between 1962 and 1968.

INDEX OF FIRST LINES

INDEX OF TITLES

ALPHABETICAL INDEX OF POETS

MORE ABOUT PENGUINS AND PELICANS

Penguinews, which appears every month, contains details of all the new books issued by Penguins as they are published. From time to time it is supplemented by *Penguins in Print*, which is a complete list of all books published by Penguins which are in print. (There are well over three thousand of these.)

A specimen copy of *Penguinews* will be sent to you free on request, and you can become a subscriber for the price of the postage. For a year's issues (including the complete lists) please send 30p if you live in the United Kingdom, or 60p if you live elsewhere. Just write to Dept EP, Penguin Books Ltd, Harmondsworth, Middlesex, enclosing a cheque or postal order, and your name will be added to the mailing list.

Some other books published by Penguins are described on the following pages.

Note: *Penguinews* and *Penguins in Print* are not available in the U.S.A. or Canada

PENGUIN NEW ART

Penguin New Art is unique in offering a series of monographs to introduce the work of younger artists who have already made an acknowledged contribution to contemporary art.

Each volume will trace the development of the artist's own style, emphasizing the effect of his work and the viewer's response to it within the prevailing cultural environment.

Already published:

Patrick Caulfield by Christopher Finch
Frank Stella by Robert Rosenblum
Robyn Denny by David Thompson

To be published

Anthony Caro by Richard Whelan
Bernard Cohen by Anne Seymour
Dan Flavin by Barbara Reise
Richard Hamilton by Lawrence Alloway
David Hockney by Henry Geldzahler
Howard Hodgkin by Richard Morphet
Donald Judd by William C. Agee
Phillip King by Charles Harrison
Kenneth Noland by William Rubin
Claes Oldenburg by Ellen H. Johnson
Richard Smith by Kynaston McShine
Andy Warhol by Barbara Rose

CHILDREN OF ALBION

Poetry of the 'Underground' in Britain

EDITED BY MICHAEL HOROVITZ

Here at last is the 'secret' generation of British poets whose work could hitherto be discovered only through their own bush telegraph of little magazines and lively readings. These are the energies which have almost completely dispelled the arid critical climate of the 'fifties' and engineered a fresh renaissance of 'the voice of the bard' –

The anthology contains many of the best poems of

Pete Brown
Dave Cuncliffe
Roy Fisher
Lee Harwood
Spike Hawkins
Anselm Hollo
Bernard Kops
Tom McGrath
Adrian Mitchell
Edwin Morgan
Neil Oram
Tom Pickard
Tom Raworth
Chris Torrance
Alex Trocchi
Gael Turnbull

– and *fifty* others – from John Arden to Michael X –

It is edited by Michael Horovitz, with a Blakean cornucopia of 'afterwords' which trace the development of oral and jazz poetry – the Albert Hall Incarnation of 1965 – the influences of the great American and Russian spokesmen – and the diverse lyric, political, visioning and revolutionary orientations of these new poets.

A Penguin Classic

THE JEWISH POETS OF SPAIN

TRANSLATED BY DAVID GOLDSTEIN

Ha-Levi's yearning for the land of Israel, Gabirol's communion with his own soul, Moses ibn Ezra's grief in his exile, and the extraordinary martial character of Samuel ha-Nagid, Vizier to the Moorish king of Granada: each of these poets is represented in this anthology of Hebrew verse in Spain from the tenth to the thirteenth centuries. Their subjects range from a wine-feast in a beautiful hanging garden to the arcane treasures of immortality; and they bring together two strands of the civilization of the Jews, one the unbridled sensuality of the Song of Songs, the other the unshakeable faith of the Prophets.

PENGUIN MODERN EUROPEAN POETS

This series now includes selected work by the following poets, in verse translations by, among others, W. H. Auden, Lawrence Ferlinghetti, Michael Hamburger, Ted Hughes, J. B. Leishman, Christopher Middleton and David Wevill:

Akhmatova
Amichai
Apollinaire
Bobrowski/Bienek
Ekelof
Enzensberger
Four Greek Poets:
Cavafy/Elytis/Gatsos/Seferis
Grass
Herbert
Holan
Holub
Kovner/Sachs
Montale
Pavese
Popa
Prevert
Quasimodo
Rilke
Three Czech Poets:
Nezval/Bartusek/Hanzlik
Ungaretti
Weores/Juhasz
Yevtushenko